Social Entrepreneurship

Included with *Social Entrepreneurship: An Evidence-Based Approach to Creating Social Values* are PowerPoint slides and sample text questions for each chapter. You can download them from www.wiley.com/college/guo

Essential Texts for Public and Nonprofit Leadership and Management

Understanding and Managing Public Organizations, 5th Edition, by Hal G. Rainey

Leading Forward: Successful Public Leadership Amidst Complexity, Chaos, and Change, by Tim A. Flanagan and John S. Lybarger

Smart Communities: How Citizens and Local Leaders Can Use Strategic Thinking to Build a Brighter Future, 2nd Edition, by Suzanne W. Morse

Creating Value in Nonprofit-Business Collaborations: New Thinking and Practice, by James E. Austin and M. May Seitanidi

Visual Strategy: A Workbook for Strategy Mapping in Public and Nonprofit Organizations, by John M. Bryson, Fran Ackermann, and Colin Eden

Human Resources Management for Public and Nonprofit Organizations: A Strategic Approach, 4th Edition, by Joan E. Pynes

The Handbook of Nonprofit Governance, by BoardSource

Strategic Planning for Public and Nonprofit Organizations, 5th Edition, by John M. Bryson

The Effective Public Manager: Achieving Success in Government Organizations, 5th Edition, by Steven Cohen, William Eimicke, and Tanya Heikkila

Handbook of Human Resources Management in Government, 3rd Edition, by Stephen E. Condrey (ed.)

The Responsible Administrator, 6th Edition, by Terry L. Cooper

The Jossey-Bass Handbook of Nonprofit Leadership and Management, 3rd Edition, by David O. Renz, Robert D. Herman, and Associates (eds.)

The Ethics Challenge in Public Service, 3rd Edition, by Carol W. Lewis and others

Managing Nonprofit Organizations, by Mary Tschirhart and Wolfgang Bielefeld

Social Media in the Public Sector: Participation, Collaboration, and Transparency in the Networked World, by Ines Mergel

Meta-Analysis for Public Management and Policy, by Evan Ringquist

The Practitioner's Guide to Governance as Leadership: Building High-Performing Nonprofit Boards, by Cathy A. Trower

Measuring Performance in Public and Nonprofit Organizations, by Theodore H. Poister

Hank Rosso's Achieving Excellence in Fundraising, 3rd Edition, by Eugene R. Tempel, Timothy Seiler, and Eva Aldrich (eds.)

Handbook of Practical Program Evaluation, 3rd Edition, by Joseph S. Wholey and others (eds.)

Social Entrepreneurship

AN EVIDENCE-BASED
APPROACH TO CREATING
SOCIAL VALUE

Chao Guo
Wolfgang Bielefeld

JB JOSSEY-BASS™
A Wiley Brand

Published by Jossey-Bass
A Wiley Brand
One Montgomery Street, Suite 1200, San Francisco, CA 94104-4594—www.josseybass.com

Library of Congress Cataloging-in-Publication Data

Guo, Chao.
    Social entrepreneurship : an evidence-based approach to creating social value / Chao Guo and Wolfgang Bielefeld.
        pages   cm
    Includes bibliographical references and index.
        ISBN 978-1-118-35648-7 (pbk); 978-1-118-84417-5 (ebk); 978-1-118-84413-7 (ebk)
        1. Social entrepreneurship.   I. Bielefeld, Wolfgang.   II. Title.
    HD60.G7556 2014
    658.4'08—dc23
                                                                                            2013048860

Printed in the United States of America
FIRST EDITION

PB Printing   10 9 8 7 6 5 4 3 2 1

CONTENTS

TABLES, FIGURES, AND EXHIBIT

EXHIBIT

Chao Guo, Ph.D., is associate professor of nonprofit management in the School of Social Policy and Practice at the University of Pennsylvania. Previously, he was on the faculties of Indiana University, the University of Georgia, and Arizona State University. He received his Ph.D. in public administration from the University of Southern California.

Guo's research interests focus on the intersection between nonprofit and voluntary action and government. More specifically, he conducts research on representation, advocacy, governance, collaboration within and across sectors, social entrepreneurship, and volunteerism. He has many published articles in prestigious journals. In 2005, Guo received the David Stevenson Faculty Fellowship from the Nonprofit Academic Centers Council. In 2008, he was selected as a recipient of the inaugural IDEA Award for research promise by the entrepreneurship division of the Academy of Management. In 2012, he was selected as a recipient of the Top Research Paper Award by the public relations division of the National Communication Association.

Guo is actively involved in professional and community service activities. He currently serves on the boards of directors of the Association of Research on Nonprofit Organizations and Voluntary Action and the *Nonprofit Quarterly*, and he is the senior vice president of the International Council of Voluntarism, Civil Society, and Social Economy Researcher Associations. He also serves on the editorial boards of leading journals of nonprofit studies, such as *Nonprofit and Voluntary Sector Quarterly* and *Nonprofit Management and Leadership*. He has consulted with various nonprofit organizations on board governance and organizational change. In 2013, he was selected as a finalist for the Indiana

Public Service Award by the Indiana Chapter of the American Society for Public Administration.

Wolfgang Bielefeld, Ph.D., is professor emeritus at the Indiana University School of Public and Environmental Affairs and the Lilly Family School of Philanthropy at Indiana University-Purdue University Indianapolis. He has taught at the University of Texas at Dallas, the University of Minnesota, and Stanford University. He is a former coeditor of the *Nonprofit and Voluntary Sector Quarterly* (from 2005 to 2010) and has served on the editorial board of *VOLUNTAS: International Journal of Voluntary and Nonprofit Organizations*. He has served on the board of the Association for Research on Nonprofit Organizations and Voluntary Action and was the program chair for several annual conferences of that organization. His professional experience includes serving on the board of Lutheran Child and Family Services of Indiana/Kentucky. Professor Bielefeld earned his Ph.D. degree in sociology from the University of Minnesota. He also holds an M.A. degree in marketing, an M.A. degree in sociology, and a B.S. degree in engineering. In addition to social entrepreneurship, his research interests include the relations between nonprofit organizations and their environments and the dynamics of the nonprofit sector. He has authored numerous articles and coauthored a number of books, including *Managing Nonprofit Organizations* and *Nonprofit Organizations in an Age of Uncertainty: A Study of Organizational Change*. The latter book won the 2001 ARNOVA Best Book Award, the 1999 Independent Sector Virginia A. Hodgkinson Research Prize, and the 1999 Academy of Management, Public and Nonprofit Division, Book of the Year Award.

INTRODUCTION: UNDERSTANDING AND USING SOCIAL ENTREPRENEURSHIP

E ven a cursory look at the daily news will be enough to convince the viewer that pressing challenges present themselves at all social levels. We are all familiar with issues such as neighborhood crime and struggling schools, city-wide poverty and unemployment, lack of funding for state services, and the global problems brought about by overpopulation. Moreover, our ever more connected and more rapidly changing world is making these issues far more complex and difficult to solve. Stephen Goldsmith and William Eggers echo the views of many observers:

> In many ways, twenty-first century challenges and the means of addressing them are more numerous and complex than ever before. Problems have become both more global and more local as power disperses and boundaries (when they exist at all) become more fluid. One-size-fits-all solutions have given way to customized approaches as the complicated problems of diverse and mobile populations increasingly defy simplistic solutions.[1]

This makes the root causes of many problems difficult to identify.[2] In addition, addressing these problems may also require changes in values, beliefs, roles, relationships, and approaches to work. Moreover, solutions to these problems usually require change in numerous places, and often across organizational boundaries. Finally, these solutions are also likely to require experiments and new discoveries. This situation can give rise to frustration, cynicism, and power struggles for what are seen as finite and shrinking resources. The current gridlock in the U.S. Congress and the grassroots demonstrations against the 1 percent of the wealthiest Americans are striking examples.

We are, however, also seeing a much more positive development—the rise of social entrepreneurship. Social entrepreneurs in both the private and public sectors are working to develop innovative solutions to our most difficult problems. In his international bestselling book *The World Is Flat: A Brief History of the Twenty-First Century*, *New York Times* columnist Thomas L. Friedman wrote:

> One of the newest figures to emerge on the world stage in recent years is the social entrepreneur. This is usually someone who burns with desire to make a positive social impact on the world, but believes that the best way of doing it is, as the saying goes, not by giving poor people a fish and feeding them for a day, but by teaching them to fish, in hopes of feeding them for a lifetime. I have come to know several social entrepreneurs in recent years, and most combine a business school brain with a social worker's heart. The triple convergence and the flattening of the world have been a godsend for them. Those who get it and are adapting to it have begun launching some very innovative projects.[3]

Social entrepreneurship is clearly in fashion. Until recent years, we were used to carving society into three sectors: government, business, and nonprofit. Each sector seemed to be clearly defined, easily understood, and conveniently stereotyped. This segmentation allowed us to frame and solve problems in our society according to the sector boxes we created for them, and there had yet to be a mechanism to disrupt this trifecta. However, faced with a tougher financial environment, unprecedented competition, stronger accountability expectations, and accumulating social demands, public and nonprofit leaders today are increasingly called to be innovators and entrepreneurs, whereas business leaders and entrepreneurs are increasingly expected to be socially responsible. A host of factors have eroded the boundaries between the nonprofit, government, and business sectors. In the absence of these boundaries, ideas, values, roles, relationships, and capital now flow more freely between sectors.[4] In response, we increasingly see the three sectors joining forces to tackle the social problems that affect us all.

It is against this backdrop that social entrepreneurship has become one of the most popular mechanisms in the public, nonprofit, and for-profit sectors. "Social entrepreneurs are mad scientists in the lab," says Pamela Hartigan, director of the Skoll Centre for Social Entrepreneurship at Oxford University. "They're harbingers of new ways of doing business."[5]

Social entrepreneurs work in all three sectors.[6] They are developing innovative social ventures in their own sector and creative new ways for the sectors to collaborate. In addition, although social entrepreneurship can be launched through individual efforts, it will eventually be carried out by a group, network, organization, or alliance. The following are a few examples of innovative social entrepreneurial programs and organizations.[7]

• *City Year* (www.cityyear.org): City Year's mission is to build democracy through citizen service, civic leadership, and social entrepreneurship. City Year's citizen service vision is that citizens of all ages and backgrounds will unite to serve their community, nation, and world. City Year's civic leadership vision is that one day every citizen will have the skills, values, and inspiration to be a leader for the common good.

• *College Summit* (www.collegesummit.org): College Summit's mission is to increase the college enrollment rate of low-income students by ensuring that every student who can make it in college makes it to college, and by putting college access know-how and support within the reach of every student.

• *KickStart* (www.kickstart.org): KickStart is a nonprofit organization that develops and markets new technologies in Africa. These low-cost technologies are bought by local entrepreneurs and used to establish highly profitable new small businesses.

• *Teach for America* (www.teachforamerica.org): Teach for America is a national, highly selective service corps of outstanding recent college graduates of all academic majors who commit two years to teach in underserved urban and rural public schools. The mission is to eliminate educational inequity by enlisting our nation's most promising future leaders in the effort. Since its founding, Teach for America has become the nation's largest provider of teachers for low income communities.

Entrepreneurship for commercial gain, or the creation of economic value in for-profit organizations, has been discussed and studied since the early 1800s. However, the systematic study of entrepreneurship for the creations of social value is in its infancy. The term "social entrepreneurship" was first used in the

1980s to refer to the development of new and innovative nonprofit programs. Since then, nonprofits have increasingly been called upon to become more innovative and to enhance the social value they create.

In addition, as noted earlier, government agencies and for-profits are also being called upon to enhance their creativity and responsiveness to social issues. Government has responded with a series of reforms that seek to create more effective and efficient services and to empower citizens. Business has responded by broadening their conception of the corporation's role in society. The term "corporate social responsibility" (CSR) has been in wide use since the 1960s. It has often been practiced by corporations donating to worthy causes. In the late 1980s, however, companies like the Body Shop, Ben & Jerry's, and Patagonia embraced a more active vision of CSR that "regarded their businesses both as a vehicle to make money and as a means to improve society."[8] This vision of CSR is gaining wider acceptance.

Our book will provide readers with an understanding of the exciting and dynamic field of social entrepreneurship. Our goal is to help current and future social entrepreneurs create social value in innovative ways. We are part of a rapidly growing trend in universities, which have also responded to the increased need for and use of social entrepreneurship.

There has been a dramatic increase in demand for courses in social innovation and social entrepreneurship over the past few years. The first social entrepreneurship class was taught at Harvard University in the mid 1990s and the first European course at the University of Geneva in Switzerland in 2003.[9] A comprehensive scan of the field in 2008 identified over 100 courses in 35 countries and over 350 professors who are actively teaching or doing research on social entrepreneurship.[10] At that time, there were also over 30 national and international social entrepreneurship competitions, 800 different published articles about social entrepreneurship, and 200 written cases used in social entrepreneurship courses.[11] An update of the scan in 2011 identified more than 148 institutions globally teaching some aspect of social entrepreneurship on their campuses.[12] It also found a greater diversity in institutional types, including "2- and 4-year institutions, online universities, continuing and executive education programs and undergraduate and graduate schools across diverse disciplines, including engineering, design, law, social work, and education. In addition, social entrepreneurship education is moving outward from its popularity at elite colleges and universities to institutionalization at other universities and colleges worldwide."[13] We are pleased to be part of this growing field and to contribute to the education of a new wave of social entrepreneurs.

PLAN OF THE BOOK

In this section we present a short outline of the major sections of the book and the chapters they contain. Our goal is to provide social entrepreneurs and innovators with the knowledge, tools, and skills they need to meet the challenges that they will face.[14] Management of social entrepreneurship is unique in a number of ways. In the chapters to follow we will discuss how social entrepreneurs can develop the skills needed for the management of:

• Distinctive and complex issues of accountability: Depending on the sector they are in, social entrepreneurs may be accountable to donors, investors, owners, the public, and those they seek to help.

• Double and triple bottom lines: Social entrepreneurship entails social, commercial, and environmental objectives. This can create tensions within ventures, as these bottom lines may need to be traded off against one another.

• Complex identity issues: Social entrepreneurial organizations may need to be presented in ways that garner legitimacy for actors in both the public and private sectors.

We also stress that social entrepreneurs need a deep understanding of how social problems are rooted in institutionalized beliefs, values, and ideas, as well as in existing social practices and structures. Along with this, social entrepreneurs need to understand that social transformation is inherently political, and they must become adept in the use of political skills to overcome resistance from entrenched interests that may resist change.

In Part One, we introduce the concept of social entrepreneurship and the context in which it is practiced. Chapter One describes what social entrepreneurship is, who social entrepreneurs are, why they practice social entrepreneurship, and where social entrepreneurship occurs. In Chapter Two we examine how social entrepreneurship is expressed in organizational behavior. This includes how organizations may be oriented toward social entrepreneurship and how the extent, or intensity, of their social entrepreneurial activities can be described.

Part Two delves into social entrepreneurship in more detail and describes how the social entrepreneurial process can be understood and managed. In Chapter Three we examine how the recognition of an opportunity to create social value begins the process. The chapter provides an understanding of what social entrepreneurial opportunities are, how they are distinctive, and how they are discovered or created. Chapter Four explains how social entrepreneurs take the next step in the process: turning opportunities into action. Social ventures need to be based on a viable theory or expectation of the social benefits they will provide. This theory is used to establish the venture's operating model, which links venture inputs to outputs and impacts. The operating model is then assessed in light of feasibility, business planning, and further supporting analysis. Chapter Five discusses the payoff to social entrepreneurship; that is, how we can determine the results that social ventures produce. We define social venture effectiveness and different approaches to its assessment. We next consider the evaluation of venture outcomes and impacts and how these impacts can be scaled to produce greater social value. All ventures need funding, which is the subject of Chapter Six. Social ventures can be funded by government funds, philanthropy, and self-generated income. Each source has particular characteristics. Moreover, the funding available for social ventures in the public and private sectors varies.

Social entrepreneurship occurs through both the establishment of new organizations and the development of programs within existing organizations. The latter is usually referred to as "social intrapreneurship." Part Three describes how the social intrapreneurial process can be understood and managed. In Chapter Seven we clarify what social intrapreneurship is, including its dimensions, antecedents, and consequences, and the challenges of social intrapreneurship. Chapter Eight delves into the details of the social intrapreneurship process. We describe a social intrapreneurship management model and discuss the different roles that different levels of management have in the social intrapreneurship process.

Social entrepreneurship is a rapidly growing field of study and practice. In the final part of the book, we consider a number of emerging trends and issues. In response to citizen pressure, the public sector in the United States has instituted a number of innovations. In Chapter Nine we discuss the nature of public sector entrepreneurship. Recent initiatives include the new public management, reinventing government, the new public service, and others.

Social entrepreneurship often takes place in cooperative relationships. This is the topic of Chapter Ten. We consider this at two levels: first, how organizations work together in social ventures, and second, how organizations in different sectors need to work together to deal with the most complex problems. Finally, developments are under way to establish new legal forms that span sectors. In our final chapter, we discuss how new media are being used by social entrepreneurs. New media can be used for information sharing, fundraising, and stakeholder engagement. The implications of these developments are discussed.

OUR APPROACH

In recent years, management scholars have drawn increasing attention to the consequences that can occur when management decision making does not make use of the best available evidence. The *Harvard Business Review* summarized the opinions of Jeffrey Pfeffer and Robert Sutton on the problem:

> The good news? Evidence abounds to help us make the right choices. The bad? Many of us ignore it—relying instead on outdated information or our own experience to arrive at decisions. Some of us fall victim to hype about "miracle" management cures, or we adopt other companies' "best practices" without asking whether they'll work just as well in our organizations. Result? Poor-quality decisions that waste time and money . . . [15]

The solution is for managers to use "evidence-based management" in decision making. This includes demanding evidence of the efficacy of proposed actions, clarifying the logic behind that evidence, encouraging managers to experiment with new ideas, and insisting that managers stay current in their field—and provide continuing professional education opportunities to help them do so.[16] Denise Rousseau explains further:

> Evidence-based management means translating principles based on best evidence into organizational practices. Through evidence-based management, practicing managers develop into experts who make organizational decisions informed by social science and organizational research . . . This links how managers make decisions to the continually expanding research base on cause-effect principles underlying human behavior and organizational actions.[17]

While there are challenges to this approach, including the difficulties in interpreting scientific evidence and the need to adapt principles to specific settings, we firmly believe that when solid principles are available they should be the basis of management action. Fortunately, in the social entrepreneurship field we have a growing body of theory and research to draw on to help managers.

Evidence-based management plays a critical role in the development of managers as *reflective practitioners*. Donald Schön defines reflective practitioners as those who can draw upon both the technical knowledge of their fields and their own action as they engage in their practice.[18] This is especially important for social entrepreneurs, as they need to both understand the limitations of past solutions and develop their own new approaches to social value creation.

As they do this, they are likely to encounter the three types of professional practice situations that Schön describes, and they will also need the types of knowledge appropriate to deal with them. The first are familiar or identifiable situations that can be solved by the application of knowledge derived from the body of professional knowledge. This will involve "the application of theories and techniques derived from systematic, preferable scientific research to the solution of the instrumental problems of practice."[19] Throughout our book, we provide this type of knowledge by explaining the theories and research that have been used to advance our understanding of social entrepreneurship.

A second type of situation described by Schön will involve problems that initially are not clear and have no clear link between the problem and available theories and techniques. This situation is particularly likely to arise as social entrepreneurs work on developing new approaches to problems that have defied solution in the past. In these situations, practitioners should engage in rule-governed inquiry. According to Schön, this will involve "following rules for data gathering, inference, and hypothesis testing, which allow him to make clear connections between presenting situations and the body of professional knowledge, where such connections are initially problematic."[20] Our approach also fosters an appreciation of this approach. The grounding in the literature of the field of social entrepreneurship that we provide will instill in social entrepreneurs an appreciation of modes of inquiry used by management scientists and standards by which to judge both established and proposed approaches.

Finally, Schön notes that in any field of practice there are situations when practitioners not only follow rules of inquiry but also sometimes respond to surprising findings by inventing new rules in order to "make new sense of uncertain, unique, or conflicting situations."[21] In these situations, practice is more artistry than technique. In this sense, the critically important applied science and research-based techniques are augmented by "an art of problem framing, and art of implementation, and an art of improvisation."[22] These arts are best-taught in real-life practicums or internships. In this book, we use cases to provide readers with examples of how social entrepreneurs responded to the situations they found themselves in and developed innovative processes and solutions. We hope that these practical examples will provide guidance to social entrepreneurs as they encounter their own novel situations.

PART ONE

Social Entrepreneurship: Concept and Context

The Many Faces of Social Entrepreneurship

In this chapter, we provide a survey of the many faces of social entrepreneurship, summarized as four Ws: What is social entrepreneurship? Who are the social entrepreneurs? Why social entrepreneurship? Where does it occur?

WHAT IS SOCIAL ENTREPRENEURSHIP?

The term "social entrepreneurship" was used first in the literature as early as the 1960s, but it was not until the term was adopted by Bill Drayton in the early 1980s that it began to come into widespread use. Despite a recent growth of interest in social entrepreneurship, researchers have yet to reach consensus on the definition of this emerging concept. For example, the terms "social entrepreneurship" and "social enterprise" are sometimes used interchangeably, which leads to confusion. To illustrate the variety of the understanding of the concept, we provide a sample of definitions of social entrepreneurship in Table 1.1.

The wide variety of existing definitions can be roughly categorized as broad and narrow. A narrow definition of social entrepreneurship refers mainly to earned-income strategies for nonprofit organizations,[1] or what Dees and Anderson call the "social enterprise" school of thought.[2] Enterprise, as the name suggests, is the main topic of concern in the social enterprise school of thought. It is defined as an entrepreneurial, nonprofit project that helps generate revenue as well as serve the society. This perspective focuses on producing income flows other than collecting revenue from grants and subsidies. Also, it endorses the scheme of business techniques to improve the working of nonprofits in order to make them more entrepreneurial. Social enterprise school has a commercial

Table 1.1
Definitions of Social Entrepreneurship

Author(s), Year	Definition
Austin, Stevenson, & Wei-Skillern (2006)[3]	Innovative, social value creating activity that can occur within or across the nonprofit, business, or government sectors (p. 2).
Brinckerhoff (2000)[4]	Social entrepreneurs have the following characteristics: • They are willing to take reasonable risk on behalf of the people their organization serves; • They are constantly looking for new ways to serve their constituencies, and to add value to existing services; • They understand that all resource allocations are really stewardship investments; • They weigh social and financial return of each of these investments; • They understand the difference between needs and wants; and • They always keep the mission first, but know that without the money, there is no mission output (p. 12).
Center for the Advancement of Social Entrepreneurship (2008)[5]	Innovative and resourceful approaches to addressing social problems. These approaches could be pursued through for-profit, nonprofit, or hybrid organizations.
Dees (1998)[6]	Social entrepreneurs play the role of change agents in the social sector, by: • adopting a mission to create and sustain social value (not just private value); • recognizing and relentlessly pursuing new opportunities to serve that mission; • engaging in a process of continuous innovation, adaptation, and learning; • acting boldly without being limited by resources currently in hand; • exhibiting a heightened sense of accountability to the constituencies served and for the outcomes created (p. 4).

Author(s), Year	Definition
Frumkin (2002)[7]	Social entrepreneurs have a combination of the supply-side orientation and the instrumental rationale, providing a vehicle for entrepreneurship that creates enterprises that combine commercial and charitable goals (p. 130).
Light (2006a)[8]	A social entrepreneur is an individual, group, network, organization, or alliance of organizations that seeks sustainable, large-scale change through pattern-breaking ideas in what governments, nonprofits, and businesses do to address significant social problems or how they do it.
Martin & Osberg (2007)[9]	Social entrepreneurship has the following three components. 1. Identifying a stable but inherently unjust equilibrium that causes the exclusion, marginalization, or suffering of a segment of humanity that lacks the financial means or political clout to achieve any transformative benefit on its own. 2. Identifying an opportunity in this unjust equilibrium, developing a social value proposition, and bringing to bear inspiration, creativity, direct action, courage, and fortitude, thereby challenging the stable state's hegemony. 3. Forging a new, stable equilibrium that releases trapped potential or alleviates the suffering of the targeted group, and through imitation and the creation of a stable ecosystem around the new equilibrium ensuring a better future for the targeted group and even society at large (p. 35).
Mort, Weerawardena, & Carnegie (2003)[10]	1. Social entrepreneurs are first driven by the social mission of creating better social value than their competitors which results in them exhibiting entrepreneurially virtuous behavior. 2. They exhibit a balanced judgment, a coherent unity of purpose, and action in the face of complexity. 3. Social entrepreneurs explore and recognize opportunities to create better social value for their clients. 4. Social entrepreneurs display innovativeness, proactiveness, and risk taking propensity in their key decision making process.

(Continued)

Table 1.1 *Continued*	
Author(s), Year	**Definition**
Peredor & McLean (2006)[11]	Social entrepreneurship is exercised where a person or group:
	• aims at creating social value, either exclusively or at least in some prominent way;
	• shows a capacity to recognize and take advantage of opportunities to create value;
	• employs innovation, ranging from outright invention to adapting someone else's novelty, in creating and/or distributing social value;
	• is willing to accept an above average degree of risk in creating and disseminating social value; and
	• is unusually resourceful in being relatively undaunted by scarce assets in pursuing their social venture (p. 64).
Pomerantz (2003)[12]	Social entrepreneurship can be defined as the development of innovative, mission-supporting, earned income, job creating or licensing ventures undertaken by individual social entrepreneurs, nonprofits, or nonprofits in association with for-profits (p. 25).
Thompson, Alvy, & Lees (2000)[13]	Social entrepreneurs are people who realize where there is an opportunity to satisfy some unmet need that the state welfare will not meet, and who gather together the necessary resources (generally people, often volunteers, money, and premises) and use these to "make a difference" (p. 328).
Young (1986)[14]	Nonprofit entrepreneurs are the innovators who found new organizations, develop and implement new programs and methods, organize and expand new services, and redirect the activities of faltering organizations (p. 162).

knowledge foundation similar to the social innovation school. The social enterprise school is rooted in commercial entrepreneurship practice, which believes that entrepreneurship is a method of creating and administrating organizations.

A broad definition of social entrepreneurship tends to include all types of innovative, social-value-creating activities that can occur within or across sectors,[15] or what Dees and Anderson call the "social innovation" school of thought, which sees social entrepreneurs as people who attempt to solve societal problems and meet its needs in a novel way. This school aims to find new and improved methods to deal with society's problems or meet its needs. This can be done if social entrepreneurs launch a nonprofit or a profitable company. The private foundations that encourage planned growth of the sector and their creators have contributed a lot to the basics of both schools of thought within the American tradition. The social innovation school of thought takes its roots from profit-making businesses regarding discovery, evaluation, and exploitation of opportunities—opportunities obtained, in the case of social entrepreneurship, through fulfillment of social needs in novel ways.[16]

Opponents of the narrow definition emphasize that earned income is only a means to a social end, and that the fundamental driver of social entrepreneurship is innovation and social impact. On the other hand, opponents to the broad definition are concerned that it confuses innovation with entrepreneurship, and that it "becomes a convenient label for almost any new approach that has a social outcome."[17]

For the purpose of this book, we follow Tschirhart and Bielefeld to define social entrepreneurship as *the pursuit of social objectives with innovative methods, through the creation of products, organizations, and practices that yield and sustain social benefits.*[18]

A better understanding of the social entrepreneurship concept also requires that we examine the similarities and differences between social entrepreneurship and commercial entrepreneurship. Austin, Stevenson, and Wei-Skillern provide a detailed examination of this question.[19] They hold that differences between social and commercial entrepreneurship are the results of four major variables:

- Market failure—creates different entrepreneurial opportunities for social entrepreneurship and commercial entrepreneurship
- Mission—results in fundamental differences between social entrepreneurship and commercial entrepreneurship
- Resource mobilization—requires different management approaches in social entrepreneurship and commercial entrepreneurship
- Performance measurement—social entrepreneurship necessitates the measurement of social value in addition to commercial value

Austin and colleagues discuss the management implications of social entrepreneurship based on Sahlman's PCDO model, which states that the management of entrepreneurship necessitates the creation of a dynamic fit between People (P), Context (C), the Deal (D), and the Opportunity (O). They argue that social entrepreneurship differs from commercial entrepreneurship in each of the four elements. The most distinct difference is in Opportunity, due to differences in organizational missions and responses to market failure. The impact of Context varies due to the way that the interaction of mission and performance measurements influences management. The role of People varies due to differences in the difficulties of resource mobilization. Finally, the terms of the Deal are fundamentally different, due to the way resources must be mobilized, as well as the ambiguities of performance measurement.

To facilitate the distinction between these two types of entrepreneurship, Austin, Stevenson, and Wei-Skillern recommend that the Deal be replaced with what they term the "social value proposition"—a conceptualization of the social value or benefits produced—and People be replaced with economic and human resources.

Moreover, due to its difference from commercial entrepreneurship, they maintain that the management of social entrepreneurship should take into account the following issues:

- The centrality of social value—this must be the first and foremost consideration.
- Attention to organizational alignment—both internal and external alignment will be needed to deliver social value.
- Organizational boundaries—they may need to be more flexible, because social value may be enhanced by cooperation instead of competition.

WHO ARE THE SOCIAL ENTREPRENEURS?

We know who the social entrepreneurs are: Susan B. Anthony (United States), William "Bill" Drayton (United States), Florence Nightingale (U.K.), Vinoba Bhave (India), Y.C. James Yen (China), Muhammad Yunus (Bangladesh)—the list goes on. Of course, it is one thing to identify the famous ones, and quite another thing to try to provide a definition that can capture the key aspects shared by these and many other social entrepreneurs. In some way social entrepreneurs are like the arts: they seem to defy definition; they refuse to share a common denominator. This perhaps explains why scholars and practitioners alike are having trouble settling on the "best" definition for social entrepreneur.

However, the effort to find common denominators has never stopped. Researchers have hypothesized that there are certain individual qualities that make up a social entrepreneur. Social entrepreneurs share many of the same qualities that regular entrepreneurs share: their ventures are typically of high risk, they are characteristically skilled at stretching resources more efficiently, and typically they have a new idea that fills a niche in the market. What separates them from regular entrepreneurs is their drive for social change and the "potential payoff, with its lasting, transformative benefit to society, that sets the field and its practitioners apart."[20] Their visions include a permanent change to the status quo. In addition to changing the social landscape, social entrepreneurs do not operate in the current system, optimizing the current possibilities, but "instead find a wholly new way of approaching the problem." Social entrepreneurs are not merely trying to make the best out of the current situation, but instead create a wholly new situation in which to operate. A social entrepreneur, therefore, has a business and social mission, and through that mission changes the way the system functions.

The following are some common behavior categories found in existing definitions of social entrepreneurship:

• **Balanced Judgment**: The social entrepreneur literature often refers to balance, as in judgment and in managing the interest of multiple stakeholders. The relationships that social entrepreneurs manage are complex, and this balance assists the manager with serving both the mission and the financial needs of the organization.[21]

• **Opportunistic**: Experts point out that social entrepreneurs excel at recognizing and taking advantage of opportunities to deliver in a way that provides social value and honors the mission.[22] Social entrepreneurs "act boldly" and are not limited by resources they currently control.[23]

• **Virtuous**: The social entrepreneur has to be or become entrepreneurially virtuous in both behaviors and actions, such as integrity, compassion, and inclusiveness.[24]

• **Risk Endurance**: When discussing the term social entrepreneur, it is understood that these individuals are engaging in a social enterprise that involves risk.[25]

Young identifies seven types of social entrepreneurs that each display a combination of traits and motivations:[26]

- *Independent* entrepreneurs, who search and find an entry into small organizations where it is relatively easy to get in
- *Searchers*, who want to get away from rigid rules and awkward organizations
- *Power seekers*, who give credit to larger organizations for providing opportunities for advancement
- *Conservers*, who want security and well-set traditions and seek established and stable organizations for providing them with that
- *Professionals*, who want to follow their career and search for organizations that can provide them with the platform
- *Artists*, who search for organizations that can sustain the work they want to do and can help them get recognized
- *Income-seekers*, who have no goals other than to enhance their income potential, be it in a large or small organization[27]

Based on a review of the existing literature, Mair and Noboa summarize the unique characteristics of social entrepreneurs in terms of:

• Traits and skills, including: vision and fortitude, creativity, a collective style of leadership, the ability to pounce on opportunities, the capability of working as a team, and a community-oriented motivation factor.[28] Other characteristics might include passion, a clear purpose, bravery, values, commitment, and a business style of thinking. Along with this there should be planning, flexibility, willingness to plan, and customer focus.[29]

• Behavioral attributes, such as openness to others' feelings, good communication skills, determination, less concern about failure, ingenuity, trustworthiness, competence to satisfy the needs of the customers, guts to accept social criticism, a good working capacity, and a target orientation.

• Context and background, such as social, moral, and educational background; previous entrepreneurial experience; social entrepreneurs' involvement with the social sector or their exposure to social issues; and the like.[30]

Helpful as it is, research on the traits and characteristics of social entrepreneurs alone may be insufficient and potentially misleading. Researcher William Gartner draws an interesting equivalence between the problem of a trait approach to entrepreneurship and that of recruiting baseball players based on their personality profiles:

Based on upbringing and experience we could document a baseball player's locus of control, need for achievement, tolerance of ambiguity, and other characteristics that we thought must make for good baseball playing . . . Yet, this type of research simply ignores the obvious—that is, the baseball player, in fact, plays baseball. Baseball involves a set of behaviors—running, pitching, throwing, catching, hitting, sliding, etc.— that baseball players exhibit. To be a baseball player means that an individual is behaving as a baseball player. A baseball player is not something one is, it is something one does, and the definition of a baseball player cannot stray far from this obvious fact without getting into difficulty.[31]

WHY SOCIAL ENTREPRENEURSHIP?

Why does social entrepreneurship occur? We identify both motivation- and capacity-related reasons. We also discuss briefly the impact social entrepreneurship may have in social value generation. Figure 1.1 illustrates how the factors work together to trigger social entrepreneurship.

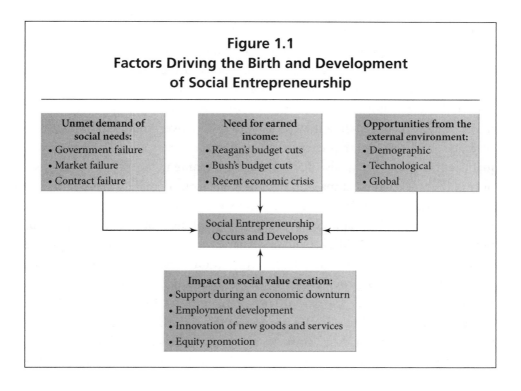

Figure 1.1
Factors Driving the Birth and Development of Social Entrepreneurship

Unmet demand of social needs:
- Government failure
- Market failure
- Contract failure

Need for earned income:
- Reagan's budget cuts
- Bush's budget cuts
- Recent economic crisis

Opportunities from the external environment:
- Demographic
- Technological
- Global

Social Entrepreneurship Occurs and Develops

Impact on social value creation:
- Support during an economic downturn
- Employment development
- Innovation of new goods and services
- Equity promotion

The *first and foremost* reason is the fact that the demand in terms of social needs is not yet fully met. In other words, the demand, such as the need to feed and house the homeless in a big city, outstrips the ability of existing individuals and organizations to meet this demand. The desire to do more to meet pressing social needs than is possible with existing resources motivates entrepreneurial behavior. In a 2012 commentary in *New York Times*, columnist David Bornstein wrote, "Today, as problems have grown increasingly complex, a big question is how we can reorganize the problem-solving work of society so it is more responsive to needs. Three generations ago, the federal government could address many forms of injustice through legislation—mandating a 40-hour workweek, instituting a minimum wage, establishing housing codes. Today, our societal challenges—in education, health, or the environment—demand innovation from many directions."[32]

Several theories explain why there always have been and may increasingly be social needs that are unaddressed or underaddressed. First, market failure and government failure theories are concerned with collective action problems around the provision of public goods or collective goods. A public good is a good that is both nonexcludable (that is, there is no easy way to prevent nonpaying customers from accessing the good once it is produced) and nonrival (that is, its consumption by one person does not diminish the simultaneous consumption by another). Examples of public goods include national defense and clean air. A collective good (for example, the performing arts) is a good that is excludable but still nonrival. Public goods and collective goods may lead to market failure, and therefore they provide roles for government, nonprofit organizations, and social entrepreneurs. Government can step in to correct market inefficiencies, but it may also fail, because government provides public goods only at the level that meet majoritarian, homogeneous demand (that is, that satisfy the median voter). Thus nonprofits and social entrepreneurs step in to meet residual unsatisfied demand for public goods resulting from the heterogeneous preferences of citizens. Market inefficiencies also occur in the case of private goods: according to contract failure theory, information asymmetry between customers and service providers leads to the breakdown of ordinary contractual mechanisms; nonprofits and social entrepreneurs arise in situations in which consumers feel unable to evaluate accurately the quantity or quality of the service a firm produces for them. In such situations, consumers may find nonprofit organizations to be more trustworthy than for-profit businesses because of the nondistribution constraint (that is, a nonprofit is prohibited from distributing its net earnings among individuals who oversee the organization).[33]

The *second* broad reason why social entrepreneurship occurs is that, for nonprofits, there is a need for enhanced revenue generation or greater internal efficiencies to financially sustain operations. Nonprofits have a long history of earning income. For decades nonprofits had been carrying out traditional commercial activities, such as gift shops and secondhand clothing stores, to provide services to their constituencies. Nonetheless, since the early 1980s the picture has changed. During the Reagan administration, due to the economic recession and budget cuts in social services, numerous nonprofits were forced to consider or initiate earned-income ventures to make up for lost government funding. In 2000, when the George W. Bush administration threatened a series of budget cuts, nonprofits had to embark on a new round of revenue-seeking efforts. Conservative outlooks, both within and outside of the government, further urged nonprofits to invest in market-based solutions to social problems, which included paying more attention to earned income as a source of nonprofit sustainability. The early 2000s recession triggered by the burst of the dot-com bubble, and most recently the Great Recession triggered by the collapse of the housing bubble and the failure of financial institutions, had significant impacts on federal and state economies and changed priorities of government expenditures. Diminished political support for social welfare spending at the federal level, combined with state budget deficits, resulted in significant budget cuts in many nonprofits. Because government funding has become increasingly unpredictable or even unreliable, nonprofits have substantially changed the way they do business and have been forced to find more innovative ways to carry out their missions.[34]

The *third* reason for social entrepreneurship is related to changes in the external environment, which provide social-value-creation opportunities that did not previously exist. We identify four factors in the external environment in which changes may introduce opportunities to serve broader social needs and create new forms of value. These factors are demographics, technology, globalization, and potential impact on social value creation.

Demographics

Demographic factors refer to the characteristics of a human population, such as age, gender, level of education, level of income, family, race/ethnicity, and geographic distribution. The demographic profile of the United States has undergone some important changes since the 1950s: in addition to growth in sheer numbers, the U.S. population is growing disproportionately older and becoming more racially and ethnically diverse.[35] Similar trends are observed in Europe.[36] These trends will likely lead to newly emerging social needs and open up opportunities for social entrepreneurs. In many developing countries, with more access to education and the growth of the middle class in recent years, a markedly increasing number of people now have the capacity to be change makers and initiate social entrepreneurial activities.

As an integral part of this demographic transition, women are playing a more significant role in the movements of social entrepreneurship. In the United States, women account for over two thirds of the nonprofit workforce, and the percentage of women in leadership positions (for example, chief executives, fiscal officers) in nonprofit organizations has been greater than the percentage of men.[37] This overrepresentation of women in nonprofit employment suggests that the nonprofit sector might provide a more robust supply of aspiring women social entrepreneurs than do other sectors. In the United Kingdom, there is evidence that women are more likely to be social entrepreneurs than commercial entrepreneurs, and that the difference between male and female levels of entrepreneurship is much smaller for social entrepreneurs than it is for their commercial counterparts.[38] This increasingly important role of women in social entrepreneurship can be partially attributed to the fact that more women are now receiving education from professional schools (business, public affairs, social work, and so on), which are fostering an ecosystem for women students. Take Wharton San Francisco as an example. According to Wharton San Francisco's COO Bernie Birt, the school is working toward attracting highly talented women to their programs, and the 2014 class of the school's MBA for Executives program is up to 19 percent female. Even if this is not close to the 50 percent mark, compared to prior years, it is moving in the right direction.[39] Moreover, as discussed in the Introduction, there is also growing interest in professional schools around the world for a more engaging social entrepreneurship curriculum.

Technological Factors

The technological environment refers to innovations, institutions, and activities associated with creating new knowledge and translating that knowledge into new products and services.[40] In the United States, a milestone event in the technological environment was the passage of the Bayh-Dole Act in 1980. Bayh-Dole allows a university, small business, or nonprofit institution to retain property rights of inventions funded by the federal government and to commercialize their research advances.[41] Prior to this act, it was difficult to transfer inventions produced by universities and research institutions using government funding to the industry or the public, as the government retained the licenses to all patents from government-funded research. This law significantly increases inventors' incentive to pursue innovation and entrepreneurship.

Moreover, the Internet and social media have provided an unprecedented arsenal of resources for the success and collaboration of many social entrepreneurs. The U.S.-based nonprofit peer-to-peer microfinance organization Zidisha is a good example. Capitalizing on the rapid diffusion of internet and mobile technologies in developing countries, Zidisha provides an eBay-style microlending platform where computer-literate, low-income entrepreneurs in developing countries (borrowers) can engage in direct dialogue with individual web users worldwide (lenders) without intermediaries, thus making small business loan transactions at a lower cost than has ever before been possible in most developing countries.[42]

Globalization

Globalization provides opportunities for entrepreneurs to make better use of the resources of some countries to address social needs common to many countries. VisionSpring offers a good example: a social enterprise with a mission to ensure access to equitable and affordable eyeglasses for people in the developing world, VisionSpring provides eye tests and eyeglasses to lower-income customers in more than twenty countries, including Bangladesh, El Salvador, India, and South Africa.

Although globalization provides a lot of opportunities, it also requires enormous localization efforts from social entrepreneurs in order to solve local problems. Proximity Designs is a social venture that aims to reduce poverty for rural families in Myanmar (Burma) by designing and delivering low-cost products and services. To customize the delivery of agricultural-development services in rural Myanmar, Proximity Designs established a local design lab in Myanmar where a team of ethnographers and product designers worked closely with low-income farmers to develop such products as foot-powered irrigation pumps, water storage tanks, and solar-lighting systems. To ensure that farmers can afford to use its products and services, Proximity Designs developed a financing program that make small loans available to farmers at modest rates. They also offered after-sales support and repair services to user households.[43]

Potential

Finally, social entrepreneurship is further spurred by its potential to contribute significantly to our fight against economic downturns and social value generation. Among the few major impacts generated by social entrepreneurship are (1) support during an economic downturn, (2) employment development, (3) innovation, and (4) equity promotion.

1. Support During an Economic Downturn Social entrepreneurship becomes especially important during an economic recession, helping to address the widening gap between capitalized needs and social needs. In a bad economy, many become homeless or struggle to survive on a reduced income. Adults as well as children must adapt and cope, and various organizations must meet an increasing demand for cash or in-kind donations to support these families. Personal counseling, career counseling, and job training become particularly important to help these families remain stable. Social entrepreneurs, with their passion for solving social problems, have a critical role to play.[44]

2. Employment Development Social entrepreneurship creates jobs and employment—a major and vital economic value in itself. Estimates suggest that anywhere from 1 to 7 percent of workers are employed in the social entrepreneurship sector.[45] For example, based on a population survey of 22,500 individuals across the U.K., a Global Entrepreneurship Monitor (GEM) study reported that about 3.2 percent of the working-age U.K. population could be classified as social entrepreneurs (defined in the survey as being involved in founding and running a social venture younger than forty-two months).[46] The GEM study found that social entrepreneurs are disproportionately more effective at job creation than other businesses. On average, all forms of socially oriented organizations create more jobs than mainstream entrepreneurial enterprises. Specifically, those social enterprises with mixed revenue streams create five times as many jobs as mainstream entrepreneurial businesses; however, it is worth noting that they also have over six times the amount of turnover as mainstream entrepreneurial businesses.[47]

3. Innovation   Innovation is often instrumental in improving social welfare and promoting social development. Social enterprise can excel in this area, as it is more free to innovate in developing new services and goods without financial expectations from shareholders or the red tape of government. With the increase in social entrepreneurial initiatives, issues like mental health, crime, HIV, drug abuse, and illiteracy are being handled in innovative ways.[48]

4. Equity Promotion   Social entrepreneurship, if appropriately designed and implemented, fosters a more equitable society. It does so by disrupting what is currently unjust and deficient and by addressing social issues more creatively and effectively. Moreover, some of the most vulnerable populations that have particular difficulty finding employment (homeless, disabled, unemployed people, women facing gender discrimination, at-risk youth) benefit from both the employment and the job training offered by social enterprises.[49]

WHERE DOES SOCIAL ENTREPRENEURSHIP OCCUR?

Social entrepreneurship can occur in all three sectors: public, business, and nonprofit. It can also occur in networked settings, in which public, nonprofit, and business organizations work together toward common goals. Below we provide a set of examples of social entrepreneurship in public, business, and nonprofit sectors respectively and their intersection areas.

In the *public sector*, social entrepreneurship is closely related to innovation and can mean different things in different contexts. It might indicate new ways of organizing work (such as Public Private Partnerships), new ways of rewarding employees (such as pay for performance), or new ways of communicating with the public (such as government blogs and social media sites). It might take the form of policy innovations, service innovations, and innovations in other fields like democracy (such as e-voting) or international affairs (such as the International Criminal Court). Some innovations are so radical that they are regarded as systemic (such as National Health Service in the U.K. and Obamacare in the U.S.).[50]

Garbage collection in the city of Phoenix, Arizona, offers a good example of social entrepreneurship in the public sector at the local level. In the 1990s, the city of Phoenix put out their contract for garbage collection to public bid. The public works department, which is responsible for providing external services to Phoenix residents as well as internal support functions for other city departments, bid along with the private sector. At first, public works lost most of their business, but over time they learned how to compete and win. Though it is a government agency, public works' garbage collection business is "an enterprise function with all services supported by service fees charged to residential and commercial customers."[51]

Some governments in the United States have recently made efforts to institutionalize innovation and to foster entrepreneurial initiatives. At the federal level, the Obama administration established the Office of Social Innovation and Civic Participation to support projects that combine public and private resources to solve social problems. In New York, the state and city partnered to support the Center for Court Innovation, a nonprofit organization aiming at experimenting with innovative approaches to public safety problems.[52]

Governments in European and Asian countries have taken similar steps. For example, Denmark's Ministry of Finance set up a unit to promote new creativity—such as the creation of a single account for financial transactions with citizens. The Economics and Business Affairs Ministry has restructured itself to be project-based rather than function-based, and has established its own internal consultancy, MindLab, that provides a systematic approach to public sector innovation. Singapore has provided funding for innovations in public service delivery through the so-called "Enterprise Challenge" program, which was run through the Prime Minister's office. One project of the program is the "virtual policing center" through which non-urgent inquiries are routed to the Singapore Police Force, and teleconferencing for incarcerated individuals to interact with their relatives. It is reported that these initiatives could achieve savings ten times greater than their costs.[53]

Public sector unions can be sources of innovation and champions for faster adoption. Public sector unions primarily represent the interests of employees within public sector organizations. Unions representing professionals and manual workers are sometimes perceived as resisting innovations, particularly those that involve changes to demarcations between industries. However, unions have often helped drive innovation: the Fire Brigades Union in the U.K., for example, helps firemen find part time employment as benefits advisors alongside their roles as firemen; the local branch of Unison—one of the U.K.'s largest trade unions—in Newcastle upon Tyne was key to the introduction of a new IT system for the Council. In Norway, the Model Municipalities initiative brings together multiple stakeholders including politicians, management, and trade unions in a program for upgrading public services.[54]

Social entrepreneurship in the *business sector* goes beyond "doing well by doing good," emphasizing the combination of business and ethics, particularly corporate social responsibility. In this sector, social entrepreneurship is conducted by a for-profit organization that has clear charitable causes or even operates a nonprofit subsidiary to distribute its products or services or redistribute its revenue and profit. An excellent example is TOMS Shoes, a shoe company with a charitable cause: "to create a better tomorrow by taking compassionate action today." Their approach is simple: for every pair sold, a new pair is donated to a child in need of shoes. Since TOMS launched in 2006, over ten million pairs of shoes have been given to children in more than sixty countries. Recently TOMS has begun selling eyewear: similar to their shoes, with every pair of glasses sold, TOMS helps give sight to an individual in need.[55]

Pura Vida Coffee is a Seattle-based company that sells fair-trade certified organic coffee from third world countries. While this business model is not really that "entrepreneurial," the company makes itself different by using its profits to help coffee growers and producers of the third world. Before founding the company, cofounder John Sage worked at Microsoft and was already one of Microsoft's early millionaires. But he felt "money wasn't enough for him" and "there had to be more." He thought, "Americans spend somewhere between $15 billion and $20 billion every year on coffee, and if there's an opportunity to just get some small piece of that . . ." The idea was developed into a venture when he talked to his college friend Chris Dearnley, who had been struggling to find steady funding for charitable programs in Costa Rica. The company sells coffee mainly on college campuses and churches. With its slogan, "Create Good," it provides living wages to farmers and producers of coffee and donates money (including its own profits and contributions it encourages from its distributors and private donations) to help the education and healthcare programs in coffee growing countries. It has grown into one of the largest distributors of fair-trade organic coffee in the country, and has been able to attain significant social and environmental outcomes, demonstrating that financial bottom line and social performance can go hand in hand.[56]

Fifteen was founded by English celebrity chef Jamie Oliver in 2002. It began as an ambitious effort to offer disadvantaged youths (ages eighteen to twenty-four) an opportunity to develop a career path for themselves through the art of cooking and hospitality. The restaurant initiative was named for the fifteen young people who originally entered this apprenticeship program funded by Jamie's restaurant. Since the first establishment opened, in London, *Fifteen* has:

- Delivered delicious dishes to diners and opened two other restaurants in Amsterdam and Cornwall
- Trained hundreds of unemployed young people to be chefs and inspired many of them to pursue successful careers in the restaurant business
- Reinforced the value of local produce and cooking techniques[57]

Two examples are offered to illustrate social entrepreneurship in the *nonprofit sector*. *Real Change* is a weekly street newspaper based in Seattle, Washington. It is written by professional staff and sold or delivered by vendors, most of whom are poor or homeless, as an alternative to panhandling. The paper covers a variety of social justice issues, including homelessness and poverty and also mainstream news. Each copy costs the vendors about 35 cents; they sell these to customers for a $1 "donation" and keep the difference, plus any tips. A 501(c)3 nonprofit organization, *Real Change* has been operating since 1994. According to *Real Change*'s 2012 Annual Report and survey, 43 percent of vendors are currently homeless and 49 percent were previously homeless. Of those surveyed, 44 percent are housed (of which over half are in subsidized housing), 17 percent are sleeping outdoors, 11 percent are sleeping in shelters, 8 percent are "staying with friends or family," and 6 percent are sleeping in cars. Less than 8 percent of vendors have never been homeless.[58]

OneWorld Health is the first nonprofit pharmaceutical company in the United States. It was founded by Drs. Victoria Hale and Ahvie Herskowitz in 2000, and received 501(c)(3) tax-exempt status in 2001. The mission of the organization is to discover, develop, and deliver safe, effective, and affordable new treatments and interventions for people in developing countries, with an emphasis on diseases that disproportionately afflict children. OneWorld Health has established its unique strength by utilizing and integrating the scientific and manufacturing capacity of the developing world. Working with partners across the world, the organization identifies potential new medicines for neglected infectious diseases afflicting the most vulnerable populations, assesses the safety and effectiveness of investigational drugs, follows international ethical standards for research, collaborates to manufacture and distribute new medicines, and works to ensure their affordability and availability for distribution. The model of OneWorld Health challenges the traditional profitability thinking of the pharmaceutical industry and redesigns the entire value chain of drug delivery. The model is sustainable because it manages to create value for everyone involved. As researchers Seelos and Mair note, "Biotechnology companies have found an appealing outlet for idle intellectual property, and compassionate research and development efforts have attracted scientists and volunteers to donate time, effort, and knowledge to the project."[59] The organization has received funding from a number of influential donors, including the Bill & Melinda Gates Foundation (the Institute received 96 percent of its funding from the Foundation as of 2006), Amgen, Chiron Corporation, Gap, Lehman Brothers, Pfizer, Vital Spark Foundation, and Skoll Foundation.[60]

The interface between public and private/nonprofit sectors is a fertile ground for innovation and social entrepreneurship. Relatedly, public-private partnerships are a common form of venture. One of the earliest examples is a partnership between Marriott (a hospitality company) and the March of Dimes (a public charity that works to improve the health of mothers and babies) to conduct a cause-focused campaign in 1976. For Marriott, the goal was to generate highly cost-effective public relations and media coverage for the opening of their two-hundred-acre family entertainment center, Marriott's Great America in Santa Clara, California. For the March of Dimes, the goal was to fundraise for its cause. The campaign was highly successful: it provided 2.5 million dollars in donations to the March of Dimes, while stimulating the record-breaking opening of Great America and providing hundreds of thousands of dollars in free publicity.[61]

Another example is a joint venture between American Express and the Statue of Liberty Restoration Fund in 1983. During this period, the Statue of Liberty was undergoing extensive renovations, and the company came up with the idea to donate to the renovation. The promotion spanned the fourth quarter of the year, and the agreed-upon amount was one cent for each use of its cards and one dollar for every new card issued. The campaign succeeded in increasing the profits of American Express; the company saw a 28-percent increase in card usage and issued numerous new cards. A total of $1.7 million was donated to the Statue of Liberty-Ellis Island Foundation. (Note, however, that more than $6 million was spent on campaign promotions.[62])

Social entrepreneurship can also occur *inside or outside an existing organization*. It occurs when individuals identify an idea for social innovation and take the risk to implement the idea by establishing a new organization (that is, an independent start-up). A prominent example is the Grameen Bank, which grew from a project undertaken by Dr. Muhammad Yunus at Chittagong University in 1976 and became a groundbreaking social business that provides collateral-free micro loans for self-employment to millions of women villagers in Bangladesh.[63] Another example is Kiva, an online microfinance organization with a mission to connect people through lending to alleviate poverty and an innovative approach that leverages the Internet and a worldwide network of microfinance institutions. Social entrepreneurship also occurs when individuals develop innovative initiatives aimed at social causes *within* established organizations (that is, social intrapreneurship). For example, in his role as the chief information officer of the American Red Cross, Steve Cooper guided the introduction of a first-ever national call center during Hurricane Katrina to provide emergency financial assistance to the more than four million people displaced from their homes.[64]

CONCLUDING THOUGHTS

Social entrepreneurship occurs when there is a new problem to be faced, new technology available that would make things more efficient, or new research discovers a different cause of a social malady or a new treatment for a social issue. Social entrepreneurship does not always have to be novel; it could even be a resurgence of an old technique. For instance, Hassan Fathy, an Egyptian architect working in the 1950s, attempted to revive ancient Egyptian techniques of building using adobe to build clean, safe, spacious, private homes for the poor with almost no material costs.[65] Fathy's work came as a response to governmental housing projects that were small, unventilated, and very costly due to the use of foreign materials such as cement and steel. Although Fathy's attempted housing project failed due to several reasons, his approach was novel and entrepreneurial at a time when progress was defined by western standards.

EXERCISES

Exercise 1.1

This chapter reviews two dominant schools of thought on the definition of social entrepreneurship: the "social enterprise" school and the "social innovation" school. Please identify an example of social entrepreneurship based on each definition, and then use the examples to discuss the merits and limitations of these definitions.

Exercise 1.2

What unique characteristics do social entrepreneurs tend to display? Use a real example to describe the unique traits and/or behavioral patterns of a social entrepreneur.

Exercise 1.3

Why does social entrepreneurship occur? Please describe the factors that lead to the birth and prevalence of social entrepreneurship. In particular, find a social enterprise in your local community that was created during the last economic downturn, and explain how it has addressed a community need.

Social Entrepreneurship as Organizational Behavior

PaperSeed Foundation is a 501(c)(3) non-operating foundation dedicated to strengthening education for children and young people in underserved and resource-lacking communities around the globe. The Foundation was founded in 2001 by Michel Robert, a former executive of CellMark Paper—one of the world's largest providers of supply chain services to the pulp and paper industry— and his fellow employees. The name of the Foundation reflected the founders' vision that, similar to the transformation and growth from seeds, education ("words on paper") will plant seeds of knowledge into young minds and help them grow into a better person. Since then, PaperSeed has been working closely with CellMark, business partners of CellMark, and community-based partners in a dozen countries spanning four continents.

During its first ten years, PaperSeed focused its work on Latin America and funded numerous projects and initiatives. In Argentina, for example, PaperSeed donated a house to Casa del Niño (Child's Home) so that elementary school children could have a place to have breakfast and a hot lunch, while high school students could come in for lunch, snacks, and school activities. Other funded projects included the construction of a pre-K facility and playgrounds in Brazil, the construction of elementary and junior high schools in Peru, and many others. Having no full-time staff, PaperSeed was very shoestring and relied entirely on donations and volunteer work.

Across all the projects and initiatives, PaperSeed has relied on the strong support from CellMark to maximize the outcome and impact that it desired to achieve. More specifically, the Foundation has harnessed CellMark's global connections to keep costs low (for example, shipping at a reduced rate or low-cost notebooks/sanitary pads, and the like from the paper/pulp industries). In their Kenyan project, they worked with a customer of CellMark, MegaSoft, which provided a reduced cost for sanitary napkins; received free shipping from a business partner of CellMark, Fr. Meyer's Sohn, from the Philippines to Kenya; received assistance in customers' processing and clearing in Kenya from a CellMark customer, East Africa Packaging; and partnered with a network/social enterprise called ZanaAfrica for distribution.

Over a decade later, PaperSeed had a moment of celebration as the board decided to hire a full-time executive director in 2011 to keep up with expanded global needs and an expanded vision of the Foundation. Aliyya Shelley Mattos, the new figurehead of the Foundation, along with a new board of directors, has ambitious plans to further expand their work. In particular, they consider China an ideal country to include in their portfolio. With educational disparity and needs, in addition to a robust business network, they are hoping to create a network of public, private, and nongovernmental organizations to create innovative solutions for educational opportunities in China.[1]

In the previous chapter, we argued that social entrepreneurship occurs in all types of organizations: social entrepreneurial activities can be found in public, nonprofit, for-profit, and even hybrid organizational forms; they can take place in start-ups as well as in established organizations. Like commercial entrepreneurship, the essential act of social entrepreneurship is *new entry*. In some cases, new entry entails entering a new market or serving a new group of constituencies with an existing product or service; in other cases, it entails entering an established market or serving existing constituencies with a new product or service.

However, all organizations are not created equal in terms of their degree and amount of social entrepreneurship: a job training agency in a local community that extends its current services to a neighboring community that is demographically similar demonstrates some degree of social entrepreneurship, but it certainly does not seem to be as social entrepreneurial as another job training agency that explores an innovative approach to placing the hardest-to-employ individuals into sustainable jobs. It is therefore very important to understand why and how some organizations are more social entrepreneurial than others.

In this chapter, we address this question by conceptualizing social entrepreneurship as organizational behavior. Following prior research, we extend the concepts of "entrepreneurial orientation" (EO)[2] and "entrepreneurial intensity" (EI)[3] into the context of public and nonprofit organizations. The EO construct identifies three key dimensions of entrepreneurial orientation in organizations: risk taking, proactiveness, and innovativeness. The EI construct posits that risk taking, proactiveness, and innovativeness can be termed as the degree of entrepreneurship, and that degree and frequency combine to form EI. However, the two constructs capture the "entrepreneurial" part more effectively than the "social" part of social entrepreneurship, and therefore should be understood in conjunction with the social mission of the organization. We then introduce the concept of "social entrepreneurial orientation" (SEO), which incorporates mission alignment as an independent and dynamic dimension. We conclude the chapter by presenting an approach for measuring SEO.

ENTREPRENEURIAL ORIENTATION

One emerging stream of research has focused on the role of social entrepreneurship as organizational behavior.[4] In particular, several researchers have taken advantage of the progress made in the sister field of commercial entrepreneurship and applied the construct of "entrepreneurial orientation" (EO) to the nonprofit context.

In the field of commercial entrepreneurship, Danny Miller and his colleagues pioneered this line of work by introducing the notion of firm-level entrepreneurship. In a seminal article published three decades ago, he argued that a firm is entrepreneurial when it "engages in product-market innovation, undertakes somewhat risky ventures, and is first to come up with 'proactive' innovations, beating competitors to the punch."[5] Since then, the EO construct has been proposed to conceptualize the processes, practices, and decision-making activities that lead to the act of entrepreneurship.[6] It is a firm-level attribute that is recognizable through the presence of sustained behavioral patterns in terms of three common features:

- Risk taking, which is defined as "the firm's proclivity to engage in risky projects and managers' preference for bold versus cautious acts to achieve firm objectives."

- Innovativeness, which refers to "a firm's tendency to engage in and support new ideas, novelty, experimentation, and creative processes that may result in new products, services, or technological processes."

- Proactiveness, which refers to "processes aimed at anticipating and acting on future needs" by pursuing new opportunities and strategically introducing new products and eliminating old operations.

Researchers disagree over whether EO is a unidimensional or multidimensional construct.[7] If the former, then only firms that exhibit high levels of all EO dimensions (that is, innovativeness, risk taking, and proactiveness) should be regarded as entrepreneurial.[8] If the latter, then the different dimensions of EO can vary independently of each other; that is, entrepreneurial firms can differ along these EO dimensions, depending on the type of entrepreneurial opportunities they pursue.[9]

Extending the EO construct into the context of nonprofit and voluntary organizations, Mort, Weerawardena, and Carnegie argue that social entrepreneurs' decision-making behaviors are premised on the same three key dimensions that are identified for commercial entrepreneurs, that is, tolerance for risk taking, proactiveness, and innovativeness.[10] Later, Weerawardena and Mort propose a multidimensional model that presents social entrepreneurship as a combination of the three aforementioned EO dimensions under the constraints of three conditions within which nonprofit organizations operate: the external environment, their mission, and the necessity to achieve sustainability.[11] According to this model, the organization that most adeptly demonstrates the three EO dimensions while adapting to the constraints of the three conditions is most likely to achieve and sustain success.

This understanding of proactiveness and innovativeness is similar to what is found in the entrepreneurship literature. Social entrepreneurs must be proactive both in anticipating internal and external forces that will affect their work and in strategically responding to opportunities afforded to them. Their analyses and predictions of future conditions give way to strategic plans that adapt to and capitalize on emerging trends. Social entrepreneurs also must be innovative by seeking to discover new approaches to achieving their goals, often taking advantage of emerging trends as an asset rather than a liability. Although not all innovations are necessarily good innovations, it is worthwhile to collect numerous ideas so that one can choose the best from among them. Fostering an organizational culture of creativity and innovation gives the organization the flexibility to find better solutions to problems.

However, the third EO dimension that Weerawardena and Mort propose is risk management instead of risk taking. Although any new initiative or program involves a certain amount of risk, social entrepreneurs are believed to generally avoid taking big risks. Social entrepreneurs are less likely to take risks because their resources are limited: nonprofit organizations must be cautious about the programs and projects to which they commit, as funding is scarce and often received based on success of work currently being done. Their risk aversion is also likely to be due to the fact that they must manage and balance the competing demands of multiple stakeholders (such as clients, members, donors, sponsors, government, employees, and volunteers). In a more recent study, which examines the EO of social enterprises and commercial enterprises, Cools and Vermeulen find significant differences between the two types of enterprises in their level of proactiveness, innovativeness, and risk taking.[12] More specifically, they find that social enterprises are significantly less innovative and less likely to take risks than their commercial counterparts, and that there is no significant difference between the two in terms of proactiveness.

The divergence between social enterprises and their commercial counterparts in terms of risk taking propensity, however, may be due to the manner in which the risk-taking dimension is conceptualized. In commercial entrepreneurship literature, although the focus has been on financial risks such as making large resource commitments or incurring heavy debt, scholars also consider nonfinancial risks (such as social or psychological risks associated with venturing into the unknown). In contrast, existing social entrepreneurship literature appears to focus solely on financial risks; the discussion of nonfinancial risks is very limited. As an exception, Emerson identifies several nonfinancial risks, including damaged external reputation, damaged internal morale, loss of political leverage, missed opportunities, mission drift, and negative (or severely disappointing) social returns.[13] Considering the fact that nonprofit organizations are driven by a social mission rather than a financial bottom line, the risks of mission drift and negative or disappointing social returns seem to be particularly important.

Using PaperSeed Foundation (the organization introduced at the beginning of the chapter) as an example, the innovativeness of the organization is manifest in how it operates: PaperSeed donates 100 percent of its funds to projects, whereas CellMark sponsors the foundation and provides all operating expenses. PaperSeed is certainly not the only organization to do this, but it is still a fairly rare practice, especially among nonoperating foundations. PaperSeed is also innovative in how it mobilizes resources to achieve organizational goals: as the case illustrates, PaperSeed has managed to leverage CellMark's core competence in supply chain management and its global network in a creative way to minimize the costs and maximize the impact. In terms of risk taking, the leadership of PaperSeed does not shy away from taking the necessary risk in the design and implementation of its programs. A unique type of risk involved in PaperSeed's development work is looking for partner organizations that often have limited established presence online and are in remote areas of the country, where communication is difficult and a lot of trust is required. As the executive director recognized,

> Another example, of learning the hard way, was partnering with a very grassroots organization in Kenya that we believed in, but ultimately was more heart than head and wasn't able to commit to our standards of transparency, monitoring, and evaluation. It was tough to lose a partner at the ultimate hour and scramble for another, but we ended up finding a far better partner organization that was more in line with our values and mission. It worked out well in the end, but there were some fraught sleepless nights wondering how five hundred thousand sanitary napkins would get to the girls that most needed them. Of course, traveling to remote areas as a woman always presents some degree of risk.[14]

PaperSeed is also proactive in reaching out and spreading its programs to different parts of the world. PaperSeed is looking to China as the next target of its programs, and the leadership team is doing research, baseline surveys, and analysis to see what currently exists and how PaperSeed might be able to create opportunities for positive change and collaboration.

Trinity Effect offers another good example. This religiously inspired microfinance organization is devoted to "eliminating global poverty by partnering with existing organizations and ministries that are reaching out to the working poor in rural communities all across the world."[15] Trinity Effect demonstrates a high level of EO according to the criteria discussed earlier. This organization is innovative in that it takes a proven existing platform for alleviating poverty (online microfinance) and brings it to a new donor-lender base (the church). Also, though microfinance is not brand new, it is certainly not a mainstream activity yet. So participation in an innovative charity model such as microfinance also contributes to Trinity Effect's innovativeness. Trinity Effect is most certainly proactive, in that its founders are seeking out existing connections and microfinance institutions in the third world that need help but are currently underfunded. Rather than reacting to an obvious crisis, Trinity Effect is targeting areas plagued by systemic poverty and seeking to support and encourage microfinance efforts in these communities. Trinity Effect qualifies as a risk-taking organization because it seeks to compete with existing microfinance institutions and similar existing services like Kiva (a very successful online microfinance organization). It is also clear that it is taking risks, because transferring money into developing countries and then back out again can lead to fund losses. Finally, there is a risk that the first loans could be poorly managed and the promise of 98-percent returns could be seen as misleading.

Goodwill Industries serves as yet another example of the concept of EO. A well-established nonprofit agency, Goodwill provides job training, employment placement services, and other community-based programs for people who face employment challenges, lack education or job experience, or have disabilities. Goodwill is funded by operating a massive network of retail thrift stores worldwide. In 2010, Goodwill Industries of Lane and South Counties opened a Prosperity Center in Eugene, Oregon, that would allow low-income people to work with a financial planner, free of charge, and come up with their own long-term financial plan.[16] In late 2011, Goodwill Industries of Northwest North Carolina, in partnership with Consumer Credit Counseling Service and the United Way, opened the Career Connections and Prosperity Center.[17] At each of these centers, participants are offered opportunities to talk to financial professionals about their financial goals and how to design a personal plan to meet those goals, which may include paying their bills on time, reducing personal debt, saving enough for education, or investing in a major purchase like a car or home.

By launching such initiatives, Goodwill Industries bears a fair amount of risk because, on the one hand, operating costs go up with increased staff members and duties, and on the other hand, it will take a long time for these programs to attract enough donors. With regard to the level of innovativeness, the Prosperity Center presents a coaching model to help people achieve success and generate financial capability, which is the first of its kind. Therefore, Goodwill Industries is innovative in that it has changed the service delivery model from helping people find jobs, to a more innovative and expansive model that helps people get not only jobs, but better jobs, and to increase not only their income, but also their income sustainability. Finally, the proactiveness of Goodwill Industries is evident in the fact that, in order to sustain the new model, it reaches out to other community organizations and aggressively develops partnerships to pool resources and capitalize on complementary competencies.

MEASURES, DETERMINANTS, AND OUTCOMES OF EO

EO is a latent construct that cannot be observed or measured directly. Therefore, researchers must identify directly observable indicators that represent the underlying construct. To measure EO among business organizations, Miller and Friesen develop a fifteen-item scale that examines proactiveness, innovativeness, and risk taking.[18]

Morris and Joyce adapt the scale of Miller and Friesen to the nonprofit sector context.[19] Criteria include "a high rate of new program and service development compared to other organizations in our field/area," "risk-taking by key managers or administrators in seizing and exploiting new opportunities," "the seeking by managers of unusual, novel solutions to problems," and "active searches for major new opportunities," among others.

Based on the EO methods proposed by business scholars, Helm and Andersson develop an original scale to measure social entrepreneurship in nonprofit organizations. They first provide the following operating definitions for innovativeness, proactiveness, and risk taking:

• *Innovation*: The internal creation and use of new programs, services, processes, policies, or any other organizational output—from the original combination of existing inputs or the application of an existing activity to a new area.

• *Proactiveness*: The implementation of a program, service, policy, or process before other organizations in the industry, sector, or community, in response to opportunities that cannot be proved in the present but are expected to influence change in the future.

• *Risk taking*: The willingness to engage in behavior that disrupts internal or external operating norms. The behavior can, but need not, be financial; in fact, financial risk is often borne by a third-party financier such as a foundation.[20]

In line with the operating definitions, a scale is formulated that measures nonprofit organizations' social entrepreneurship behavior along a continuum. Helm and Andersson use data of 145 Kansas City Metropolitan Area nonprofit organizations to validate the underlying constructs represented in the scale and find significant behavioral differences between entrepreneurial and nonentrepreneurial nonprofits.

A review of existing literature reveals several important factors that have implications for levels of EO:

- *Organizational structure.* A number of organic structural elements, including fewer layers or levels in the organizational structure, broader spans of management control, a general orientation toward a more horizontal and less vertical design, and a more active board of directors, tend to lead to higher levels of EO.

- *Leadership style.* EO is consistent with transformational leadership, a leadership style that transforms and motivates followers by inspiring them with mission, vision, and identity.

- *Organizational control systems.* Informal control, flexibility, and resource discretion allow an organization to achieve higher levels of EO.[21]

The positive relationship between EO and organizational performance is well documented in the commercial entrepreneurship literature.[22] In a recent study, researchers Rauch, Wiklund, Lumpkin, and Frese undertook a meta-analysis to examine the existence and magnitude of the EO-performance relationship.[23] Their analysis of 53 samples from 51 studies with an N of 14,259 companies shows that the positive correlation of EO with performance is moderately large and moreover, this relationship is robust to different operationalizations of the EO construct and different measures of performance (perceived financial performance, perceived nonfinancial indicators of performance, and archival financial performance). The meta-analysis thus supports the contention that EO has positive performance implications. Their findings also indicate that the EO-performance relationship is equally significant across different countries and that the strength of the relationship is moderated by such factors as business size and technological intensity of the industry.

In the public and nonprofit sector context, the relationship between EO and organizational performance is less clear. There are several possible reasons for this lack of empirical evidence. First, although there are a number of EO studies on business enterprises, there are very few studies explicitly looking at EO in nonprofits. Second, because nonprofit scholars have used a wide range of measures to capture the major EO constructs, it becomes difficult, if not impossible, to compare results across different studies. Third, it is less intuitive to measure performance in nonprofit organizations. Whereas business enterprises focus on economic performance (that is, market share, profitability, ROA, and ROI), nonprofit organizations value economic performance and, more important, social performance. These two aspects of performance may or may not be correlated with each other, thereby making it difficult to interpret EO's impact on overall nonprofit effectiveness.[24]

Among the existing empirical studies on the association of EO and performance, the results are mixed. A study of religious congregations over a three-year period shows that higher levels of EO lead to better performance in terms of growth in church attendance and donations by church members.[25] A study of Australian public sector entities reveals a positive association between EO and a composite measure of perceived nonfinancial performance.[26] Similarly, another study of nonprofit arts organizations finds that EO is positively associated with social performance but not with financial performance.[27] The finding that EO has no significant relationship with financial performance is confirmed in two additional studies. A research study of nonprofit organizations in the Kansas City metropolitan area shows that EO is not significantly correlated with total revenues.[28] In a sample of 145 nonprofits in upstate New York, researchers find no relationship between EO and various financial performance measures including total expenses, total revenues, change in assets, and net revenues obtained from the agencies' tax returns.[29] Findings from these studies suggest that higher levels of EO do not necessarily translate into better organizational (financial) performance.[30] It is likely that EO does not directly affect financial performance because the social entrepreneurial efforts of public and nonprofit organizations are directed more toward social goals and objectives.

ENTREPRENEURIAL INTENSITY

In an effort to expand the concept of EO, researchers Morris and Sexton argue that the overall EO of an organization should be understood as a function of both the *degree* ("how much?") and *frequency* ("how often?") of entrepreneurship that the organization demonstrates over time. They have relabeled this expanded concept of EO as "entrepreneurial intensity" (EI). The EI concept thus contains two essential aspects:

- *The degree of entrepreneurship.* An organization's entrepreneurial behavior may differ in terms of its levels of innovativeness, proactiveness, and risk-taking characteristics. Consistent with the unidimensional view of EO, the degree of entrepreneurship can be understood as a conceptual continuum, on which one extreme represents conservative behavior and the other extreme represents entrepreneurial behavior.

- *The frequency of entrepreneurship.* This refers to the number of times an organization acts entrepreneurially. Examples of such entrepreneurial acts include new products or services, higher quality products or services, new methods of production or service delivery, and entry into a new market.[31]

Combining both aspects, Morris and Sexton then create a two-dimensional matrix, with the vertical axis capturing the frequency of entrepreneurship and the horizontal axis denoting the degree of entrepreneurship. This matrix, referred to as the "entrepreneurial grid," is illustrated in Figure 2.1.

As visualized by five designated points in the grid, five possible scenarios have been highlighted. The scenarios—labeled periodic/incremental, continuous/incremental, periodic/discontinuous, dynamic, and revolutionary—reflect the variable nature of EI. For example, an organization responsible for numerous entrepreneurial events that are highly innovative, risky, and proactive will

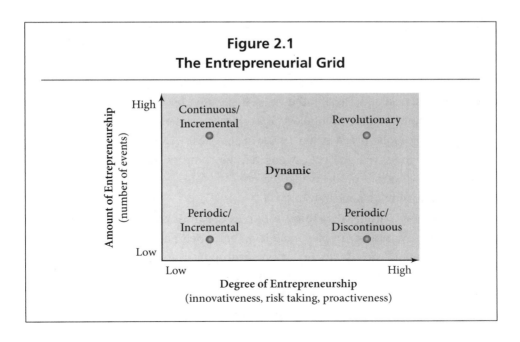

Figure 2.1
The Entrepreneurial Grid

fit into the revolutionary segment of the entrepreneurship matrix (located at the top right corner of the grid) and will exhibit the highest levels of EI. In contrast, when few entrepreneurial events are produced and these events are only nominally innovative, risky, and proactive, the organization can be described as periodic/incremental; that is, characterized by a low level of Entrepreneurial Intensity (located at the bottom left corner of the grid).

To better understand the grid, we provide a few examples of the five scenarios based on the explanations of Morris and colleagues.[32] A franchise operation, such as opening a franchised unit of McDonald's or Pizza Hut, is an example of periodic/incremental entrepreneurship. Because the primary operating format has already been offered by the headquarters, each franchised unit needs only to respond to changing environmental trends on a periodic and incremental basis, such as offering low-calorie meals or online ordering service. Since 1955, the Coca-Cola Company has been adding a wider variety of beverage selections for consumers at a fairly constant pace. Most new products are just variants of the original Coca-Cola, including the caffeine-free version, diet cola, additional fruit flavors, and Coca-Cola served in various portion sizes. The Coca-Cola Company's entrepreneurship can be considered continuous/incremental. Another example of this scenario is Procter & Gamble (P&G), the well-known consumer goods company, which produces a continual flow of consumer packaged goods innovations. In contrast with Coca-Cola and P&G, Polaroid represents an opposite scenario. Because Polaroid introduces new products only periodically but the new products are featured by technological discontinuities, the company should be best described as periodic/discontinuous. Minnesota Mining and Manufacturing (3M) is a good example of dynamic entrepreneurship. 3M has long enjoyed a reputation as a hothouse of innovation because it has a unique talent for developing a given technology into dozens of marketable forms and finding novel applications for these products. In the 1990s, 3M sold more than 6,800 consumer and industrial products. Moreover, the company set a goal of producing 30 percent of sales from products that did not exist four years earlier, as an effort to accelerate away from incrementalism.[33]

Revolutionary entrepreneurship should, as the most entrepreneurial type, be rare in reality. Possible examples include AT&T's Bell Labs, which is known for its continuous and steady stream of breakthrough innovations in telecommunication, and IBM, which has twelve research laboratories worldwide, invested enormously in basic research, and held the record for most patents generated by a company for twenty consecutive years (as of 2013).

Although Figure 2.1 depicts five distinct scenarios, it should be noted that these scenarios are arbitrarily defined to provide an example of how EI may vary. Amounts and degrees of entrepreneurship are relative; there are no absolute standards. Further, it is possible for any given organization to operate at more than one point in the space. An organization could be highly entrepreneurial at some times and not very entrepreneurial at others; consequently, it could occupy different segments of the matrix at different points in time.[34]

There is reason to believe that the level of entrepreneurial intensity may positively affect performance outcomes in an organization. Morris and Sexton predict that levels of EI are significantly associated with measures of organizational performance. Their survey findings provide evidence in support of a positive relationship between EI and various performance measures. The findings also indicate that the EI-performance relationship is strongest when more weight is placed on the degree of entrepreneurship rather than the frequency.[35]

LIMITATIONS OF EO AND EI

Implicit in the EO and EI constructs is the assumption that these concepts can be applied to any type of organization, not just for-profit businesses. Prior research,[36] however, has identified three important differences between public and nonprofit organizations and their counterparts in the business sector:

- *Motivations.* In the for-profit context, the organization exists to create wealth for owners and investors. Yet the primary purpose of a public or nonprofit organization is not to make profit or generate wealth, but to create social value for multiple stakeholders; it needs to remain financially sustainable, but this need should not distract the organization from serving its social mission. Lacking a profit motive, the organization loses a principal driver for supporting innovation, risk taking, and proactiveness—a driver that motivates for-profit organizations to engage in entrepreneurial activities.

- *Processes.* Public and nonprofit organizations differ from for-profits in their key processes and activities, especially in the set of activities through which cash flow is generated. In particular, nonprofit organizations rely on a much wider variety of funding sources (such as donations, grants, program service charges, and so on) than their for-profit counterparts, and have to dedicate significant resources to fund-raising processes.

- *Outcomes.* The outcomes of public and nonprofit organizations include both social performance measures, such as clients served, and financial performance measures, such as revenues and assets. It is often the case that an organization's social performance does not go hand in hand with its financial performance.

Given these differences in terms of motivations, processes, and outcomes, it is questionable whether the constructs of EO and EI can be readily applied to the public and nonprofit sector contexts. These constructs seem to capture the "entrepreneurial" part of social entrepreneurship more effectively than the "social" part. They say little about the observation that social entrepreneurial behavior may vary significantly in the degree to which it is motivated by a social cause (in the case of an independent start-up) or relevant to the social mission of the organization (in the case of an established organization). This is a significant oversight. As Peter Frumkin points out, the range of social entrepreneurial activities may range "from activities closely related to mission, all the way to those completely unrelated to mission."[37] In light of the centrality of mission in public and nonprofit organizations, it is therefore necessary to incorporate the consideration of mission alignment into the EO and EI constructs when they are applied to the context of social entrepreneurship.

Continuing the Goodwill Industries example discussed earlier in this chapter, the addition of a fourth dimension of "social mission" or "social value" might be helpful to distinguish the impact of EO within Goodwill. Their innovative strategies must be seen in the context of achieving the mission (helping people obtain employment) and how these strategies improve social impact. The expansion and new service delivery model of the Prosperity Center helped people find jobs; however, the truly innovative impact was that Goodwill went beyond placement numbers to track results: the percentages of members of the Prosperity Center who increased their income, increased their savings, reduced debt, monitored a monthly budget, and gained access to a financial institution. Taken together, the documentation of these results helps us to understand the long-term impact of this innovative program on the mission of the organization.

SOCIAL ENTREPRENEURIAL ORIENTATION

Public and nonprofit organizations differ from their counterparts in the business sector in that their mission goes beyond the financial bottom line. Nonprofit organizations in particular must rely on the social mission to attract financial and human resources and guide decision making. In light of the centrality of mission in public and nonprofit organizations, social entrepreneurship should give higher priority to creating social value than to capturing economic value.

Although prior research acknowledges that organizations must keep their mission and social value central to their entrepreneurial activities, it often treats mission as a constraint rather than an independent dimension. For example, Weerawardena and Mort suggest that nonprofit organizations that adapt to these constraints of an external environment, mission, and necessity to achieve sustainability, while also demonstrating EO, are the most likely to be successful. Although they should be innovative in the way they operate and obtain funds, they should not allow this to detract from their organizational goals.

The choice to not add a separate dimension of "social mission" is based in part on the logic that the EO dimensions are conceptualized in terms of sustained behavioral patterns (reflecting risk taking, innovativeness, and proactiveness) rather than goals and objectives. Following this rationale, researchers Morris, Webb, and Franklin have reconceptualized the three EO dimensions by taking into consideration the importance of mission (see Figure 2.2).

As illustrated in Figure 2.2, Morris and colleagues distinguish three subtypes of "innovativeness": mission-related (Innovativeness 1), revenue-related (Innovativeness 2), and a hybrid type that aims at enhancing both social mission and financial viability (Innovativeness 3). Similarly, they distinguish three subtypes of "proactiveness": mission-related (Proactiveness 1), revenue-related (Proactiveness 2), and stakeholder-based (Proactiveness 3). And they also distinguish three subtypes of "risk taking": mission-related (Risk taking 1), revenue-related (Risk taking 2), and stakeholder-based (Risk taking 3).

Such distinctions are helpful for incorporating social purpose or social mission into the conceptualizations of EO dimensions. Empirically, however, the picture gets cloudy when it comes to measuring and assessing the EO dimensions of a given organization. For example, consider two organizations, one of which scores high on mission-related innovativeness but low on revenue-based innovativeness and the other of which is just the opposite. Which organization is more innovative? The aforementioned conceptualization of innovativeness cannot answer this question, as it mingles innovation and mission.

In view of this limitation, we introduce the notion of "social entrepreneurial orientation" (SEO) by adding "social mission" as a separate dimension. We

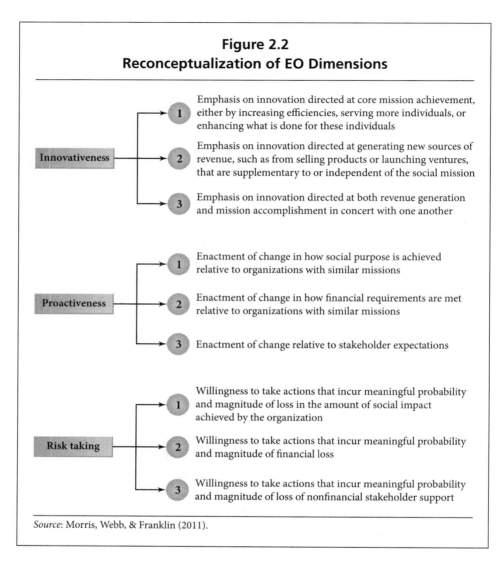

Figure 2.2
Reconceptualization of EO Dimensions

Innovativeness

1. Emphasis on innovation directed at core mission achievement, either by increasing efficiencies, serving more individuals, or enhancing what is done for these individuals

2. Emphasis on innovation directed at generating new sources of revenue, such as from selling products or launching ventures, that are supplementary to or independent of the social mission

3. Emphasis on innovation directed at both revenue generation and mission accomplishment in concert with one another

Proactiveness

1. Enactment of change in how social purpose is achieved relative to organizations with similar missions

2. Enactment of change in how financial requirements are met relative to organizations with similar missions

3. Enactment of change relative to stakeholder expectations

Risk taking

1. Willingness to take actions that incur meaningful probability and magnitude of loss in the amount of social impact achieved by the organization

2. Willingness to take actions that incur meaningful probability and magnitude of financial loss

3. Willingness to take actions that incur meaningful probability and magnitude of loss of nonfinancial stakeholder support

Source: Morris, Webb, & Franklin (2011).

define SEO as a set of distinct but related behaviors that demonstrate an organization's propensity to engage in social entrepreneurship. SEO is conceptualized as a three-dimensional construct (see Figure 2.3). It consists of three relatively independent dimensions: the degree of entrepreneurship; the frequency of entrepreneurship; and the alignment with social mission. There can be significant variation by dimension. For example, an organization can score high on the degree and frequency of entrepreneurship dimensions but low on the alignment with social mission dimension, or vice versa.

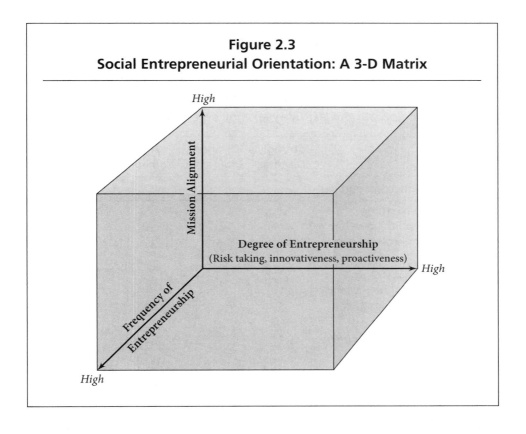

Figure 2.3
Social Entrepreneurial Orientation: A 3-D Matrix

High

Mission Alignment

Degree of Entrepreneurship
(Risk taking, innovativeness, proactiveness)

High

Frequency of Entrepreneurship

High

The three-dimensional matrix of SEO presents what an organization's social entrepreneurial orientation looks like in three-dimensional graphical form. Any organization can be placed somewhere in this three-dimensional space. With the SEO matrix, organizations can now benchmark themselves and track changes in SEO over time.

Consistent with the three-dimensional matrix and drawing upon prior research, we developed a SEO Instrument that contains fifteen questions (see Exhibit 2.1). Nine of the questions are designed to measure an organization's degree of entrepreneurship: three questions each for the assessment of innovativeness, proactiveness, and risk taking. Three questions are designed to measure an organization's frequency of entrepreneurship. The rest of the questions measure the extent to which the processes, policies, products, or services of an organization are relevant to its core mission. This scale aims to determine the SEO level of an organization and help differentiate between those organizations with higher social entrepreneurial propensities and those that are less social entrepreneurial.

Exhibit 2.1
Social Entrepreneurial Orientation Instrument[38]

Complete the survey by circling your response for each item.

Presently and during the last five years, my organization:

	Strongly Disagree	Disagree Somewhat	Agree Somewhat	Strongly Agree
Degree of Entrepreneurship				
1. Has placed a strong emphasis on the development of new products or services	1	2	3	4
2. Has placed a strong emphasis on the development of new organizational processes	1	2	3	4
3. Has made major changes in processes, policies, products, or services	1	2	3	4
4. Is very often the first organization to introduce new products/services, administrative techniques, operating technologies, and the like	1	2	3	4
5. Has exploited changes in the field	1	2	3	4
6. Has provided the lead for similar service providers	1	2	3	4
7. Has conducted itself in conflict with the behavioral norms of the operating environment, industry, or sector	1	2	3	4
8. Has selected projects that may alter the organization's public image	1	2	3	4

	Strongly Disagree	Disagree Somewhat	Agree Somewhat	Strongly Agree
9. Has made decisions that created changes in staff stability	1	2	3	4
Frequency of Entrepreneurship				
10. Has introduced many new products or services	1	2	3	4
11. Has introduced many new organizational processes	1	2	3	4
12. Has made many changes in processes, policies, products, or services	1	2	3	4
Alignment with Social Mission				
13. Has regularly reviewed our processes, policies, products, or services to ensure their relevance to its core mission	1	2	3	4
14. Has developed new processes, policies, products, or services that are most relevant to its core mission	1	2	3	4
15. Has culled existing processes, policies, products, or services that are least relevant to its core mission	1	2	3	4

CONCLUDING THOUGHTS

Why are some organizations more social entrepreneurial than others? In this chapter, we have addressed this question by conceptualizing social entrepreneurship as organizational behavior. Building on the existing constructs of entrepreneurial orientation (EO) and entrepreneurial intensity (EI) from the entrepreneurship literature, we have introduced the concept of social entrepreneurial orientation (SEO) as a set of distinct but related behaviors that demonstrate an organization's propensity to engage in social entrepreneurship. SEO consists of three key dimensions: the degree of entrepreneurship ("how much?"); the frequency of entrepreneurship ("how often?"); and the alignment with social mission ("how relevant?"). The SEO concept and the accompanying instrument provide a balanced tool that public and nonprofit leaders can apply to perform a reality check on the social entrepreneurial propensities of their organizations.

EXERCISES

Exercise 2.1

What are the connections between "entrepreneurial orientation" (EO) and "entrepreneurial intensity" (EI)? Why is it challenging to apply the constructs of EO and EI to the setting of public and nonprofit organizations?

Exercise 2.2

Based on the Entrepreneurial Grid in Figure 2.1, suggest a social venture that could best be described as periodic/incremental entrepreneurship. Suggest one that could be described as continuous/incremental entrepreneurship. Can you find an example of a social venture that can be depicted as revolutionary entrepreneurship?

Exercise 2.3

Select an organization that you are familiar with and assess its SEO based on the three key dimensions: the degree of entrepreneurship, the frequency of entrepreneurship, and the alignment with social mission.

PART TWO

Understanding and Managing the Social Entrepreneurial Process

chapter THREE

Discovering and Creating Social Entrepreneurial Opportunities

Founded by Muhammad Yunus, the Grameen Bank ("Bank of the Villages" in the Bengali language) is a microfinance organization and community development bank started in Bangladesh that makes small loans to the impoverished without requiring collateral. The story of the Grameen Bank began in 1974, three years after the independence of Bangladesh as a country, when Yunus, then a professor of economics at the University of Chittagone, witnessed widespread famine in the rural northern region of his country. Yunus recalls, "[Refugees] started showing up at the train stations and bus terminals—people withered to skeletons . . . They were everywhere. Soon the first corpses were lying in the streets."

Distressed by the suffering and starvation of his people, Yunus wanted to understand the causes of poverty and its possible solutions. Two years later, Yunus launched an action research project to study the economic situation in Jobra, a village near the university. Together with some colleagues and students, he talked to villagers and learned the struggles of these hardworking people. "There was, for example, the twenty-one-year-old mother Sufia Begum . . . She wove chairs from bamboo. She bought the material from a trader for five taka— about twenty-two U.S. cents a chair. Because this was not her money, she was obliged to sell the trader the chair in the evening for a price

47

that left her two cents . . . Because no institution was concerned about the very poor, loan sharks in the villages could do what they pleased and charged interest rates of up to 10 percent per day. Sufia's trader left her just enough profit so that she would not starve but would need to keep on borrowing from him and working for him."

Yunus and his team later identified 42 villagers in the same situation as Sufia. Together, these people needed a total of just US$27 to break out of the poverty cycle. Yunus loaned these villagers the money from his own pocket and started negotiating with commercial banks, trying to get the established financial institutions to lend money to the poor. The banks rejected his request, based on the rationale that the poor have no collateral and are not creditworthy. Refusing to give up, Yunus decided to establish a new financial institution that provides banking services targeted to the rural poor. The system of this new institution is different from traditional banks in several important ways. First, it targets the poorest and weakest of the poor, especially women, who account for the overwhelming majority (98 percent) of the borrowers. Second, whereas conventional banking is based on collateral, Grameen system is collateral-free. Third, Grameen takes a group-based credit approach: credit applicants must form groups of five, attend orientation sessions, and pass a test on the fundamentals of their loan. Everyone must pass the test, and when the entire group passes, only two of the five get a loan. The rest of group becomes eligible only after the first two pay their installments faithfully. As such, the peer pressure within the group serves to ensure repayment from the borrowers. Fourth, whereas conventional loans require that the borrower pay in full with interest by a set date, at the Grameen Bank the borrower pays back a small amount of installment on a weekly basis. Finally, the bank is owned by its borrowers: Borrowers own 90 percent of its shares, while the remaining 10 percent is owned by the government.

The Grameen Bank was a huge success: the vast majority of the borrowers repaid their loans on time. With the sponsorship of the central bank and support of the commercial banks, the project was eventually extended to the other regions of the country. In 1983, Grameen became an independent bank. In 2006, Muhammad Yunus and the

Grameen Bank were jointly awarded the Nobel Peace Prize. Today, the Grameen model of microfinance is replicated in over a hundred countries.[1]

This chapter focuses on the social entrepreneurial opportunity. Leading entrepreneurship researchers have argued forcefully that entrepreneurship operates at the nexus of opportunities and enterprising individuals, and that future research focuses on the discovery and exploitation of entrepreneurial opportunities.[2] A recent literature review article confirms the importance of opportunity by proclaiming: "Without an opportunity, there is no entrepreneurship."[3] In a similar vein, social entrepreneurship scholars have established that opportunity is at the heart of social entrepreneurship.[4]

Recent research has shifted the focus away from the characteristics and functions of individual entrepreneurs and focused on the nature and characteristics of the entrepreneurial process itself.[5] Researchers have called for the development of a process-oriented model to "capture the dynamics of the entrepreneurial process itself to explain how innovative opportunities are recognized and innovation-supporting behaviors are generated and directed within entrepreneurial organizations."[6] In the context of social entrepreneurship, the entrepreneurial process can be understood as the sequences of functions, activities, or behaviors associated with identification of opportunities, leading to a social entrepreneurial event—creation of a new program, venture, or organization.[7]

Opportunity identification is the first, and arguably the most important, stage in the social entrepreneurial process. As the story of the Grameen Bank illustrates, a social entrepreneur first identifies an opportunity that has the potential to create social value; next, he or she gathers resources and bears all the risks to pursue that opportunity; then the entrepreneur reassesses the opportunity continually in order to stay afloat. Without the recognition and/or creation of an opportunity, the rest of the process falls apart. Yet opportunity and opportunity development are also poorly understood concepts. What exactly is a social entrepreneurial opportunity? In what ways do opportunities in social entrepreneurship differ from those found in for-profit ventures? How are social entrepreneurial opportunities discovered, recognized, or even created? Why are some people able to see opportunities that the rest of us overlook? In this chapter, we aim to gain a better understanding of these questions.

DEFINING OPPORTUNITY

There is little consensus on the definition and nature of entrepreneurial opportunities. In one popular definition, opportunity is defined as "those situations in which new goods, services, raw materials, and organizing methods can be introduced and sold at greater than their cost of production."[8] Another definition sees opportunity as "an idea or dream that is discovered or created by an entrepreneurial entity and that is revealed through analysis over time to be potentially lucrative."[9] A recent literature review has examined the various conceptual and operational definitions of entrepreneurial opportunity in extant research.[10] From this review emerge six composite conceptual definitions that reflect a wide variety of conceptual definitions found in the literature:

1. An opportunity is the possibility of introducing a new product to the market at a profit.

2. An opportunity is a situation in which entrepreneurs envision or create new means-ends frameworks.

3. An opportunity is an idea that has developed into a business form.

4. An opportunity is an entrepreneur's perception of a feasible means to obtain or achieve benefits.

5. An opportunity is an entrepreneur's ability to create a solution to a problem.

6. An opportunity is the possibility to serve customers differently and better.

Behind this heterogeneity of definitions are two philosophical views of entrepreneurial opportunity: the "discovery view" and the "creation view." The discovery view is based on the assumption that opportunities are objective realities that exist independent of alert, skillful, or fortunate entrepreneurs who discover them. In this view, opportunities are formed by exogenous shocks caused by imperfections in a market or industry; they exist objectively as "hidden treasures" just waiting to be discovered and exploited. Examples of exogenous shocks include changes in technology, consumer preferences, policies and regulations, and social demographics, among others. The creation view assumes that opportunities do not exist independent of the entrepreneurs but are enacted through social construction: they are created through the enactment process between an entrepreneur and the environment. In other words, opportunities would not exist without the entrepreneur's actions.[11] Researchers Sharon

Alvarez and Jay Barney illuminate the difference between the two views with the metaphors of "mountain climbing" and "mountain building." According to the discovery view, opportunities are objective phenomena, like mountains standing somewhere waiting to be climbed; it is the entrepreneur's job to climb the mountains; that is, to search for opportunities that already exist. According to the creation view, however, opportunities are *not* like mountains; there are no mountains to climb, so the entrepreneur must build the mountains: "entrepreneurs do not search—for there are no mountains to find—they act, and observe how consumers and markets respond to their actions."[12]

In a recent empirical study, researchers Gartner, Carter, and Hills analyzed the discourse of nascent entrepreneurs to see whether and how the discovery and creation perspectives are reflected in the vocabularies of the entrepreneurs. They asked 433 nascent entrepreneurs an open-ended question: "Briefly, how did the original idea for starting a business develop?" Such "discovery verbs" as "saw," "find" or "found," and "looking" and "notice" were found in a very small percentage of the entrepreneurs' statements (less than 10 percent). The word "discovery" did not appear in any of the statements. Even more interesting are the answers to the following question: "Which came first to you, the business idea or your decision to start some kind of business?" Thirty-five percent of the respondents indicated that a business idea or opportunity came first, but nearly 45 percent of the respondents indicated the decision to start a business came before the "recognition" of an opportunity. The remaining 20 percent of the respondents noted that the idea or opportunity and the desire to have a business came at the same time.[13]

Findings of this study thus suggest that the discovery and creation views be combined to provide a better understanding of opportunity. The discovery view applies to situations where the entrepreneurial process begins with the recognition of an opportunity, whereas the creation view applies to situations where a sensemaking process between entrepreneurs and their contexts leads to the formation of an opportunity. The discovery view emphasizes the pursuit of opportunities regardless of resources, whereas the creation view focuses on what can be done with what is currently under control. Taken together, these indicate that some opportunities are discovered whereas others are created.

The late management guru Peter Drucker identified seven sources for innovative opportunity: unexpected occurrences—successes, failures, or other outside events; incongruities—between reality as it actually is and reality as it is assumed to be or as it "ought to be"; process needs—if the problem is understood, knowledge is available and made to fit with the way it is done; changes in industry structures or markets; demographic changes (populations changes); changes in perception, mood, and meaning; and new knowledge, both scientific and nonscientific.[14]

Similarly, there is considerable lack of agreement about the definition of opportunity in the context of social entrepreneurship (see Table 3.1 for a sample of existing definitions). Some define an opportunity as "the desired future state that is different from the present and the belief that the achievement of that state is possible." Others define an opportunity as "a feasible situation that exploits market inefficiencies, and provides an innovative product or service that creates social value in a less-than-saturated market." Still others suggest that an opportunity takes the form of a social problem or an unmet social need.[15]

Table 3.1
Definitions of Social Entrepreneurial Opportunity

Definition	Source of the Definition
The desired future state that is different from the present and the belief that the achievement of that state is possible.	Austin, Stevenson, & Wei-Skillern (2006)[16]
An opportunity that has sufficient potential for positive social impact to justify the investment of time, energy, and money required to pursue it seriously.	Guclu, Dees, & Anderson (2002)[17]
A feasible situation that exploits market inefficiencies, and provides an innovative product or service that creates social value in a less-than-saturated market.	Clarkin, Deardurff, & Gallagher (2012)[18]
A market opportunity that, when exploited, will allow the entrepreneur(s) to create enhanced social value.	Monllor (2010)[19]

Guclu, Dees, and Anderson suggest that opportunities in social entrepreneurship tend to be created rather than discovered. They write, "Despite popular sayings, attractive entrepreneurial opportunities do not come knocking at the door fully formed. Nor are they out there, like lost treasures, simply waiting to be discovered by the lucky or observant. Rather, they have to be conceived, developed, and refined in a dynamic, creative, and thoughtful process."[20]

In a similar vein, Paul Light also points out the socially constructed nature of opportunity in social entrepreneurship. He notes, "[T]he notion that ideas might emerge before champions is a staple of both business and nonprofit thinking. Social entrepreneurship might follow a very similar track in which ideas find champions, or vice versa, or in which solutions find resources, or vice versa. If true, the most effective social entrepreneur might be one who simply ties the streams together and stands aside."[21]

Taking an economic perspective, researcher Monllor attributes social entrepreneurial opportunities to market and government failures. Five primary types of market failure are identified: imperfect information, monopoly power, public goods, externalities, and flawed pricing mechanisms. Three types of government failure are identified: pursuit of self-interest by politicians and civil servants, short-term solutions, and imperfect information. These forms of market and government failures result in inefficient resource allocations and Pareto suboptimal outcomes, but they provide sources of opportunity for social entrepreneurs.[22]

Following and extending economist Joseph Schumpeter's ideas, J. Gregory Dees identifies seven types of innovative opportunities in social entrepreneurship:[23]

- *Creating a new or improved product, service, or program.* One example is the Grameen Bank's micro loan program, which makes small loans to the impoverished without requiring collateral.

- *Introducing a new or improved strategy or method of operating.* The practice of social franchising among some nonprofit organizations as a strategy for replicating their projects falls into this category.

- *Reaching a new market, serving an unmet need.* For example, Grameen Bank has opened an office in the United States to provide loans to people who have traditionally had no access to the regular banking system.

- *Tapping into a new source of supply or labor. Street News*, a street newspaper published in New York City, employs homeless individuals to write, produce, and sell the newspaper.

- *Establishing a new industrial or organizational structure* through mergers, spin-offs, alliances, and other contractual arrangements.

- *Framing new terms of engagement* with clients, consumers, suppliers, funders, or employees.

- *Developing new funding structures.* An example is Susan G. Komen for the Cure's partnership with Yoplait on an annual campaign called "Save Lids to Save Lives" to raise money for breast cancer research.

HOW ARE SOCIAL ENTREPRENEURIAL OPPORTUNITIES DIFFERENT?

A number of scholars have explored the differences between opportunities in social entrepreneurship and their counterparts in commercial entrepreneurship.[24] Several themes have emerged from this line of research.

- *Focus.* The focus of a social entrepreneurial opportunity is on creating social value rather than making profit. The potential of a possible opportunity to create enhanced social value is an important factor to determine whether the opportunity is worthy of pursuing. This focus on social value creation ensures that the opportunity would benefit society as a whole rather than owners and investors (as is usually the case in commercial entrepreneurship). This focus, however, poses a challenge for the pursuit of a social entrepreneurial opportunity, because social value is often difficult to define and measure. Moreover, it is more difficult to stay focused on social value creation and enhancement when a social entrepreneurial entity has owners and investors. Some entrepreneurs choose to adopt the form of for-profit organizations and include some social entrepreneurial elements in their business models. For example, TOMS is a for-profit company that operates the nonprofit subsidiary Friends of TOMS. Founded in 2006 by a Texas entrepreneur Blake Mycoskie, TOMS designs and sells shoes based on the Argentine Alpargata design, as well as eyewear. TOMS creates social value primarily in two ways: when TOMS sells a pair of shoes, a pair of shoes is given to an impoverished child, and when TOMS sells a pair of eyewear, part of the profit is used to save or restore the eyesight of people in developing countries. For such a business model, tradeoffs may exist between maximizing value for owners and investors (that is, maximizing profits) and creating social value (that is, donating goods and services to others).

- *Context.* A social entrepreneurial opportunity is deeply embedded in the local context. Embeddedness—defined as the nature, depth, and extent of an individual's ties to the environment—has been considered by some researchers as a configuration element of the entrepreneurial process: "Being embedded within the social structure of the area provides the entrepreneurs with intimate knowledge, contacts, sources of advice, resources, information and support. This indicates that by being embedded it is easier to recognize and understand what is required and available."[25]

- *Stakeholders.* The discovery or creation of a social entrepreneurial opportunity often happens in collectives and involves a wider array of stakeholders than that of a commercial entrepreneurial opportunity. In particular, stakeholder buy-ins are important to the successful development of a social entrepreneurial opportunity.

HOW ARE SOCIAL ENTREPRENEURIAL OPPORTUNITIES DISCOVERED OR CREATED?

As with all nonprofit and voluntary activities, social entrepreneurship is fundamentally driven by two forces: demand and supply. It can be understood as a response to an unmet demand in the community, or an important supply function that generates its own demand. On the demand side, social entrepreneurship "exists by virtue of the broader social context within which it is embedded and that its activities are responsive to the demands of the public or its members." On the supply side, social entrepreneurship is driven by "the resources and ideas that flow into it—resources and ideas that come from social entrepreneurs, donors, and volunteers."[26]

Ardichvili, Cardozo, and Ray have developed an entrepreneurial opportunity recognition theory that is widely accepted in the field.[27] Their theory suggests that there are five major factors that influence the opportunity recognition and development process: entrepreneurial alertness, information asymmetry and prior knowledge, social networks, personality traits, and the type of opportunity itself. Ardichvili and colleagues' theory points out that opportunity recognition is a combination of factors and characteristics, and not just one particular thing that makes entrepreneurs see what the rest of us tend to pass over.

The opportunity recognition process involves a perception of market needs, recognizing a fit between market needs and specified resources, and then creating a new model to fit the recognized needs. For example, Project 7—a cause-related company that makes everyday consumer goods—recognizes that there are seven different types of fundamental human needs (clean water, medicine, housing, education, and so on) around the globe. Their organization sells existing products that individuals buy (coffee, gum, mints, and the like) and then uses the revenue from those products to fulfill one of the seven "areas for good" by supporting nonprofit partners in that area. This is a simple idea, but Project 7 has recognized the opportunity and then capitalized on it in an original way.

Ardichvili and colleagues argue that some individuals are more sensitive to these perceptions, seeing market opportunities in every setting, while others nearly fail to see them at all. Ardichvili and colleagues' multidimensional model requires that individuals have some innate capabilities for creating and recognizing potential value. Their model is based on the recognition that individuals can see past individual facts and put them together mentally in order to create a feasible opportunity. This theory provides a basis for research moving forward, but does not in itself give us a full picture of opportunity recognition.

Guclu, Dees, and Anderson provide another useful framework to guide social entrepreneurs through the process of creating a worthwhile opportunity. Their framework breaks down the opportunity creation process into two major steps. First, a social entrepreneur generates a promising idea. Second, the social entrepreneur attempts to develop that idea into an attractive opportunity.[28]

Building on these frameworks, we provide a two-phase model of the opportunity recognition process (see Figure 3.1).

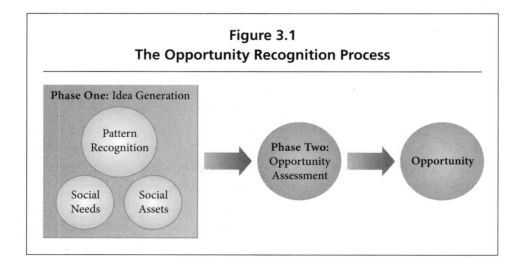

Figure 3.1
The Opportunity Recognition Process

PHASE ONE: IDEA GENERATION

During this phase, the generation of a promising idea results from the interplay of three important factors: social needs, social assets, and pattern recognition.

Social Needs

Social needs can be understood as the gaps between socially desirable conditions and the existing reality. For example, *The Big Issue* is a British street newspaper written by professional journalists and sold by homeless individuals. It was founded in September 1991 as a response to a social need: the increasing numbers of homeless people in London. It is entrepreneurs' perception of the need to help homeless people (or individuals at risk of homelessness) return to mainstream society that triggers the innovative idea of launching a street newspaper and hiring homeless people to sell it.

Changes in social needs can also open up new possibilities and inspire the development of promising new ideas. One example is a recent change in the American workforce: in the United States today, nearly one in three workers are in nonstandard jobs, including freelancers, consultants, independent contractors, temp workers, part-timers, contingent employees, and the self-employed.[29] Because they are employed in nontraditional arrangements, these independent workers do not have access to employer-based insurance. Therefore, Working Today, a 501(c)3 nonprofit organization, launched the Freelancers Union in 2001 to meet this need.

Social needs alone, however, draw only an incomplete picture of opportunity development. Researchers Seelos, Mair, Battilana, and Dacin note that "if the extent of obvious . . . social needs seemingly defines a natural opportunity space for SEOs, then we need to address the question of why these obvious opportunities are not systematically picked up by entrepreneurs."[30] Indeed, an unmet social demand alone does not form a viable opportunity unless a social entrepreneur (or a group of social entrepreneurs) finds an innovative and feasible way to meet the demand. Moreover, in some cases the demand is unformed and thus nonexistent in an articulated form: this "inchoate demand" can be met only through entrepreneurial action to provide a new good or service.[31]

Social Assets

Although some leading theorists argue that social entrepreneurs relentlessly pursue new opportunities without regard to resources currently controlled, a good understanding of the scope and level of tangible and intangible assets in a community is key to developing promising ideas that aim at addressing social needs. City Year offers an excellent case in point. Founded in 1988 by Michael Brown and Alan Khazei, then-roommates at Harvard Law School, City Year is based on the understanding that young people in service could be a powerful resource for addressing America's most pressing issues. Therefore City Year was established not to serve young people, but to engage young people to serve others. Since its inception, the organization has mobilized young people to work on community rehabilitation, beautification of neighborhoods, developing community awareness, and, most recently, finding solutions to the dropout crisis.

Pattern Recognition

Robert A. Baron defines pattern recognition as the cognitive process through which individuals identify meaningful patterns in complex arrays of events or trends. According to his pattern recognition theory, new business opportunities are identified when entrepreneurs, using relevant cognitive frameworks, "connect the dots" between seemingly unrelated events or trends and then detect patterns in these connections suggestive of new products or services. More specifically, individuals notice various events in the external world (such as changes in technology, economic, political, social, and demographic conditions) and then utilize cognitive frameworks they have developed through experience to determine whether these events are related in any way—in short, whether they form a discernible pattern.

An example of pattern recognition in the context of social entrepreneurship is the Diamond Empowerment Fund (DEF), a nonprofit organization that works with jewelry retailers to sell DEF products, with portions of the proceeds going to benefit children in diamond mining countries like Botswana and South Africa. They work with diamond retailers to have them donate a portion of their profits from sales of diamonds from these countries to help fund scholarships, with the intention of eradicating poverty. DEF was founded by Russell Simmons, an entrepreneur with ventures in music, jewelry, clothing, and productions. He knows how to go about looking for opportunities and the necessary connections to leverage his resources. His prior knowledge has proven to be a factor in how his organization has gone beyond surviving, to thriving and expanding.

Pattern recognition has played a serious role in the success of DEF. As discussed earlier, pattern recognition is a complex process whereby a person perceives links or connections between unrelated events or changes in order to find an opportunity for business. As consumers become more conscious of how the products they buy are made, and how their production impacts those who produce them, there is a general movement to seek out "clean" products. Diamond trade has long been established, but more people are now looking at how these diamonds are being produced and how the money is being used in the countries of their origin, due in large part to popular media, like the movie *Blood Diamond*, which have brought this information to the mainstream. DEF saw that there could be a way to use this need for clean products along with the enduring desire for diamonds to push diamonds traders and retailers to participate in donating some portions of their proceeds back to the countries they come from, through DEF, and to also expand by creating their own jewelry line, from the high end "Green Bracelets" to more affordable charms, that could work to further their mission while still earning the company a profit. Having also seen this change in consumer preferences, many other entrepreneurs have started ventures in their respective markets; some (for example, TOMS Shoes) have proven to be very successful.

A question every entrepreneur may ask is: how do we learn to be better at recognizing different patterns that would eventually lead to an opportunity? Baron and other scholars outline several factors that contribute to pattern recognition.

• *Active information search.* Opportunities, often hidden and unobtrusive, can be recognized by individuals who are actively searching for them.

• *Alertness.* Any recognition of opportunity is preceded by a state of heightened entrepreneurial alertness to information.[32] Sometimes opportunities are recognized by individuals who possess "a unique preparedness to recognize them" when they appear. This is a matter of not necessarily searching out opportunities, but rather being open to recognizing them when they arise—potential social entrepreneurs are active observers. A potential entrepreneur needs to be alert to market demands and actively seek ways to connect his or her skills and resources to fulfill that need. Muhammad Yunus founded the Grameen Bank, which gives out micro loans. He recognized the need for alternative methods of credit for the extremely poor (alertness) and then harnessed his resources to fulfill that need.

• *Prior experience.* In addition to "an active search," most "highly experienced entrepreneurs" (those with four or more ventures) restrict their search to areas and disciplines in which they already have expert knowledge and experience.

- *Social networks.* An individual's social networks are considered to be one of the important antecedents of entrepreneurial alertness to business opportunities.

Based on these factors, scholars have provided a number of practical suggestions. For example, learning how to be "alert" would consist of asking questions such as "Is this serving its purpose effectively?" "How could this be done better?" "How could I do this better?" These questions may not lead to an "Aha!" moment every time, but perhaps they would help create the mindset of asking questions and training the thinking in a way that recognizes those potential opportunities. Dees and colleagues argue that opportunity recognition is a skill, not an innate ability.[33] In order to become better at recognizing opportunities for social entrepreneurship, they give some practical tips: look at the situation from a different perspective, change the basic assumptions, brainstorm with colleagues and the competition, brainstorm with the customer, and look for opportunities to partner with existing organizations. These are practical skills that anyone can apply to improve their recognition in any field.

To better understand the "how" question, we focus on two factors that may play a crucial role in the process of pattern recognition: (1) prior experience and (2) social networks.

Prior Experience

There is abundant research from the commercial entrepreneurship field showing that prior experience or knowledge contributes to pattern recognition. Specifically, working within an industry or having had the experience, successful or not, of setting up a business venture increases the chances that one will find opportunities. Researchers Baron and Ensley compare the "business opportunity" prototypes of novice (first-time) and repeat (experienced) entrepreneurs—their cognitive representations of the essential nature of opportunities.[34] They find that the prototypes of experienced entrepreneurs are more clearly defined, richer in content, and more concerned with factors and conditions related to actually starting and running a new venture than the prototypes of novice entrepreneurs. Shane and Venkataraman argue that discovery of opportunities is dependent on the possession of prior knowledge necessary to identify an opportunity and the cognitive abilities of individuals.[35] Any given entrepreneurial opportunity is not obvious to all potential entrepreneurs; rather, any given entrepreneur will discover only those opportunities related to his or her prior knowledge.

Two examples show that promising ideas often arise from the personal experience of the social entrepreneur. Back on My Feet is a Philadelphia-based nonprofit social venture that promotes self-sufficiency of homeless people by engaging them in running as a means to build confidence, strength, and self-esteem. Founder Anne Mahlum started running at the age of sixteen and has been an avid runner ever since. She originally used running as an outlet to deal with family issues, including her father's obsessive gambling habit, which was crippling the family. As Anne grew older and continued to run, she would frequently pass a homeless shelter where she developed a friendly rapport with some of the residents. Running past the shelter each day, Anne realized there was an opportunity to use running to assist the homeless men and women, who frequently reminded her of her father. She realized that running was her outlet and that it could be theirs as well. Anne then contacted the homeless shelter and asked if she could invite the men to join her on her runs. The first run took place on Wednesday, July 3, 2007. Later that year, Back on My Feet was born. Clearly, Anne's personal experience (her running, family issues) was crucial to generating the idea of improving the physical and spiritual health of homeless people through running.

Another example is Sara Horowitz, who founded Working Today and Freelancers Union, leading organizations of independent workers. Before founding Working Today–Freelancers Union, Horowitz was a labor attorney in private practice and a union organizer. Her grandfather was vice president of the International Ladies Garment Workers Union in New York, and her father was a union lawyer.

Although the importance of prior experience is empirically confirmed in the setting of commercial entrepreneurship, it is not clear whether such a positive impact can be corroborated in social entrepreneurship. Several recent projects by Professor Peter Roberts of Emory University conclude that this is not the case. Using a sample of social entrepreneurs who applied to participate in the 2010 or 2011 summer accelerator programs run by the Unreasonable Institute, he examines whether entrepreneurs with prior entrepreneurial experience outperform those who have never launched a new enterprise. The findings show that experienced social entrepreneurs do not enjoy more superior social performance, more commercial success (early revenue, investment results), or larger online followings.[36]

Exploring the possible reasons for the insignificant impact of prior experience in social entrepreneurship, Roberts speculates that social entrepreneurs are launching what some call hybrid organizations, which follow neither straight-up for-profit nor nonprofit models. Instead, hybrid organizations use for-profit techniques in order to meet the concrete social and/or environmental aspirations of traditional nonprofits. Entrepreneurial experience from either domain may not help founders navigate the many tradeoffs that this novel model requires.[37]

Social Networks

Social networks serve as an avenue through which individuals recognize potential entrepreneurial opportunities.[38] According to social network theory, people who maintain numerous, diverse social relationships are more likely to generate new ideas and identify novel opportunities.[39] Networks contribute to the entrepreneurial process by providing access to information and advice; according to Hills, Lumpkin, and Singh's study, approximately half of the entrepreneurs obtain new ideas through their networks.[40]

The reason why some people are more successful at recognizing opportunity also stems from the nature of the network structure that they are embedded in. Within an individual's network there are strong and weak connections. Strong connections are those which are characterized by close personal relationships and high maintenance costs. Weak ties, in turn, are more casual acquaintances that require less resources and time to maintain. Overall, weak ties seem more likely to connect persons to different social circles than stronger ties.[41] Weaker ties also facilitate creativity by providing access to a wider array of people and more nonredundant information.[42] Furthermore, persons embedded in a diverse set of network ties, with a mixture of strong and weak ties and advisors with whom they have no prior relationship, are more likely to be innovative than are those who rely on only homogenous ties.[43]

PHASE TWO: OPPORTUNITY ASSESSMENT

Once an opportunity is recognized or created, the next step is to evaluate benefits and costs of exploiting the opportunity and decide whether or not to pursue it. In other words, during the phase of opportunity assessment, entrepreneurs screen recognized opportunities to judge their attractiveness for exploitation. Drawing on prior research on evaluating opportunities for new businesses, Jerry Kitzi has developed a useful model for the assessment of social entrepreneurial opportunities. The model contains three key dimensions: social value potential, market potential, and sustainability potential (see Table 3.2):[44]

Table 3.2
Three Criteria for Opportunity Assessment

Social Value Potential

Value Added	High		Low
Strategic Alignment	Service/product creates social value that is aligned with the mission	⬌	Service/product creates social value but is loosely or indirectly aligned with the mission
Achievable Outcomes	Service/product will create a significant change in user behavior, condition, or level of satisfaction	⬌	Service/product will create minimal change in user behavior, condition, or level of satisfaction or indirectly linked to changes
Partnership and/or Alliance	Additional partnership(s) would have a synergistic effect and improve or increase chances for desired results – social value	⬌	Service/product has minimal change potential and would not benefit by a partnership or alliance strategy
Organizational Benefit	Successful service/product will increase or create positive community perception of and/or political support for the organization	⬌	Unsuccessful service/product will have negative effect on community perception and/or political support for the organization

Market Potential

Demand	High		Low
User Need	Evidence of social need and an open window of opportunity	⬌	No data or other evidence of social need or a closing window of opportunity

(Continued)

Table 3.2 *Continued*

Market Potential

Demand	High		Low
User Desire	Evidence of user interest or evidence of success of similar services in other communities	⬅➡	No data or other evidence of user interest available, declining participation in services in other communities
Funder Interest	Evidence of interest, or noticeable trends in grant making or government contracts for similar service	⬅➡	No data or other evidence or findings of interest for similar services
Market Share	Evidence of an open market with little competition	⬅➡	Evidence of highly competitive market or no data or other evidence of competition's interest or involvement in the market

Sustainability Potential

Capital Needs	High		Low
Idea Development	Research and development resources are available or easily accessible	⬅➡	No funding or staff time available or readily accessible
Startup	Low cost of startup and/or easily accessible funding for startup	⬅➡	High cost of startup and/or scarcity of available resources or interest
Cost-to-Benefit Ratio	Low total program costs compared against high public benefit	⬅➡	High total costs compared against low to marginal public benefit
Organizational Capability	Board, staff, or volunteer capability is present and aligned with potential service or project	⬅➡	Absence of capability among existing board, staff, or volunteers

	Sustainability Potential	
Capital Needs	**High**	**Low**
Income Potential	Target population with discretionary income potential and/or evidence of ability/desire to pay fees	⟷ Target population has little discretionary income or evidence of ability/ desire to pay minimal fees
Organizational Capacity	Internal structures, space, technology, etc. are in order or easily adjusted for new services or expansion of services	⟷ Internal structures are limited or in need of substantial upgrade to support presenting opportunity
Funder Interest	Trends or other evidence of funder interest for three-to-five-year horizon	⟷ Funder interest unknown or evidence of declining interest over the last three to five years

In a more recent study, Shaker Zahra and colleagues suggest five criteria for assessing opportunities in social entrepreneurship:[45]

• *Pervasiveness.* The pervasiveness of an opportunity refers to the extent to which the social need that the opportunity aims to address is widely prevalent or salient.

• *Relevance.* The relevance of an opportunity refers to the match between the opportunity's salience to the entrepreneur and his or her personal experiences, expertise, skills, resources, and demographics.

• *Urgency.* The urgency of an opportunity is inherent in its unpredictability (as in the case of a natural disaster). An unpredictable event generates a sense of urgency and creates a window of opportunity to address a particular social need in a timely manner.

• *Accessibility.* The accessibility of an opportunity refers to the level of perceived difficulty in addressing a social need through traditional welfare mechanisms, such as government or philanthropy. To the extent that an opportunity is inaccessible to traditional welfare mechanisms, it creates a market niche for social entrepreneurs to search for innovative solutions.

- *Radicalness.* The radicalness of an opportunity refers to the extent to which a major innovation or social change is necessary to address a particular problem. To the extent that an opportunity is radical and innovative, it differentiates the entrepreneurial organization from other established mechanisms.

CONCLUDING THOUGHTS

In this chapter, we discussed the processes by which social entrepreneurs discover or create opportunities, and we presented a process model of opportunity development that includes two phases: idea generation and opportunity assessment. In the next chapter, we discuss how social entrepreneurs capitalize on opportunities and turn them into successful ventures.

EXERCISES

Exercise 3.1

What is opportunity? How do the "discovery view" and "creation view" advance our understanding of opportunity in social entrepreneurship?

Exercise 3.2

The opportunity recognition process of social entrepreneurs involves two major phases: idea generation and opportunity assessment. What are the three core elements of the first phase? Describe each of them.

Exercise 3.3

Where do entrepreneurial opportunities come from? Describe the factors that would influence the probability for particular social entrepreneurs to discover particular opportunities. Be specific.

From Opportunity to Action

Berkeley Oakland Support Services (BOSS) was founded in Alameda County, California, in 1971 to provide a continuum of care from emergency shelter to transitional and permanent housing.[1] BOSS recognized that employment was a key factor for successfully obtaining housing. In 1988 BOSS began an employment program that counseled program participants on activities such as goal clarification, resume preparation, job search techniques, confidence-building workshops, and individualized referrals and placements. The program was designed to assist clients in obtaining and keeping jobs and supported BOSS's own practice of hiring qualified program participants as paid staff. This employment support effort was expanded in 1991 to two new programs to employ program participants: one to clean streets and the other to remove graffiti. The programs provided homeless people with six-month paid training positions that would serve as stepping stones to other employment in the open market. Between 1991 and 1995 these programs were well received by both business and the City of Berkeley, which gave BOSS over $500,000 in contracts.

To capitalize on this success and move its program to a higher level, BOSS decided to move from employment development into enterprise development. The goal was to establish profitable businesses that would yield earned income for BOSS while also training the homeless. This could facilitate expanding into other geographic areas and markets. In addition, it was consistent with BOSS's strategic plan to increase innovation in programs, upgrade capacity, and enhance sustainability. To develop this, the board of directors initiated a focused, step-by-step planning effort by a venture committee. Support was obtained from the San Francisco Foundation to explore the idea of establishing enterprises. This entailed looking into the experiences of other agencies which had started enterprises and reading background material about the subject. This resulted in more organizational commitment to proceed and support from the Roberts Foundation's Homeless Economic Development Fund (HEDF) for feasibility research and the creation of a business plan. Feasibility research selected two businesses through a "focusing" process. This entailed (1) establishing criteria for successful BOSS enterprise development, (2) brainstorming options by external stakeholders and BOSS participants, and (3) matching and narrowing criteria and options. Through this process, a list of ninety-one possibilities in twenty-two categories became three businesses in the property maintenance category. This was followed by a business planning process that entailed marketing, operations, finance, and values dimensions of enterprises. The business plan was approved by the board, and HEDF gave BOSS a startup grant in 1996 to establish its enterprise.

In Chapter Three we developed a robust view of the processes by which social entrepreneurs discover or create opportunities. It is important to note, however, that every opportunity does not necessarily mean a successful attempt at social entrepreneurship. While opportunity recognition is a necessary start, following through on that recognition is an important part of social entrepreneurship. In this chapter we discuss how social entrepreneurs capitalize on opportunities and turn them into successful ventures. The opening story of BOSS illustrates this process. It is clear that the homeless need employment, and BOSS recognized an opportunity to provide employment services to its clients. BOSS developed this opportunity into a series of increasingly significant programs. For other social entrepreneurs to do this, a number of questions must be addressed. How can an opportunity be further developed and clarified in order to enhance the prospects for the creation of the benefits envisioned? What factors should be taken into account when planning the programs or services needed to for social impact?

This chapter discusses the process of turning a social entrepreneurial opportunity into a viable program or organization. The basic elements involved in this process are summarized in Figure 4.1.

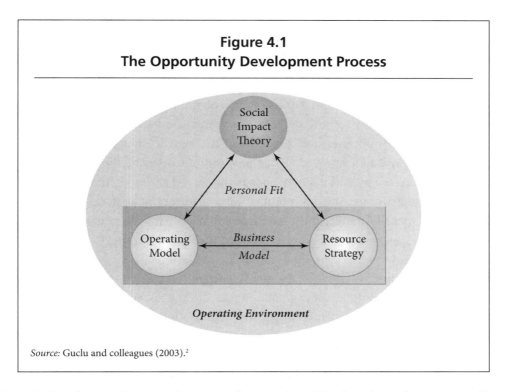

Figure 4.1
The Opportunity Development Process

Social
Impact
Theory

Personal Fit

Operating
Model

Business
Model

Resource
Strategy

Operating Environment

Source: Guclu and colleagues (2003).[2]

In brief, a *social impact theory* is a theory, or model, about how the venture will achieve its intended social impact. This theory will drive the strategy of the new venture and demonstrate the mission and values of the organization. The articulation of the theory should include a clear understanding of the social value to be created as well as a convincing sequence of activities which will lead from program inputs to ultimate outcomes. In addition, the opportunity needs to be supported by a plausible business model that includes an effective *operating model* and a viable *resource strategy*. These two elements of the business model work closely together to bring the social impact theory to life. These elements are described further in this chapter and techniques for accomplishing them are presented.

ELABORATING THE OPPORTUNITY WITH SOCIAL IMPACT THEORY

Social entrepreneurs need to have a clear idea of what they want the outcome of their venture to be. The social benefits to be created should be articulated in a social value proposition. This, in turn, should be grounded in a realistic notion, or theory, of how desired changes in individual behavior or social conditions can be successfully brought about.

The Venture's Value Proposition

Austin and colleagues note that the creation of value underlies and forms the basis for the operations of any organization.[3] This can be expressed in a value proposition, which outlines how the lives of the beneficiaries of the organization's activities will be improved. Value propositions describe the type of value that is being created by addressing who is being served and how. The value proposition is essentially the starting point of the organization, as it will determine the strategic focus of the organization and significantly influence the structures, processes, and resource allocations established to attain the strategy.

For social entrepreneurship, a *social value proposition* should be developed that should in some way involve "attaining socially desirable outcomes that are not spontaneously produced by private markets."[4] The social value proposition should be about the social mission of the organization. Wie-Skillern and colleagues describe how the social value proposition plays the central role by linking the opportunity, people, capital, and context.[5] It is only in the alignment of these elements that the desired social value can be created. The goal of planning and organizational design is to ensure this alignment, as shown in Figure 4.2.

In constructing their value propositions, social entrepreneurs should answer the "who is being served?" question by addressing what the mission is, who the beneficiaries are, and what their values are.[6] The "how are they being served?" question can be addressed by considering the social value that is being produced. As noted earlier, in this formulation, social value is the provision of value not spontaneously provided by markets. BOSS's social value proposition involved providing employment training and jobs to those having difficulty finding them on their own. In addition, however, social enterprises can generate income (economic value through sales of products or services to those who can afford to purchase them). Hence, for social enterprises, both economic value and social value should be laid out in the value proposition. A social enterprise may be able to integrate both social and economic value into a single package and provide both, thereby addressing the social and economic "double bottom line"[7] and creating "blended value."[8] For example, it can grant substantial discounts on sales made to poor customers, thereby reducing their service barriers. BOSS expanded its value proposition to establishing a profitable enterprise to further its mission.

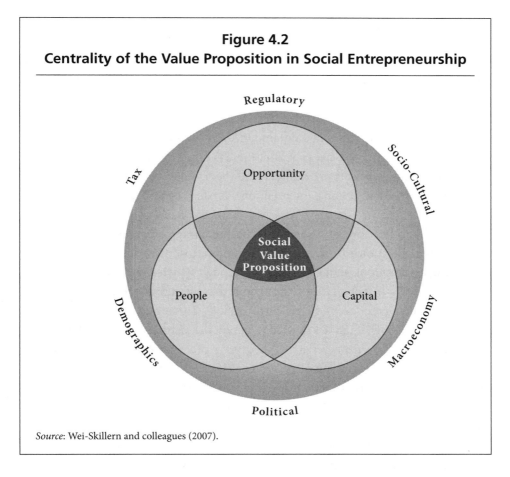

Figure 4.2
Centrality of the Value Proposition in Social Entrepreneurship

Regulatory

Tax

Socio-Cultural

Opportunity

Social
Value
Proposition

People

Capital

Demographics

Macroeconomy

Political

Source: Wei-Skillern and colleagues (2007).

By providing both types of values, social enterprises can operate in competitive markets in which both nonprofits and for-profits participate. In addition, including economic value in the specification of value reinforces the need to simultaneously consider both mission focus and financial sustainability concerns.

The Venture's Theory of Change

As articulated by Anderson, the theory of change is a useful tool for developing solutions to complex social problems.[9] At its most basic, the theory of change explains how desired long-term change occurs. It is based upon a model of individual or social behavior that is backed by theory and/or verified by experience or research. The model specifies how and why change is expected to happen in a particular way, by depicting how a complex change initiative will unfold in a series of steps over time. It predicts who or what is going to change, over what period of time, and by how much, at every step of the process.

A process of backward mapping can be used to develop the theory of change for a social venture.[10] The process begins by specifying the venture's long-term goal, or the results that are desired. This is, essentially, the social value that is to be produced and will require some change to take place. For example, our goal could be to lower the dropout rate among urban high school students. Among stakeholders designing a social program, there is usually a good deal of agreement about what ultimate results are desired. The theory then explains how a group of early and intermediate actions, interventions, or steps can be taken to bring about the desired long-term change. These will form the basis of program strategies. There is likely to be more, and sometimes severe, disagreement among stakeholders regarding the choice of strategies. This is due to differences in stakeholders' underlying assumptions about the process through which change will occur; specifically, the ways in which all of the required early and intermediate outcomes relate to achieving the desired long-term change. These underlying assumptions can be based on beliefs and knowledge about the nature of human behavior.[11] Knowledge can come from research, theory, or practice. Assumptions, however, may also be based on experiences, habits, or values not reflected in this knowledge. At worst, assumptions may come from dogma, misinformation, or ignorance.

For our example, should our program provide tutors for those currently not performing at grade level, more Head Start–type services, family counseling, stricter discipline in schools, or single-gender classrooms? Each of these is based on different assumptions about what drives student behavior. Each of them is, essentially, a different theory of change. One value of developing a theory of change is to surface differences among stakeholders and provide a mechanism for explicitly considering and, ideally, resolving differences among them. Although it may be challenging for the differing stakeholders to negotiate, if consensus or compromise is reached, this will enhance subsequent buy-in to program design and operation. If differences persist, at least the criterion upon which action is taken is explicit and subject to subsequent review as program results are acquired.

Following the clarification and elaboration of an opportunity as described earlier, work can begin on the development of more specific plans for creating a social venture to realize the opportunity.

PUTTING THEORY INTO ACTION: DEVELOPING THE OPERATING MODEL

The operating model describes how the social impact theory will be implemented in practice. It is a combination of specific activities, structures, and support systems designed to work together to bring about the intended impact. This should begin with the specification of a logic model, which traces how resources and program activities lead to results. In addition, the model should be analyzed to assess how social value is created within this chain of activity. Once key activities have been identified, decisions must be made about the structures needed to accomplish these activities and the support systems needed to ensure effective and efficient social value creation. Because structures and support systems are specific and likely to be different for every venture, we will restrict the discussion that follows to logic models and social value chain analysis.

In addition, the social entrepreneur may have several additional options. She may be able to choose the organizational form of the venture. As a guide, the advantages and disadvantages of adopting a nonprofit versus a for-profit organizational form will be considered. Also, the entrepreneur may have the option to launch the venture as a new organization or as a program in an existing organization. Here again, there are advantages and disadvantages to each option.

Program Logic Model

At its most basic, a program logic model is a systematic and visual way to present the relationships among program resources, activities, and results, as shown in Figure 4.3. It is a description of the sequence of activities thought to bring about change and how these activities are linked to the results the program is expected to achieve.[12]

In this model, resources include human, financial, organizational, and community inputs available to the program, including clients or others who will benefit from the social venture. Program activities are the processes, tools, events,

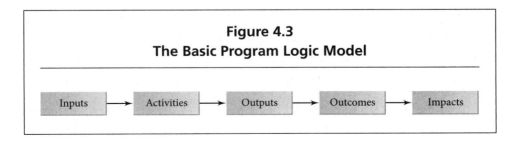

Figure 4.3
The Basic Program Logic Model

Inputs → Activities → Outputs → Outcomes → Impacts

technology, and actions intended to bring about the desired program changes or results. Outputs are the direct result of program activities, including the types, levels, and targets of services. For BOSS, program activities included job training and, later, enterprise development. Program outputs for BOSS included employable clients and, it is expected, a viable enterprise. Outcomes are changes in program participants' behavior, knowledge, skills, status, or level of functioning. These can be classified as short- or long-term, with the exact time frame varying depending on the type of change being considered. Finally, impact is more fundamental change occurring in organizations, communities, or systems as a result of program activity. For example, a community may be expected to function better if its residents are not impoverished. For the BOSS employment training program, the client outcomes would include improved life conditions resulting from employment, which would in turn contribute to community stability (impacts).

The program logic model is linked to the theory of change developed earlier.[13] The logic model starts with the results envisioned by the theory of change. These are the basis of the logic model's outcomes and impacts. The strategies and assumptions of the theory of change are used to develop the inputs, activities, and outputs of the logic model.

Given its link to the theory of change, the logic model is actually constructed from right to left, starting with impacts and outcomes. When read from left to right, however, the logic model allows you to follow a chain of reasoning connecting the program's parts. This reasoning can be expressed as a sequential series of "If . . . then" statements as follows, starting with inputs.

1. *Inputs*: Certain resources are needed to operate your program.

2. *Activities*: If you have access to them, then you can use them to accomplish your planned activities.

3. *Outputs*: If you accomplish your planned activities, then you will deliver the amount of product or service that you intend.

4. *Outcomes*: If you accomplish your planned activities to the extent you intend, then your participants will benefit in certain ways.

5. *Impacts*: If these benefits to participants are achieved, then certain changes in organizations, communities, or systems may be expected to occur.

Creating a program logic model has a number of benefits. The logic model serves as a planning tool to develop programs. It can serve as the basis for program strategy, structure, and design. In addition, it can facilitate the clear explanation and illustration of program concepts and approach for internal and external stakeholders. The logic model will also assist program implementation by helping to identify the data needed to monitor and improve performance. The logic model will focus data collection on the program aspects most critical for tracking and reporting. This can, in addition, form the basis of program evaluation and reporting.

Creating Social Value in the Value Chain

Value chains are used in business to analyze how a firm can create competitive advantage by creating value for its customers. Michael Porter developed a generic model that sees the firm as a set of value-adding activities that link inputs to outputs purchased by customers.[14] These activities can then be used to analyze their contribution to costs and profits. The model includes both primary and support activities.

Primary activities relate directly to the creation, sale, maintenance, and support of a product or service; they are generally prioritized in a sequence. Inbound logistics are processes related to acquiring inputs. Operations are activities that change inputs into outputs, which are sold to customers. Outbound logistics are activities to deliver your product or service to your customer. Marketing and sales are processes to persuade customers to purchase from you. Service relates to activities for maintaining the value of your product or service to your customers after it is purchased.

Support activities support the primary activities; they include firm infrastructure, human resource management, technology development, and procurement.

Although the model was initially developed to analyze the impact of firm activities on profit, the value chain can also be used by social entrepreneurs to analyze the impact of organizational activities on the creation of social value. Porter and Kramer propose that firms consider the social impacts of their value chains.[15] This includes both mitigating harm from value chain activities (such as reducing pollution) and transforming value chain activities to benefit society (such as using local suppliers or labor force). Sommerrock discusses a *social value chain* and describes how primary value chain activities can create social value.[16] The social value produced by any particular value chain activity could be the primary social goal of the venture. Other value chain activities should also be analyzed to see if additional social value could be created.

Social value chain activities can include:

- *Procuring supplies.* Procuring components from disadvantaged suppliers; using environmentally sustainable or supporting services.

- *Operations.* Employing disadvantaged persons (such as disabled, homeless, elderly); designing products or services that solve specific problems and in so doing acknowledge local conditions and requirements that existing products and services do not consider; making production of regular products and services more efficient or affordable for poor people.

- *Marketing and distribution.* Using modern technology or local traditional habits.

VENTURE FEASIBILITY AND PLANNING

The activities just described will clarify the mission, goals, objectives, and major activities of the social venture. More specific assessment and planning should now take place. The feasibility of the venture should be assessed. This is a check on whether the opportunity is viable against a set of initial criteria. If the venture is judged to be feasible, a more detailed business plan should be developed. This will involve more detailed analysis of internal and external considerations. In this section we review the factors that should be considered for the feasibility assessment and the business plan. In the section that follows we describe key analyses that social entrepreneurs need carry out in support of these activities.

Assessing the Venture's Feasibility

A feasibility study is designed to research the practicality of engaging in a new venture.[17] This assesses the practicality of operating the new venture. It should be completed in a relatively short time frame (four to eight weeks is recommended). Research needs to be done on the market to determine the need for the venture's output, the resources the venture will need, potential pitfalls and problems, competition, and the possibility of expansion. BOSS used its feasibility study as a focusing process that evaluated potential enterprises against criteria that became more focused as the process evolved. Clients and stakeholders were important participants in this process.

The feasibility study is not designed to promote the venture or develop specific strategic plans; rather, its purpose is to assess the advantages and disadvantages of proceeding with venture development. It should provide management and the board with an analysis of the venture's risks and rewards. If a decision is made to proceed with the venture, more detailed analyses and planning should be conducted, including a business plan.

The following are important elements to include in a social-entrepreneurial feasibility study:[18]

- *Venture description*: including a clear description of the proposed product or service and its goals for creating social and economic value
- *Industry information*: description of current industry participants, threats of new entrants, competition from substitute products, demand from users and funders, bargaining power of suppliers
- *Target and niche markets*: an initial assessment of clients or customers, basic demographics, motivators and barriers to adoption of the product or service, what competitors are doing and your competitive advantages (unique or unusual advantages your organization possesses that will make a difference to those customers and markets)
- *Resource needs to successfully create the product or service*: human, physical, financial
- *Policy or political environment*: opportunities or barriers
- *Assessment of benefits*: value-added services to the organization and community at large, growth and near-term potential
- *Financial review*: expense budget and breakeven, financial projections and risks
- *Assessment of disadvantages*: obstacles, potential negative impacts and problems, risk to investment and legal status, political complications
- *Recommendation*: whether venture development should or should not proceed, given the details of the assessment

The Venture's Business Plan

Once a decision has been made to pursue a venture, based on the feasibility assessment, a business plan is written to lay out all the details needed to explain and justify the operation of the venture. The business plan compiles information from the previous steps and adds more operational details. It normally includes descriptions of objectives, details of operations, and financial projections as well as positions the venture in its larger environment. It differs from a strategic plan, which is written to provide an internal roadmap for guiding work activities and achieving outputs. The business plan, in contrast, is also written for external audiences, to explain to outsiders the fundamentals of the venture and why the originators feel it is worthwhile and will be a success.[19] As such, it can be used to obtain allies, raise money, establish partnerships, and attract new leaders.

A Google search will reveal the many guides available for creating business plans for firms.[20] The purpose of a commercial venture in a for-profit is to generate economic value (profits) that can be distributed to the owners of the business. Hence their business plans will be focused on the profit-making prospects of the venture. As we have noted, however, while social entrepreneurs can design ventures that generate economic value, the primary goal of a social venture is the generation of social value. Social venture business plans need to address this important aspect of their goals, operations, and outcomes. So in addition to the commercial, operational, and financial considerations, social venture business plans also need to consider factors such as the social problem to be addressed, the vision and mission of the venture, its social impact theory, and how social impact will be measured.[21]

Wolk and Kreitz provide a planning guide that is particularly useful for social entrepreneurial ventures and takes advantage of the work that has already been done on opportunity development and social value clarification, as outlined earlier.[22] We have adapted their outline of a business plan as follows:

I. Executive Summary

II. Need and Opportunity

    A. Overview of Social Problem

    B. Current Trends: social, political, legal, economic trends affecting the problem

    C. Root Causes of the Problem

    D. Environmental Landscape: approaches of other organizations working on the problem

    E. Barriers: challenges to making progress in addressing the problem

    F. Opportunities: how the above information frames opportunities to address the problem

III. Social Impact Model

    A. Overview of Organization: including mission-based activities

    B. Social Impact Model: including social problem definition, mission, indicators, and vision of success

    C. Description of Operational Model: program logic model, personnel and resources needed

    D. Description of Social Impact Strategy: strategies to carry out mission, strengthen the operating model, and achieve vision of success

IV. Implementation Strategy

    A. Business Plan Timelines: pilot (phase one, twelve to twenty-four months), rollout (phase two), scaling (phase three)

    B. Phase One Strategy Goals: ground social impact strategy in a set of concrete actions

    C. Organizational Capacity Building

        1. Team and Governance: roles, responsibilities, and skills of paid staff, board members, and volunteers

        2. Financial Sustainability: including financial projections and capitalization strategy

        3. Marketing: branding, communication, target marketing, and partnerships

        4. Technology: current use, future needs, resources to obtain

        5. Public Policy: current policies that relate to problem, policies that might assist programs, opportunity to spread impact through legislation

        6. Performance and Social Impact Measurement: including indicators and targets for measurement and feedback loop to improve performance

        7. Risk Mitigation: risks that might limit success, plans to mitigate risk

V. Phase One Action Plan: assign responsibilities and establish timelines for activities

VI. Appendix: supporting documentation and assumptions made

As this outline shows, a great deal of information needs to be included in the business plan. Research and analysis are needed to acquire this information.

Much of this will be specific to the goals and operational details of the venture and will differ among organizations and ventures. Several types of analysis, however, will have similar elements between ventures. As such, we can look at their common features. We next consider several of these, particularly understanding and taking risks, understanding the market, and mobilizing resources.

SUPPORTING ANALYSIS

As part of the planning process, a number of supporting analyses should be carried out to provide information on important factors that will impact the venture. This includes assessing the risks associated with the venture and major aspects of the venture's environment, including the market, the policy field, and the resource environment.

Risk Assessment

In earlier chapters we have seen how the notion of risk is inherent in entrepreneurship. We now discuss how risk can be considered in venture planning. Any new activity involves risk in the sense that the actual results might not be as expected. According to Morris, Kuratko, and Covin, "Risk-taking involves a willingness to pursue opportunities that have a reasonable likelihood of producing losses or significant performance discrepancies."[23] They go on to note, however, that "Entrepreneurship does not entail reckless decision making. It involves a reasonable awareness of the risks involved . . . and an attempt to manage these risks."[24] Although the business world has paid more attention to risk than the nonprofit sector has, several recent works have addressed risk in social entrepreneurship.[25] These consider risk taking and have tabulated the types of risks that social ventures can become subject to. We draw upon their work to categorize risk and present some questions to ask when assessing it.

- Financial risk
  - What is the financial exposure of the venture?
  - How much donated or earned income might be vulnerable?
  - What are the financially riskiest points in the plan?
  - What would a worst-case financial scenario be?

- Organizational or operational risk

  - Management team: Are skill sets appropriate? Does the team work well together? Likelihood and consequences of members leaving?

  - Workforce: Are skills, knowledge, and abilities adequate? Are any needed supports available? Likelihood and consequences of turnover?

  - Culture: Does the culture support entrepreneurship (risk taking, innovation, proactivity)?

  - Infrastructure: Is funding adequate?

- Venture or enterprise risk

  - Concept: Is the venture strategy tested and reliable or new and uncertain? Is the venture riskier than other similar ventures? What makes it particularly risky?

  - Capitalization: Can funding for venture startup or development be obtained in a timely manner? Can any debt that is acquired be serviced?

  - Infrastructure: Are people, facilities, etc. available for the venture?

  - Mission: Is venture central to the mission? Is the organization clearly focused on its mission or are there competing agendas?

- External environment risk

  - Marketplace: How might changes in competitors; capital; the demographics, tastes, or preferences of consumers or donors; and the business cycle impact the venture?

  - Political and government: Might changes in policy, regulation, or funding affect the venture?

  - Technology: How might shifts in technology affect the venture?

  - Stakeholder backlash: If products or services are sold, will some stakeholders respond negatively? This could be the case if a nonprofit begins to charge for previously free services.

In addition, Dickson and Giglierano discuss the risk associated with the timing of ventures.[26] Two types of risk, with different time trajectories, are considered:

- *"Sinking the boat" risk*: The risk of failure due to launching a venture that does not work, due to poor concept, bad timing, or an inadequate marketing. This risk starts high and decreases over time as better information is acquired. For BOSS, conducting hurried or poor feasibility or marketing analyses may lead it to launch an enterprise in an unprofitable market.

- *"Missing the boat" risk*: The risk of not starting a venture that would have succeeded, due to delaying acting on a concept too long and competitors launching the venture first or the market undergoing a change. This risk starts low and increases over time as delay accumulates, perhaps while acquiring more information. BOSS considered ninety-one possible enterprises and needed to evaluate these in a timely manner in order to mitigate this risk.

- *Total risk* is the sum of both types of risk.

When taking both types of risk into account, total risk starts high due to high "sinking the boat" risk and low "missing the boat" risk. Total risk will decrease over time as "sinking the boat" risk falls and "missing the boat" risk rises. Total risk then rises again, as "missing the boat" risk rises above "sinking the boat" risk. The social entrepreneur needs to be aware of these consequences of timing and determine when total risk rises above a problematic level.

Market Analysis

Nonprofit marketing is a well-established field, and many good texts are available to guide practitioners.[27] Marketing uses a mix of controllable elements to create value for both consumers and the organization. These elements are commonly termed the *marketing mix* or the 4P's: product (including service), price, place, and promotion. Several marketing ideas are particularly relevant for the creation of new ventures. As shown in Figure 4.4, products or services have predictable life-cycles. Of particular concern for us at this point are the product development and introduction stages.

The activities we have discussed regarding the development of the opportunity, the theory of change, and the social value proposition take place during the development stage of the product life cycle. During this stage, the expected beneficiaries of the social venture and the products or services they are to receive will be identified. In marketing terminology, these are called target audiences, and marketing research and market segmentation are useful for specifically identifying them. Marketing research can be done using a variety of data gathering techniques, including existing information, focus groups, surveys, observation, and test marketing. Segmentation is the identification of groups of users

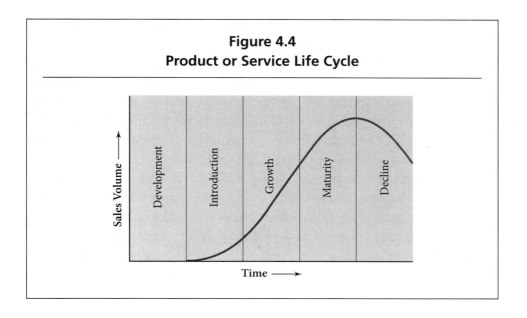

Figure 4.4
Product or Service Life Cycle

Sales Volume →

Development | Introduction | Growth | Maturity | Decline

Time →

or consumers based on some meaningful criteria. In this case, segmentation criteria are related to the social value that will be produced. Segmentation will tell you whether the target audience is homogeneous or, more likely, portions of the target audience differ and, if so, on what basis they differ. Market segments should be clearly different from each other, likely to respond differently to messages, and sufficiently large to be worth different marketing approaches.[28] Segmentation could be based on demographic criteria (such as age or gender), geographic criteria (such as where people live), product or service criteria (such as the benefits needed), or psychographic criteria (such as lifestyle or values).

Once the most relevant market segment(s) for the venture are identified, the marketing mix will be developed to appeal to them. Several broad strategic targeting choices are possible.[29] An undifferentiated (mass) marketing strategy goes after the whole market with one offering and marketing mix. On the other hand, a differentiated marketing strategy would go after several market segments with an offering and market mix for each. Finally, a concentrated marketing strategy goes after one market segment with a unique offer and marketing mix.

The introduction stage of the product life-cycle involves the initial adoption of a product or service. Research on the adoption of innovation has established adopter categories. The first 2.5 percent of adopters are labeled innovators.[30] After these, the next 13.5 percent are termed early adopters, the next 34 percent early majority, the next 34 percent late majority, and the final 16 percent laggards. Innovators are characterized by venturesomeness, as they like to try new, and possibly even risky, ideas. Marketers should not focus heavily on this group, as it is very small, members are likely to find the new venture on their own, and they have little or no influence on later adopters. The lack of influence is due to other adopters' seeing innovators as having a try-anything-once attitude. Initial marketing plans should instead target early adopters. Members of this group will occupy some prominent position in the community or industry and may in fact be looked up to as opinion leaders. They will adopt an innovation if it will enhance their standing as trendsetters, and new venture promotional efforts can be designed with this in mind. This group can be identified through self-reporting or reports from others (reputation). Researchers could also map the interactions among members of a population and establish the most influential members (sociometric techniques).

Policy Field Analysis

Because they are dealing with social and public issues, social entrepreneurs often find themselves involved in areas influenced by public policy and the actions of government agencies. For example, social entrepreneurs providing educational services will inevitably and significantly be influenced by the public education system. In these arenas, social entrepreneurs could relate to public agencies in a number of ways. They may work in cooperation with, in opposition to, or independently of government agencies. No matter the relationship, however, social entrepreneurs need to understand how public policy directly or indirectly influences their environments. This can be quite complicated, as public actors from numerous levels of government may be involved in any given service area, and these public actors may play numerous—and sometimes multiple—roles, such as legislation, regulation, funding, and service provision.

Stone and Sandfort have developed a method whereby social entrepreneurs can analyze the roles that organizations play in policy fields.[31] In their framework, "Policy fields—public and private institutions in a substantive public policy or program area in a particular place—shape how state and local actors work to solve public management problems, and their pursuit of programmatic goals in turn shapes the policy field."[32] An example of the organizations and relationships in the policy field of early childhood education in Minnesota is shown in Figure 4.5. It depicts how local childhood education nonprofit organizations are

Figure 4.5
Early Childhood Education Policy Field in Minnesota, 2008

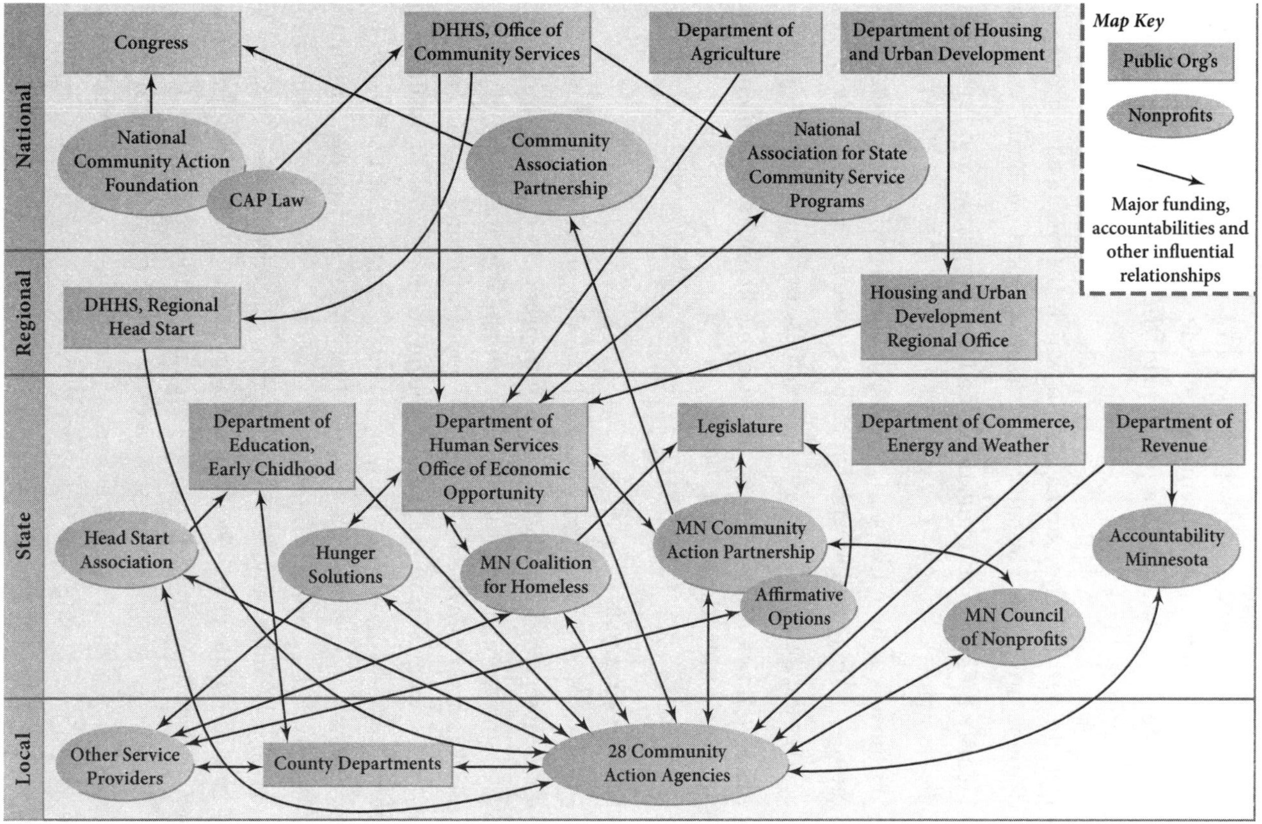

Map Key

Public Org's

Nonprofits

→ Major funding, accountabilities and other influential relationships

National

Congress

National Community Action Foundation

CAP Law

DHHS, Office of Community Services

Department of Agriculture

Department of Housing and Urban Development

Community Association Partnership

National Association for State Community Service Programs

Regional

DHHS, Regional Head Start

Housing and Urban Development Regional Office

State

Department of Education, Early Childhood

Legislature

Department of Commerce, Energy and Weather

Department of Revenue

Department of Human Services Office of Economic Opportunity

MN Community Action Partnership

Affirmative Options

Accountability Minnesota

MN Council of Nonprofits

Hunger Solutions

MN Coalition for Homeless

Head Start Association

Local

County Departments

Other Service Providers

28 Community Action Agencies

Source: Sandfort (2010, p. 640).[33]

affected by the relationships and flows of influence among public and private organizations at local, state, regional, and national levels. Connections and flows between organizations can be presented in terms of matters such as resources, administrative authority, information, or referrals.

To systematically analyze a policy field, the social entrepreneur should complete a number of tasks:

- Determine the policy domain(s) in which the organization operates. Policy domains are defined by substantive issues (education, health care, welfare).

- Identify the laws and regulations, national programs, and funding streams in the domain(s).

- Within the state and local context, determine which organizations have an interest in this problem and which have power to influence decisions.

- Specify the linkages and ties between these organizations.

- Analyze how the structure of the local field constrains and enables organizational and individual action.[34]

Resource Analysis

A wise use of resources can make all the difference for the success or failure of a business venture. All successful entrepreneurs learn how to do more with less. Resources include human capital, financing, industrial capital, structural networks, and knowledge. Once the opportunity for social entrepreneurship has been recognized, entrepreneurs begin to harness their resources and allocate them in the most effective way possible. Entrepreneurs need to be creative. For example, Shaw and Carter note that social entrepreneurs often use trading (skills, time, capital) instead of money to achieve their desired results and enhance self-sufficiency.[35] The importance placed on self-sufficiency and effective use of resources is becoming even greater as continuing government funding (in the form of grants) becomes even more uncertain.[36]

Dees suggests that the assessment of the resources a social venture needs should begin with the results desired and the organizational capabilities required to bring these about.[37] For example, to assist communities to redevelop a venture might need capability in community economic analysis, housing revitalization, and business assistance. This is in addition to capabilities needed to run the organization, such as program administration, grant writing, clerical support,

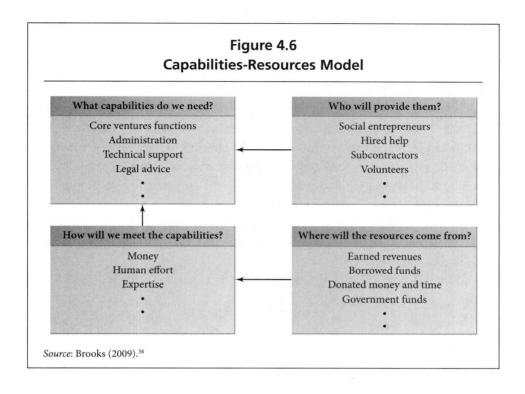

Figure 4.6
Capabilities-Resources Model

What capabilities do we need?	Who will provide them?
Core ventures functions Administration Technical support Legal advice • •	Social entrepreneurs Hired help Subcontractors Volunteers • •

How will we meet the capabilities?	Where will the resources come from?
Money Human effort Expertise • •	Earned revenues Borrowed funds Donated money and time Government funds • •

Source: Brooks (2009).[38]

and so on. These capabilities will help determine an appropriate operating structure and human resource plan. Of particular importance is whether capabilities will be developed internally, such as with staff, or via external sources such as contracting. For example, our redevelopment venture may employ administrative and support staff but contract for analytical services.

Once social entrepreneurs have determined capabilities and operations, they can develop an economic model and resource strategy. Each capability and its associated structure will require resources, such as money and time, to operate. In addition, entrepreneurs should also consider the time frame for resource needs. For example, what capabilities and resources may be needed during the first year and over a three-year period? Once they have specified resources for all capabilities, they can identify possible sources for these resources and develop a financial plan to acquire them. The process can be summarized as shown in Figure 4.6. (We consider the specifics of raising revenue and acquiring other resources in later chapters.)

CONCLUDING THOUGHTS

In this chapter we discussed the beginnings of a social venture—from the recognition of an opportunity to the establishment of a social venture to create the envisioned social value. In many ways this is the most critical stage of the social entrepreneurial process. On the one hand, a great idea will never make a difference in the world if the idea is not developed into a venture. On the other hand, ventures can be based on poor ideas and fail to live up to their promise. We have presented a systematic process for assessing how an opportunity addresses social behavior and how programs to bring about social changes can be developed.

In the next chapter we consider how a social venture can demonstrate its value and increase its impact. Most ventures begin with small-scale programs. The value of these programs needs to be tested and their potential for providing greater impact evaluated.

EXERCISES

Exercise 4.1

Consider a particular social problem (for example, low-income housing, employment assistance, addiction services). Identify a viable opportunity to improve this situation. What makes this a viable opportunity? What theory of change is this opportunity based on? What is its social value proposition?

Exercise 4.2

Propose a social venture operating model, based on the opportunity you identified in Exercise 4.1. How are activities linked to outcomes and impacts?

Exercise 4.3

What market analysis factors are relevant to this social venture? Why are they relevant? To what extent might a policy field analysis help you refine your proposed operating model?

chapter FIVE

From Action to Impact

Y ear Up was founded in 2000 in Boston with an innovative workforce development program to serve disconnected young adults from urban areas. Its premise was that if young adults from urban communities are challenged and supported to learn real job skills and gain hands-on work experience in a corporate environment, they are more likely to get good jobs and go on to college.[1] Year Up collaborates with business and educational partners to offer a comprehensive training and educational program. Year Up program includes six months of technical, communication, and professional skills training. Classes are structured so that students can earn college credit for the satisfactory completion of classes. Students then participate in a six-month internship with Year Up's corporate partners. A weekly stipend is paid during both the classroom and internship phases of the program. Student support is an important part of the program. This is provided by staff advisors, supervisors at internship sites, professional mentors outside the program, and social workers. Finally, students get assistance with the job search process and/or college enrollment upon program completion.

Year Up formulated a three-phase growth plan.[2] In Phase One (2000–2006), Year Up established the viability of its model, launched the program in several additional cities, and increased the number of students that were served. At the end of this phase, a major evaluation of program results was carried out in 2007. Using random samples, the study compared Year Up program graduates with Year Up applicants who did not go through the program (a control group).[3] The study showed that the program had a positive effect on wages. The goals of Phase Two (2007–2011) were to establish the program in more cities across the country, enhance the sustainability of the model, and generate more evidence of program impact. In Phase Three (2012–2016), Year Up will focus on influencing three of the systemic factors contributing to the problem of disconnected young adults: poor-quality workforce training, limited corporate engagement, and inadequate public policy. The growth plan will be discussed further later in the chapter.

In Chapter Four we discussed moving from the recognition of an opportunity to provide social value to the establishment of a new venture to create and distribute that value. This can be accomplished through the establishment of either a new organization or a new program in an existing organization. In this chapter, we discuss how a social entrepreneur moves forward to ensure the success of this new venture. The story of Year Up illustrates this process. As it moved through the process, Year Up answered a number of important questions that all social entrepreneurs need to address: How can a social entrepreneur assess whether the venture is effectively achieving its goals? How can the impact of a venture be determined? Finally, how can impact be increased and the venture move to a more significant level?

This chapter's discussion is outlined in Figure 5.1. The figure illustrates the process of social value provision, from the recognition of an opportunity to widespread social value provision. We have divided this process into two parts. In Phase One, the opportunity is developed into a venture (as discussed in Chapter Four) and its effectiveness established, as we discuss next. This is normally done on a small-scale or local level. If the venture is found to be successful at this level, the prospects for expanding the venture will be evaluated and, if prospects are good, provisions made for expanding impact. This is depicted in Phase Two. Figure 5.1 considers one possible route to expanding impact: scaling up. This and other methods are considered later in this chapter. At all stages in each phase, both contextual and internal factors are important and need to be considered.

SOCIAL VENTURE EFFECTIVENESS

In the most general sense, organizational effectiveness can be defined as doing well according to some kind of standard.[4] Effectiveness, therefore, always involves comparison, either between organizations or between time periods or

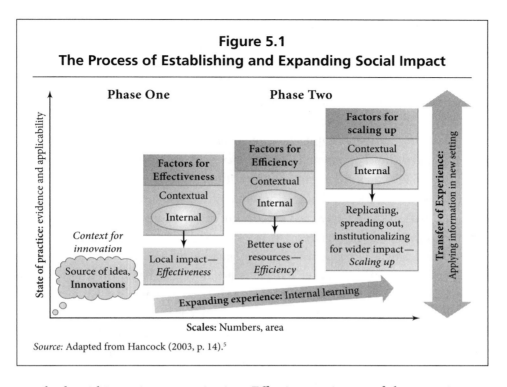

Figure 5.1
The Process of Establishing and Expanding Social Impact

Source: Adapted from Hancock (2003, p. 14).[5]

standards within a given organization. Effectiveness is one of the most important determinates of the success of an organization and, over the years, devising ways to assess or evaluate effectiveness has been a major focus for organizational scholars and practitioners. Although it sounds simple, the evaluation of effectiveness is complicated due to the variety of standards that have been proposed by for its evaluation by those inside as well as outside the organization. Moreover, these standards can be conflicting, making the assessment of effectiveness potentially divisive. Especially for nonprofit organizations with a multitude of stakeholders with different values and criteria for success, effectiveness is essentially a social construction.[6]

Framework for Venture Evaluation. Early attempts at organizational evaluation tended to focus on measuring one particular aspect of organizational performance, such as resource acquisition, internal processes, or goal accomplishment. Although each of these provides information about an important aspect of organizational functioning, each by itself is also limited.[7] Measures of inputs can reveal how successful an organization is in exploiting its environment, but they do not tell us what, if anything, the inputs get used for. Internal activities, such as the amount of work being done, can measure effort or units of output produced, but do not tell us what became of the work or the outputs. It may be tempting to rely on goal accomplishment, but this measure also has complications. Its use requires that the organization's goals be clear and stable and capable of being both prioritized and measured.[8] This poses difficulties for nonprofits, which may have multiple, abstract, shifting, or competing goals. In addition, goals may not be accomplished for a variety of reasons out of the control of the organization. For example, a large increase in community poverty might increase demands on a nonprofit and force it to cut back on the level of services it can deliver to individual clients. Consequently, although goal accomplishment should be part of the effectiveness evaluation, it should be used carefully and in conjunction with other measures.

In general, single-factor approaches to evaluation are usually inadequate, given that overall performance and effectiveness are normally based on a number of internal as well as external factors and on values as well as objective facts. This necessitates a more encompassing view of effectiveness. This was demonstrated empirically in a study of thirty-three social ventures, which found that their success in goal accomplishment and resource acquisition depended on these factors:[9]

- Previous entrepreneurial and management experience
- Capital and staff available at the establishment stage
- Standing the market test (charging fees or getting contracts)
- Venture promotion
- The venture's social network
- Long-term cooperation with other organizations
- Venture acceptance in the public discourse

As we have emphasized, a social entrepreneur's mission is to provide social value. Thus social outcome and impact are the ultimate standards that should be used to assess the effectiveness of the social venture. These, however, depend upon the successful operation of the organization's programs. Therefore, to understand reasons for venture success or failure, it will be necessary to evaluate both internal operations and external results. If the principles and procedures outlined in Chapter Four have been followed, much of the groundwork needed for these evaluations will most likely already have been laid. Of particular utility for evaluation is the development of the theory of change and logic model. As noted, these are a series of "if . . . then" expectations; for example, "if the proper organizational activities are performed, then the expected organizational outcomes will result." These expectations extend from input to impact, and evaluation can then be used to assess whether these expectations have actually come about.

These evaluations are important tests of both our internal processes and the theory of change itself. If outcomes and impacts are as expected, we can have more confidence that we understand how to positively influence human and social behavior. If outcomes and impacts are not as expected, however, we must first be sure that the programs were carried out correctly before we lose confidence in our theory of change. We can assess the way programs were designed and carried out through the evaluation of internal processes.

Figure 5.2 illustrates how a logic model relates to internal activities, external results, and types of evaluation.

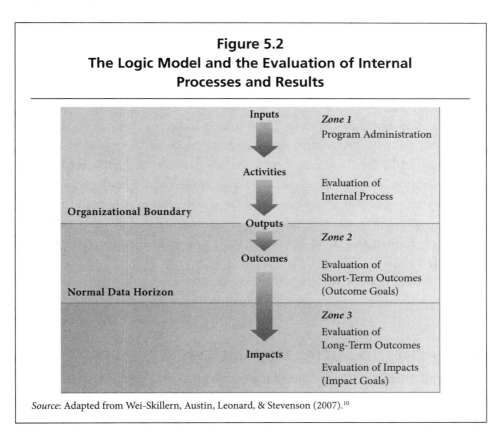

Figure 5.2
The Logic Model and the Evaluation of Internal Processes and Results

Inputs

Zone 1
Program Administration

Activities

Evaluation of
Internal Process

Organizational Boundary

Outputs

Zone 2

Outcomes

Evaluation of
Short-Term Outcomes
(Outcome Goals)

Normal Data Horizon

Zone 3

Evaluation of
Long-Term Outcomes

Impacts

Evaluation of Impacts
(Impact Goals)

Source: Adapted from Wei-Skillern, Austin, Leonard, & Stevenson (2007).[10]

Internal organizational activities take place in Zone 1. In this zone, internal process evaluation can be used to assess whether programs have been appropriately set up, based on the theory of change. For example, does an educational program have teaching staff with required expertise, and is the necessary educational material available (activities)? Also, are the needed numbers of class hours delivered to the appropriate students (outputs)? Administrative records and other data can be used for these evaluations.

The results of organizational programs take place in Zones 2 and 3. Organizational outcomes are changes brought about in program participants. Outcomes can occur in the short or long term. Impacts are more fundamental change occurring in organizations, communities, or systems as a result of program activity. Both of these should be clearly spelled out in the theory of change. An important consideration is how outcomes and impacts can be measured (we discuss this further later in this chapter). What is noteworthy here is that organizations normally gather some information on short-term outcomes; for example, student grades after the completion of an educational course. Year Up would normally collect this type of data. This is depicted as the normal data horizon in Figure 5.2. Long-term outcomes occur later in time and therefore are more difficult or costly to measure. For example, in its evaluation at the end of Phase One, Year Up compared the wages its graduates were getting versus nonparticipants. This was not data that Year Up routinely collected; hence this was outside the normal data horizon. Impacts are likely to be harder to assess, as they are further out in time and can involve factors that are more difficult to measure. For example, has the educational course resulted in students getting better jobs and attaining higher socioeconomic status? And, just as important from the standpoint of impacts, has this helped their communities? Year Up would have to conduct another, and more elaborate, study to evaluate its program's impact on these factors.

Given the framework we have outlined, we next consider a number of more specific approaches or models for the evaluation of venture effectiveness.

APPROACHES TO SOCIAL VENTURE EFFECTIVENESS

A variety of models and techniques for evaluating effectiveness have been developed that take multiple factors into account. We present a number of them here and discuss how they can be used to evaluate the effectiveness of social ventures.

They should be seen as potential alternative tools that social entrepreneurs could employ if they are appropriate to the venture's particular circumstances.

Multiple-factor models are based on the idea that for an organization to succeed, a number of internal and external factors must be taken into account and balanced. This idea can be illustrated by a triangle that represents three components of an organization: mission and mandates, internal capacity, and external support.[11] An excessive focus on any one point of the triangle will unbalance a nonprofit and lead to problems. For example, excessive concern for external support may result in mission drift. Alternatively, building excessive internal capacity will be wasteful, and a single-minded focus on the mission may result in unreasonable promises of results.[12] We next present two balanced approaches, one focusing on subjective factors (values) and the other on a variety of objective and subjective factors.

Values-Based Models

As already noted, evaluation standards have a social basis. Therefore, in assessing effectiveness, the values of important organizational constituencies and stakeholders must be taken into account. This is all the more important for social ventures, since they are based on the production of social value. One model, the *competing values framework*, sees organizational effectiveness as a value-based judgment about the performance of the organization. Research has identified the basis upon which these value-based judgments are typically made by organizational insiders.[13] As shown in Figure 5.3, the competing values framework cross-classifies two value dimensions: the value placed on flexibility versus focus, and the value placed on internal systems versus external positioning.

The quadrants of the diagram identify four models of organizational performance. Each model is characterized by a distinctive culture, orientation, leadership type, value drivers, and theory of effectiveness (our focus here). The factors underlying the models will be weighted differently by different individuals and coalitions within an organization. Each will therefore favor a particular model or model ranking and therefore favor certain criteria for effectiveness. Given the bargaining that organizational coalitions normally need to do, organizations will likely need to adopt some aspect of each model. However, the organizational model and associated effectiveness criteria favored by management will clearly be of primary importance. An examination of the four models indicates that the model in the top right quadrant is the most appropriate for entrepreneurship.

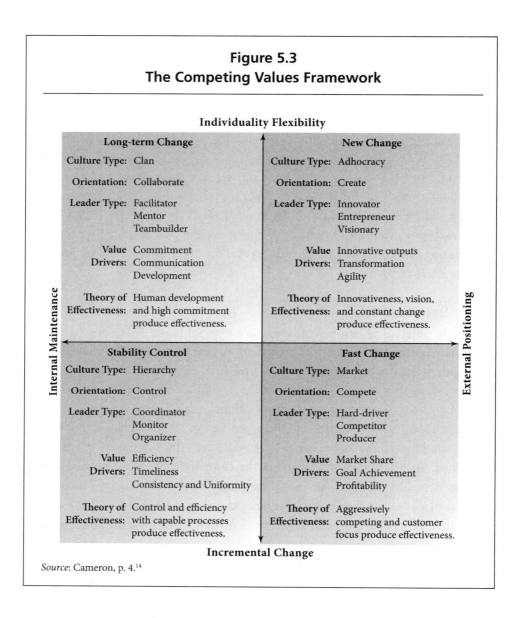

Figure 5.3
The Competing Values Framework

Individuality Flexibility

Internal Maintenance

External Positioning

Long-term Change

Culture Type: Clan

Orientation: Collaborate

Leader Type: Facilitator
Mentor
Teambuilder

Value Commitment
Drivers: Communication
Development

Theory of Human development
Effectiveness: and high commitment
produce effectiveness.

New Change

Culture Type: Adhocracy

Orientation: Create

Leader Type: Innovator
Entrepreneur
Visionary

Value Innovative outputs
Drivers: Transformation
Agility

Theory of Innovativeness, vision,
Effectiveness: and constant change
produce effectiveness.

Stability Control

Culture Type: Hierarchy

Orientation: Control

Leader Type: Coordinator
Monitor
Organizer

Value Efficiency
Drivers: Timeliness
Consistency and Uniformity

Theory of Control and efficiency
Effectiveness: with capable processes
produce effectiveness.

Fast Change

Culture Type: Market

Orientation: Compete

Leader Type: Hard-driver
Competitor
Producer

Value Market Share
Drivers: Goal Achievement
Profitability

Theory of Aggressively
Effectiveness: competing and customer
focus produce effectiveness.

Incremental Change

Source: Cameron, p. 4.[14]

This model is labeled "New Change"; it has also been referred to as an "open systems" model.[15] Organizations using this model are characterized by innovation, entrepreneurship, vision, responsiveness, and change. These will hence become standards for the evaluation of effectiveness. Therefore social entrepreneurs, with their focus on mission and social value definition and delivery, should be sure that this model is given a strong emphasis in organizational performance and evaluation.

A more general *stakeholder satisfaction model* can take the values of a variety of stakeholders into account.[16] In addition to the managers just considered, a variety of other stakeholders are likely to be important to organizations. For nonprofits, a partial listing would include employees, volunteers, board members, client groups, government regulators, donors, customers, partners, and competitors. The satisfaction of any or all stakeholders could be used to assess the effectiveness of an organization. Organizations clearly need to pay attention to important stakeholders; however, stakeholder satisfaction models become more complex as the number and diversity of stakeholders increases. Not only are there more factors to take into account, but stakeholders are also likely to have conflicting interests and make competing demands on the organization. For example, in Phase Three of Year Up's program, stakeholders would include its management, the program participants, corporate partners, and public-sector leaders. These stakeholders are likely to have differing priorities. Year Up may, for example, want to maximize its public funding, whereas public leaders are likely to want to spend as little public money as possible. Also, program graduates will want high wages, whereas corporations will likely want to keep labor costs down. To address this, organizations can profile the nature and strength of each stakeholder's interest in the organization as well as the stakeholder's ability to influence the organization. Mapping the interests and power of each stakeholder will allow the organization to identify which stakeholders merit the most attention and to prioritize its response to these.

Value-based models of effectiveness are important for social entrepreneurs. The beneficiaries of the social venture should be major stakeholders. Although they may not have much power in regard to the organization, they are the major reason for the venture, so their values and interests should be paramount considerations. This is consistent with the recommendations of Herman and Renz that the evaluation of nonprofit effectiveness should be in terms of responsiveness to the needs and expectations of stakeholders, including the interests of the least advantaged in a community or society.[17]

Besides models based on the multiple values that underlie stakeholder's assessments of the effectiveness of social ventures, evaluation approaches have been developed that consider a number of other organizational attributes, several of which we discuss next.

Multi-Attribute Approaches

A number of formulations have been developed that consider effectiveness to stem from a number of factors that need to be attended to simultaneously. For example, Kushner and Poole maintain that the assessment of organizational effectiveness must take five dimensions of performance into account, including the satisfaction of constituencies, adequacy of funding, efficiency of operations, attainment of goals, and ability to adapt to a changing environment.[18]

The *Balanced Scorecard* was formulated by Kaplan and Norton to translate organizational mission and strategy into objectives and measures that can be used to assess effectiveness. The scorecard was originally designed for for-profit organizations. It assumed that the primary goal of a business is long-rum profit maximization, which can be achieved through a balance of performance attributes. The scorecard considers organizational performance on four dimensions, or perspectives, which are seen as drivers of current and future success.[19]

- *Financial perspective.* Summarizes the readily measureable economic consequences of actions already taken. Indicates whether a company's strategy, implementation, and execution are contributing to bottom-line improvement.

- *Customer perspective.* Identifies the customer and market segments in which the business competes and measures performance in these segments. Enables the articulation of customer and market-based strategy that will deliver superior future financial returns.

- *Internal-business-process perspective.* Identifies the critical internal processes in which the organization must excel. Focuses on those that will have the greatest impact on customer satisfaction and achieving financial objectives.

- *Learning and growth perspective.* Identifies the infrastructure (people, systems, procedures) the organization must build to create long-term growth and improvement in the other perspectives.

The simultaneous use of these diverse perspectives is designed to provide a balance between short- and long-term objectives, between outcomes desired and drivers, and between objective and subjective measures. Each of the perspectives is linked to the others, and strategy should pervade and reinforce all four perspectives. For example, in a for-profit setting, return on capital employed could be a measure in the financial perspective.[20] If this is driven by sales to customers, market factors leading to those sales, such as customer loyalty in response to on-time delivery, would be included in the customer perspective. This would lead to the identification of needed internal processes, such as low production error rates, in the internal perspective. Finally, this would be supported by skills improvement in the learning and growth perspective. In this way, the perspectives can identify factors needed for strategic success, objectives for performance, and measures for evaluation and reporting.

The Balanced Scorecard has been used outside the for-profit sector. Figure 5.4 shows how the scorecard could be applied to public or nonprofit organizations.[21] The Balanced Scorecard in Figure 5.4 differs in several significant ways from those of for-profit organizations. As the figure shows, in nonprofit or public agencies, mission moves to the top of the scorecard and becomes the goal of organizational activity. This differs from the for-profit setting, where all scorecard measures should be designed to lead to improving bottom-line performance in order

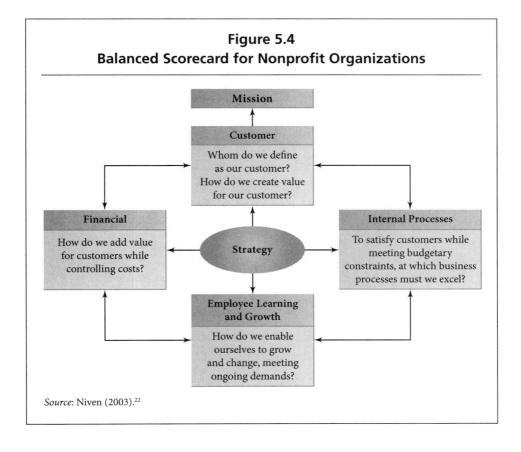

Figure 5.4
Balanced Scorecard for Nonprofit Organizations

Mission

Customer
Whom do we define as our customer?
How do we create value for our customer?

Financial
How do we add value for customers while controlling costs?

Strategy

Internal Processes
To satisfy customers while meeting budgetary constraints, at which business processes must we excel?

Employee Learning and Growth
How do we enable ourselves to grow and change, meeting ongoing demands?

Source: Niven (2003).[22]

to increase shareholder value. Although social mission, such as the eradication of hunger, is a long-term goal, and its accomplishment may be beyond the control of a single organization, it is the ultimate purpose of a nonprofit or public agency and must be included in the scorecard. The other perspectives in the scorecard are related to it, as they serve to move the organization toward the mission. They can be used to assess progress toward mission in the short and medium terms. For example, as Year Up seeks to expand in Phases Two and Three, it will be important to ensure that finances, internal processes, and learning and growth contribute to the accomplishment of strategic program (customer) goals.

This mission focus pervades the rest of the model and has significant consequences. In the for-profit model, accountability to shareholders is monitored through results in the financial perspective, which therefore attains primary importance in the scorecard.[23] In Figure 5.4, mission focus makes the customer perspective of primary importance. The mission can't be accomplished without providing social value to clients, customers, or other beneficiaries. It follows that activities and measures in the other perspectives should be designed to enhance social value and mission accomplishment.

Organizational dashboards are another balanced method for assessing effectiveness. A dashboard is a performance evaluation tool that provides a high-level overview of the progress of key activities and initiatives toward annual objectives and strategic priorities. Dashboards are designed to identify and report critical key objectives, indicators, and projects or tasks needed to steer an organization toward its mission.[24] The dashboard analogy is used because the indicators should allow management to keep its eye on what is most important to steer the organization. As such, they facilitate the management of processes needed to enhance performance and effectiveness. Paton has developed a dashboard framework for nonprofit organizations.[25] The approach assesses both the results of organizational activities and how well-run the organization is, as these are separate matters and both need to be considered to assess overall organizational performance. The dashboard includes five dimensions spanning short- to long-term measures:[26]

- Current results: Monthly checking of progress against key targets, such as summary achievements, finances, marketing

- Underlying performance: Annual reviews of appropriateness and cost-effectiveness of programs and support functions, such as service and business outcomes and external trends and comparisons.

- Risks: Monitoring ways the organization may be put in jeopardy, such as liquidity crisis, legal threats, or breakdown in key relationships.

- Assets and capabilities: Annual review of capacity to deliver future performance, such as physical and financial assets, external reputation and relationships, and expertise and process knowledge.

- Change projects: Regular reporting on initiatives the trustees or senior team are supervising directly.

Social entrepreneurs can use dashboards to provide overviews of performance to organizational leaders. They are useful for providing a snapshot of current activity and performance, change over time, and progress toward goals. Displays can also be produced that provide summary information on programs and outcomes to external stakeholders, such as funders or community leaders. Year Up has adopted a dashboard approach and tracks nineteen metrics in seven key program areas: student pipeline cultivation, consistent student support, teaching marketable skills, providing quality service to partners, student success, staff recruitment and retention, and sustainable program infrastructure.[27] Figure 5.5 shows the dashboard display for two of these elements, having to do with service to partners. The dashboard shows that the average number of apprentices per partner in three cities is growing over time. However, the latest numbers in Massachusetts and Rhode Island are in the "yellow" range (between two and four apprentices per partner), meaning that further attention is needed. Moreover, the number for the District of Columbia is in the "red" (less than two), indicating significant concern. On the other hand, the numbers for satisfaction with Year Up are all in the "green" (over 90 percent satisfaction), indicating that in this area Year Up is performing on target.

The preceding discussion stressed the need to consider both internal processes and external results in any overall organizational evaluation. We have also noted that the mission-centered nature of nonprofit organizations makes the assessment of program outcomes and impacts a primary focus. We discuss outcome and impact assessment in more detail in the following section.

OUTCOME AND IMPACT EVALUATION

Evaluating outcomes and impacts is especially important for entrepreneurial ventures. These are new programs that are designed to provide social value in

Figure 5.5
Year Up Dashboard Elements

Key

(G) • Green means that the area is performing on target

(Y) • Yellow means caution and further attention and analysis is warranted

(R) • Red means there are significant concerns and follow-up is a priority

Metric	Comments and Rules

Average Number of Apprentices Per Partner

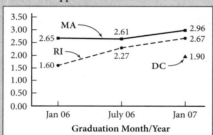

Graduation Month/Year

Consolidation among major partners in Boston and Providence continues.

In Boston, six major partners account for 53% of all apprenticeships.

(G) • > = 4 apprentices per partner

(Y) • 2< apprentices per partner <4

(R) • Apprentices per partner < = 2

Metric	Comments and Rules

Satisfaction with Year Up
Question: *Based on this apprentice's performance, would you continue relationship with Year Up?*

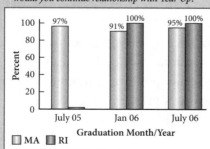

Graduation Month/Year

Apprenticeship partners remain generally satisfied with Year Up relationship.

Survey data for most recent class will be available in fall.

(G) • Yes > = 90%

(Y) • 85% < Yes <90%

(R) • Yes < = 85%

Source: Year Up.

innovative ways. The ultimate test of the theories of change that these ventures are based on is the degree to which the social value is actually delivered to beneficiaries. Programs can be designed and organizational outputs can be delivered as planned, but the question still remains whether the social benefits envisioned were forthcoming. For example, a vocational education program can be delivered, but did students actually acquire new skills, and did these new skills actually enhance their job attainment, their families, or their communities? This can be determined only by evaluating program outcomes and impacts.

Evaluating outcomes and impacts is often far from simple. As Figure 5.2 shows, it entails measuring what happens to individuals, groups, or communities after the organization's programs are delivered. As time goes by, this becomes more difficult for a number of reasons. The scope of the factors to be measured grows, and the data needed gets more difficult to collect. Short- and intermediate-term changes in program participants (outcomes) are likely to be both more specific and easier to measure than the fundamental or long-term changes in communities or systems (impacts) that result. For example, an outcome goal of an environmental awareness program might be to increase participants' knowledge of factors leading to stream and river pollution. Other desired outcomes might be a commitment by participants to cut pollution in any streams or creeks in their communities and their actual involvement in activities to do so. The impacts of this activity would be the long-term reduction of pollutants in these waterways and improvement in water quality. This would benefit the entire community. Although changes in pollution levels after a year or so could be measured, the measurement of other benefits, such as increase in recreational use of waterways or the enhancement of neighborhood quality, would pose more of a challenge.

Outcome evaluation examines the direct effects of programs on participants and should provide insight into how to improve programs. For example, the desired outcomes for the participants of an environmental education program would most likely include benefits in five areas:[28]

- Knowledge about the environment, the phenomena that shape it, and its associated problems and their potential solutions

- Thinking and action skills relevant to identifying, preventing, and addressing environmental problems

- Improved attitudes toward nature, the built environment, or how humans relate to their environment

- Intention to act in some specific way or accomplish a goal that fosters environmental protection or improvement

- Changed behavior (action) in some way that benefits the environment, such as changing lifestyle habits or participating in restoration activities

Impact evaluation seeks to assess broad, long-term changes that occur as a result of a program. An impact evaluation may, for example, show that lower rates of community-wide solid waste accumulation were the direct result of a school environmental program promoting community recycling and composting behaviors.[29] Although the outcomes of an environmental education program just listed could be evaluated fairly quickly, it will likely be much longer before the impact takes effect. For this program, there may be educational, environmental, and health impacts.[30]

- Educational impacts would contribute to meeting long-term education goals. The program could inspire student and teachers, leading to better performance in other classes. In addition, as part of the program the school's grounds could be improved.

- Environmental impacts would include some level of improvement in environmental quality and prevention of environmental harms, such as less littering in school or community recycling rates. Environmental impacts occur as a result of changes in participants' behavior

- Health impacts would include positive changes in human health and health care resulting from the program. Healthcare outcomes may include environmentally healthier facilities for health care, improved rates of correct diagnosis of environmental health problems, and greater communication of environmental health risks between doctors and patients.

Evaluation Research Designs

Outcome and impact evaluation requires data on the degree to which program goals were realized. These goals have to do with changes brought about in recipients, groups, or communities through program activities. Consequently, data on change attributable to program activity must be obtained. A variety of data collection designs are available. They compare outcomes and impacts with what would have happened without the program. Harrell and colleagues provide a good overview of these designs.[31] They vary in terms of the degree to which causation can be inferred. To show that program activity caused behavior change, it is necessary to show that the behavior change varied in tandem with the program activity (covariation), that the program took place before the behavior changed (proper time order), and that the behavior change was not caused by any other factors (nonspuriousness). The first two conditions can usually be dealt with in a fairly straightforward manner through program design. The final requirement, however, may be extremely difficult to address.

Experimental designs have been developed to explicitly address all three requirements. Individuals or groups are assigned to one of two groups at random. This is to ensure that the two groups are similar at the start of the experiment. Each group is given a pre-test, measuring the behavior of interest. One group is then subject to the experimental treatment (the program in this case). The other, or control, group does not receive the treatment. Both groups are tested again in a post-test, and any differences in the two groups can be attributed to the impact of the treatment. Although experiments are the gold standard for assessing causation, their use in real-world settings is limited. The major problem is ensuring the ability and appropriateness of random assignment to control and treatment groups. Some programs, such as youth curfews, cannot be selectively given to a subset of the target population. In addition, ethical questions could be raised against withholding benefits to the control group.

Year Up used an experimental design in the evaluation of its programs.[32] Year Up staff members recruited candidates, identified a pool of eligible young people, and submitted lists of eligible candidates to the researchers, who randomly assigned the young people to a treatment or control group. Of the 195 young people enrolled in the impact study, 135 were randomly selected to be in the treatment group and invited to take part in the Year Up program, and 60 were randomly selected to be in the control group. Those assigned to the control group were told that they were being placed on a waiting list and could reapply to the program after ten months. Because young people were randomly assigned, members of the treatment and control groups were equally qualified for the program and equally motivated to take part in the program at the time of enrollment. Therefore any differences in their employment or educational outcomes can be attributed to the treatment group's participation in Year Up. The study found that Year Up graduates had higher earnings than the control group after a year in the labor market. In addition, the Year Up experience does not deter young people from pursuing further education—program participants are just as likely to enroll in postsecondary education as control group members.

It is often difficult to meet the requirements of experimental design. Consequently, evaluations often employ *quasi-experimental designs* that relax some of the requirements of experimental designs. The most common variation is the relaxation of random assignment to treatment or control group. Usually, evaluators use existing groups that are as similar as possible for comparison purposes. For example, two classes in the same school could be used. Multivariate statistical techniques are then used to control for remaining differences between the groups. There are, in addition, a number of *nonexperimental designs*, departing further from the experimental ideal. They do not include comparison groups or individuals not exposed to the program. Although they are relatively easy and inexpensive, they have numerous methodological shortcomings. A major limitation is that they cannot estimate the full impact of the program, as no data is available for people receiving no services. These designs include:

- Before-and-after comparisons of program participants
- Time series designs based on repeated measures of outcomes before and after the program for groups that include program participants
- Panel studies based on repeated measures of outcomes on the same group of participants
- Post-program comparisons among groups of participants

For example, evaluations of the outcomes and impacts of programs to promote energy efficiency can employ before-and-after designs. These evaluations may involve obtaining a variety of estimates.[33]

- *Estimates of gross energy savings*: Changes in energy consumption or demand that results directly from actions taken by program participants, such as installing energy-efficient lighting.
- *Estimates of net savings*: The portion of gross savings that is attributable to the program. This requires separating out the impacts that are the result of other influences.
- *Estimates of co-benefits*: Co-benefits can be positive, such as the pollution that is not produced, or negative, such as increased costs of new technology.

Savings and avoided emissions can't be directly measured. They are determined by comparing energy use and demand after a program is implemented (the reporting period) and what would have occurred had the program not been

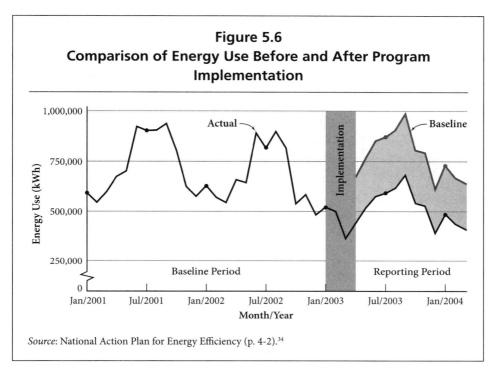

Figure 5.6
Comparison of Energy Use Before and After Program Implementation

Source: National Action Plan for Energy Efficiency (p. 4-2).[34]

implemented (the baseline). This is shown in Figure 5.6. In this figure, the graph line in the baseline period shows energy use before an energy efficiency program implementation. After implementation, the lower line in the graph shows actual energy use, and the top line shows energy use as it would have continued without the program. The shaded area between the graphs shows estimated energy savings due to the program.

MONETIZING OUTCOME AND IMPACT

Social ventures can be found in areas such as healthcare, education, social welfare, recreation, arts and culture, employment, and housing. The value of the outcomes and impacts that these ventures produce can be highly objective, such as a job, or much more subjective, such as the appreciation of the U.S. Constitution. It may be possible to assign a monetary value to some venture benefits, such as the wages from a job. There are a number of advantages to this monetization. It creates a metric that could be compared over time for one venture or between ventures, either within one organization or between different organizations. The value of several ventures could be combined into an overall monetary value. It would allow benefits to be compared to costs in standard accounting terms, resulting in a measure of efficiency as well as effectiveness. In these ways, a monetary metric can assist management decisions and other internal operations. It can also be helpful when communicating with external audiences. The terminology of financial costs and benefits is familiar to donors and investors, and expressing a venture's benefit in monetary terms helps them understand the significance of the venture's services and the return on their investment. It is important to note, however, that not all benefits can be monetized. For example, a job can provide both an income and self-esteem. The former could be monetized; the latter can't. This is not to say that one is inherently more valuable than the other, and judgments about their relative merit will still need to be made.

Sometimes it is not possible to determine the exact monetary value for a specific activity. If this is the case, it may be possible to use financial proxies to help estimate these values. Financial proxies are precalculated estimates of financial value; for example, how much higher an income a college graduate earns, on average, compared with a high school graduate. However, as program outcomes and impacts require more qualitative measurement, monetary analysis becomes increasingly difficult. When it is not possible or desirable to monetize a benefit, *cost-effectiveness* can be computed. This is a ratio of cost to nonmonetary benefit. The limitation of this method is that it is unique to each benefit considered, because it is expressed in the natural units of that benefit. For example, a nonprofit seeking to increase environmental awareness might provide educational pamphlets on recycling to the households in a given community. The cost-effectiveness of this effort might be five dollars per pamphlet delivered. This could not be directly compared to or aggregated with the cost-effectiveness of a different type of project—for example, the cost to provide waste pickup to those same households.

If it is possible to monetize benefits, several analytical approaches are available. *Cost-benefit analysis* monetizes and compares the benefits and costs of a venture and is widely used. It is the most demanding approach to analyzing costs and outcomes, as it requires a comprehensive measurement of costs and program impacts (such as primary and secondary, direct and indirect, tangible and intangible impacts), and the ability to place a dollar value on program impacts across stakeholders.[35] In this way it accounts for the net benefits to both particular stakeholder as well as society as a whole. For most programs, costs can be reasonably determined, since they are borne by the organization. The value of program outcomes or impacts, however, may be more difficult to assess. For Year Up, program benefits would include the wages of program graduates. Cost-benefit analysis can help decision-makers compare programs and allocate funds. The output from cost-benefit analysis can be measures of net benefits (benefits – costs), also known as the net present value (NPV); the ratio of benefits to cost (benefit-cost ratios); or the internal rate of return (IRR), which uses expected future costs and benefits to compute the rate of growth a project is expected to generate.[36]

Social return on investment (SROI) uses a different approach. It was originally developed in the late 1990s by Roberts Enterprise Development Fund (REDF), a San Francisco nonprofit supporting social enterprises. SROI calculates the "blended value" of a social venture. Blended value is composed of what is termed enterprise value and social purpose value. Enterprise value is the net revenue from the business side of the venture, typically sales minus costs and expenses. Social purpose value is the monetized value of the venture for society, specifically the costs saved by society or the revenues created for society by the positive impact of the venture. On the positive side, this could include gifts and grants, social cost savings, and increases in taxes. For example, a Year Up graduate who gets a job and moves off of welfare will save the public money. From social purpose value, fundraising costs and social operating costs are subtracted.[37] To allow donors to compare blended value across any ventures, REDF defined three "indices of value":

- *Enterprise index of return*: enterprise value divided by donations to the venture
- *Social purpose index of return*: social purpose value divided by donations
- *Blended index of return*: blended value divided by donations

SROI has and continues to be widely used and is currently promoted and further developed by the New Economics Foundation (http://www.neweconomics .org/), the London Business School (http://sroi.london.edu/), the SROI Network U.K. (http://www.sroi-uk.org/home-uk), and the European SROI Network (ESROIN, www.sroi-europe.org), among others.

A number of other resources for the measurement of impacts are available, including:

- The Robin Hood Foundation's Benefit-Cost Ratio: http://www.robinhood.org/metrics

- The Acumen Fund's Best Available Charitable Option Ratio: http://www.acumenfund.org/knowledge-center.html?document=56

- The William and Flora Hewlett Foundation's Expected Return: http://www.hewlett.org/uploads/files/Making_Every_Dollar_Count.pdf

- The Center for High Impact Philanthropy's Cost per Impact: http://www.impact.upenn.edu/

- The Foundation Center's Tools and Resources for Assessing Social Impact website: http://trasi.foundationcenter.org/

At some point after the effectiveness of the social venture has been demonstrated, social entrepreneurs will be faced with the question of when and how the impact of the venture can be increased. We discuss various options for increasing venture impact next.

INCREASING SOCIAL VENTURE IMPACT: SCALING

We now consider Phase Two of Figure 5.1. At this point, the social venture has been launched and an initial evaluation has shown it to be effective. Typically, a new social venture is introduced in just one or a limited number of locations, such as one city or a few neighborhood locations. If it is successful, the question of expansion naturally comes up. There are a number of reasons for wanting to increase the impact, or scale, of a social venture, including wanting to accomplish more of the mission, demands from beneficiaries, and pressure from funders.[38] Scaling should be approached thoughtfully, however, as poorly planned or unsupported scaling can result in strains in the organization or, worse, program failures, which could cast doubt on the value of the venture.

Besides evidence of venture effectiveness, scaling requires organizational capacity and resources. Paul Bloom has developed a model for assessing an organization's scaling capabilities.[39] His SCALERS model includes effectiveness in seven areas (whose initial letters form the acronym). These may be needed, depending on the details of what is being scaled and the type of scaling being considered:

- *Staffing*: filling positions needed to address any changes made
- *Communicating*: persuading key stakeholders that the change strategy is worth adopting and/or supporting
- *Alliance-building*: forging linkages to bring about desired changes
- *Lobbying*: advocating for government changes that work in favor of the organization
- *Earnings-generation*: generating earnings to support the change
- *Replicating*: reproducing the programs and initiatives that the organization has originated
- *Stimulating market forces*: creating incentives that encourage private interests

A number of specific approaches to scaling are available. Kalafatas presents an overview of techniques in Figure 5.7.[40]

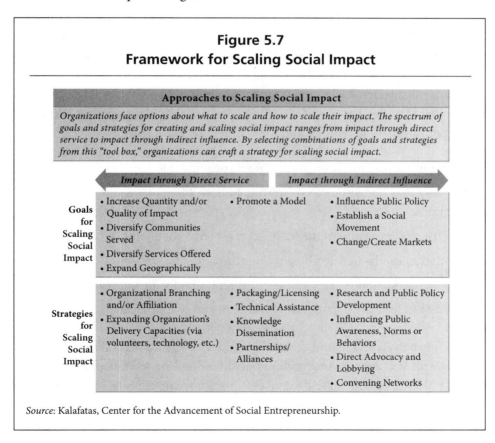

Figure 5.7
Framework for Scaling Social Impact

Approaches to Scaling Social Impact

Organizations face options about what to scale and how to scale their impact. The spectrum of goals and strategies for creating and scaling social impact ranges from impact through direct service to impact through indirect influence. By selecting combinations of goals and strategies from this "tool box," organizations can craft a strategy for scaling social impact.

Impact through Direct Service — *Impact through Indirect Influence*

Goals for Scaling Social Impact	• Increase Quantity and/or Quality of Impact • Diversify Communities Served • Diversify Services Offered • Expand Geographically	• Promote a Model	• Influence Public Policy • Establish a Social Movement • Change/Create Markets
Strategies for Scaling Social Impact	• Organizational Branching and/or Affiliation • Expanding Organization's Delivery Capacities (via volunteers, technology, etc.)	• Packaging/Licensing • Technical Assistance • Knowledge Dissemination • Partnerships/Alliances	• Research and Public Policy Development • Influencing Public Awareness, Norms or Behaviors • Direct Advocacy and Lobbying • Convening Networks

Source: Kalafatas, Center for the Advancement of Social Entrepreneurship.

As the figure shows, scaling techniques can be differentiated based on the degree to which techniques involve the provision of services or indirect methods. They also vary by how much control the originating organization retains. Indirect methods and model promotion are simpler and faster than direct service methods. Public policy can be influenced by researching and generating knowledge about an issue and proposing or opposing laws or public policies. This can be carried further to direct advocacy and lobbying. Public awareness can be raised by communication campaigns to inform, educate, and influence public awareness, opinion, or action about a social issue. Examples include public service ads on television or radio urging us to not smoke or not text while driving. Finally, organizations and individuals affected by the issue could be organized into networks or associations to advocate for shared goals. All of these methods involve promoting ideas or models and trying to motivate and engage others to bring about the beneficial changes associated with these ideas or models.

The other techniques involve more direct action on the part of the innovating organization to spread its impact to other geographic areas. This has been termed scaling out or scaling up. Dees and Anderson present a useful guide for evaluating options for this scaling.[41] We will summarize their approach. Decisions must be made about a number of questions; chiefly, should scaling out be considered at this time? As we outlined previously, scaling requires resources and organizational capabilities, and it has other costs and risks:[42]

- It can pull the organization away from its original mission, vision, and values.
- It is easy and dangerous to overestimate both the need and the demand for programs.
- Effectiveness can suffer if the focus is on growth, not quality.
- Reputation can be harmed by poor performance at a site.
- Concern about control can inflate bureaucracy and stifle innovation.
- Scaling can lead to an inappropriate cookie-cutter approach.

Careful analysis and planning should be done to ensure that these are avoided or mitigated. If it appears that scaling out should not be attempted at this time, the organization can increase its impact in its home community, or "scale deep." It can also work to enhance its future scaling prospects or seek a partner who is ready to scale or who can compensate for scaling weaknesses.

If further planning for scaling is warranted, what exactly should be scaled? The answer will depend on the core elements of the venture's theory of change. The first step is identifying what makes the approach distinctive, which elements are essential for achieving the intended impact, which elements play crucial supporting roles, and which elements could be changed without doing much harm to the intended impact. Scaling then should be done in such a way that all the crucial core elements are transferred.

Innovations can take a variety of forms, any of which may be scaled. The innovation could be in the form of an entire *organization*, such as Year Up. Year Up was scaled by establishing similar organizations in different cities. Alternatively, an innovation could be in the form of a *program*, an integrated set of activities designed to bring about particular results. For example, KaBOOM! helps communities build playgrounds. KaBOOM! promotes a model that engages and mobilizes the community in playground building and shares the knowledge and tools needed for anyone to find, improve, and/or build playgrounds on their own.[43] Finally, *principles* are guidelines and/or values for producing social benefits. For example, the Knowledge Is Power Program (KIPP) is a national network of free, open-enrollment, college-preparatory public charter schools.[44] KIPP schools share a core set of operating principles known as the Five Pillars: high expectations for academic achievement; choice and commitment by students, parents, and faculty; an extended school day, week, and year; flexibility in school administration; and focus on achievement.

The transferability of the innovation must be determined. This depends on two dimensions: how universally applicable the innovation is and how easy it will be for others to adopt it. A number of key questions need to be addressed. Will the core elements be effective in other locations or contexts? Are the core elements easy to understand? Could others easily implement or adapt the core or, for example, would unusual skills be needed?

If the innovation is transferable, a scaling mechanism should be identified. As shown in Figure 5.7, major mechanisms include promoting a venture model, affiliation, or branching. Promotion of the model to others could include providing technical assistance, training, or consulting; disseminating knowledge by sharing information; packaging or licensing the innovation; or other collaboration to deliver services or address needs. This method is the quickest and cheapest of the three, but it is also the loosest, as the originating organization normally lacks control over those adopting the model.

The other two techniques involve the most direct involvement in service delivery.

• *Branching* achieves growth by replicating the organization at other locations, under the direction of the central or headquarters office, providing the originating organization the greatest degree of control. Significant resources and effort, however, are needed for this type of expansion, including buying or leasing facilities, hiring staff, and coordinating multiple operations. This makes branching expensive and time-consuming. Year Up expansion plan entailed extensive branching.

• *Affiliated structures* are composed of multiple organizations coordinated in looser or tighter arrangements. This differs from branching in that although the organizations may share mission, brand, or standards, local offices have a substantial degree of discretion. This makes affiliation less expensive in terms of money and effort. For example, Habitat for Humanity International has grown by establishing a network of local affiliates, each an independent nonprofit, governed and operated locally.[45] Habitat for Humanity International headquarters provides information, training, and other support services to affiliates.

CONCLUDING THOUGHTS

In this chapter we discussed how, once launched, a social venture can prove its worth and increase its impact. Funders, clients, and community leaders are increasingly asking social ventures to demonstrate that they are having an impact; that is, that they are effective. There are, however, a number of ways to think about effectiveness. Social entrepreneurs need to understand how best to conceptualize and measure the effectiveness of their ventures. Social entrepreneurs also want to maximize the impacts that their ventures have. We have presented a way for them to systematically analyze whether their ventures are ready for scaling and, if so, how this might best be done.

In the next chapter we discuss a crucial requirement for all stages of social venture establishment and growth—funding. Social entrepreneurs need to marshal enough resources to launch their ventures; even if a venture is eminently scalable, a lack of financing can scuttle its chances of increasing impact.

Exercise 5.1

Why is evaluation important for social entrepreneurship? Describe a real or hypothetical social venture that would be easy to evaluate. Describe another that would be challenging or difficult to evaluate. How might you address these challenges?

Exercise 5.2

Why might it be important to consider value-based models in social entrepreneurship evaluation? Would it be enough to use these models only when evaluating social ventures? If not, what other factors might be important to include? Illustrate your points with a real or hypothetical social venture.

Exercise 5.3

Suggest a social venture that could be scaled by influencing public policy. Suggest one that could be scaled by promoting a model. Suggest one that could be scaled by geographic spread. Could any of these be scaled by more than one of these alternatives?

Funding Social
Entrepreneurship

In 1988, David Lee, chef and entrepreneur, recognized a need to serve Seattle's homeless and disadvantaged populations with nutritious and culturally appealing food. To that end, Lee founded Common Meals, a for-profit business with a social mission.[1] The business used church kitchens, delivered meals out of a truck, and sold inexpensive meals out of church basements. After four years, Lee expanded the program into job training, obtained a location, and transformed the organization into a nonprofit named FareStart. In 2003, FareStart launched the Barista Training & Education Program (in collaboration with another nonprofit), to provide at-risk youth with an opportunity to develop job skills and reconnect with their community. In 2007 the organization moved into its larger current location. FareStart's mission is to provide "a community that transforms lives by empowering homeless and disadvantaged men, women, and families to achieve self-sufficiency through life skills, job training and employment in the food service industry."[2] Its website also states: "Over the past 20 years, FareStart has provided opportunities for nearly 6,000 people to transform their lives, while also serving over 5 million meals to disadvantaged men, women, and children."[3] FareStart provides classroom and on-the-job training to the homeless and disadvantaged in addition to providing meals. FareStart provides a sixteen-week program that teaches general work skills and restaurant kitchen skill to over three hundred students a year. Over 80 percent of graduates obtain living-wage jobs in the food service and hospitality industry.

To provide on-the-job training, FareStart operates two businesses: a meals contracting service and a restaurant. To support itself, FareStart uses a combination of donations, government funds, and self-generated income. This mix is necessary to support the social mission. The decision to become a nonprofit was made, in part, because the narrow profit margin of a for-profit restaurant (typically about 3 percent) would not support the training program. In order to provide training, additional sources of funding were needed.

FareStart was able to diversify its funding to include both donated and government income. FareStart's 2007 IRS Form 990 shows that its gross receipts totaled $4,192,902. Of this, approximately 44 percent came from the income-producing activity of its meals contracts, retail café, and catering. An additional 45 percent came from charitable, in-kind, and other sources. In-kind donations came from groceries and other food-processing corporations. Grants and donations came from 80 foundations, including 38 corporate foundations, and over 150 individuals. Direct government income provided the remaining 11 percent of income. Government funding came from agencies such as the King County Workforce Development Council, the Washington State Department of Social and Health Services, and the Washington State Corrections Department. Government support, however, is more important than these figures show. If one takes into account that a large portion of the funds from income-producing activity actually originate in government, the role of government funding role is larger than shown on the 990. For example, the funds received from 80 percent of the meal contracts with child care centers and homeless shelters originate from public sources. These could be considered indirect government support. Calculated on this basis, FareStart's earned income from completely nongovernment sources would be 27 percent and income from direct and indirect government sources would be 28 percent.

All organizations need funds to finance ongoing operations, as well as capital for startup and expansion. As the story of FareStart shows, nonprofit social ventures can utilize a variety of funding sources. In addition, a mix of public and private funds may be needed to accomplish the mission. Providing meals and job training to people who cannot afford to pay for them will require subsidies from other funding sources. FareStart found that it could not accomplish its mission using only commercial revenue, and to obtain access to other funding it needed to become a nonprofit organization. This leads to a number of questions. What are the benefits and drawbacks of different funding types? Are some types better for some programs? How can social entrepreneurs decide whether a mix of funding types is best for them and, if so, which mix to pursue? The capabilities-resources analysis we presented in Chapter Four can be used by a social venture to determine the level of financial resources needed. The venture then needs to assess where these resources can be obtained. Funding needs and techniques will also vary depending on whether the social venture is carried out in the government, for-profit, or nonprofit sector.

FUNDING PUBLIC SECTOR AND FOR-PROFIT SOCIAL ENTREPRENEURSHIP

In this section we consider the funding options for social entrepreneurial ventures in public agencies and for-profits. Their funding options are somewhat more limited than those for nonprofits, which we will discuss in the section following this one.

Public Entrepreneurship

Entrepreneurship in government can be funded through the variety of normal tax-related channels that government has access to. In these cases, tax revenues would be allocated to agency budgets. New, entrepreneurial government projects could also be financed by new fees or charges. Data shows that government fees and charges amounted to $443 billion in fiscal year 2012, mostly by state and local governments.[4]

In addition, public entrepreneurship could also take the form of more market-based activity carried out by government-run businesses enterprises. Government enterprises are governmental entities that receive payments from private persons for goods and services.[5] They must maintain accounts separate from their nonenterprise accounts. For example, the expenses and receipts of a county landfill enterprise must be kept separate from the expenses and receipts of the general county government. Other examples are the U.S. Postal Service, Amtrak, and local government waste management operations. Government enterprises are treated the same as private businesses with respect to their purchases and sales to consumers.

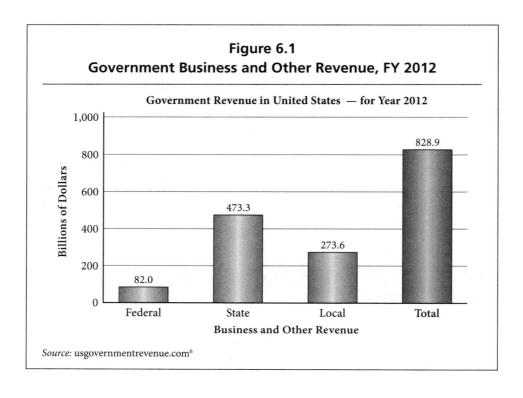

Figure 6.1
Government Business and Other Revenue, FY 2012

Government Revenue in United States — for Year 2012

Figure 6.1 shows government revenue from "business and other" sources for fiscal year 2012. It shows that all levels of government earned $829 billion in business and other income in fiscal year 2012. This represented 16 percent of total direct revenue. Over half of this income was earned at the state level and another one third was earned at the local level. Less than 10 percent was earned at the federal level.

A study of state and local government innovations provides data on the funding that these levels of government used. The data came from the Ford Foundation-Kennedy School of Government's (Ford-KSG) State and Local Government innovation awards.[7] The award program was established in 1986 and receives an average of 1,500 applications a year. In 1995 the awards program was expanded to include federal agencies.[8] A sample of the 1990–1994 award semifinalists was examined in detail, including innovation budget and financing. Although this is not a representative sample, it does provide an indication of the options used to fund government innovation. An analysis of innovation program operating budgets showed that 85 percent of the programs used government funding. It should be noted that all award applicants had to derive a majority of their funding from state and local government sources, with the consequence that the findings likely underestimate the amount of nongovernment funding. Nevertheless, 24 percent augmented their operating budgets with user fees, and these fees averaged 58 percent of program budgets. The programs most likely to use fees were environment/energy, housing/neighborhood, and economic development/transportation programs. Fees were most likely to be used when beneficiaries of programs could be identified or when business or the public were the beneficiaries. This data showed that when fees could be charged, they funded a large share—or even most—of the innovation cost.

In addition, 32 percent augmented operating budgets with donations, and these donations accounted for an average of 24 percent of their budgets. The programs most likely to obtain donations were economic development/transportation, housing/neighborhood, and social service programs. Donations were relatively small, averaging about $200,000. Although not substantial for large programs, they were crucial to small programs, especially if they were seed money. Some donations were in the form of hardware and software from IT manufacturers. Other donations were charitable contributions. For example, a foundation grant was given for start-up funding for the first year of a program in Boston that provided counseling for children who had witnessed domestic violence. Donations can be seen as partnerships between the public and private sector in fostering innovation in government.

For-Profit Social Ventures

For the social ventures of for-profits, the major question is the degree to which these initiatives are integrated into the firm's mission, vision, and strategy. A firm's orientation toward creating social value over and above its routine market-related transactions can range from making relatively routine donations to social causes to operating a social venture as an integrated part of the firm's strategy and marketing. More firms are adopting the latter orientation. A study of corporate social enterprises concluded: "In the companies we studied . . . there is a growing trend towards greater integration of diverse social initiatives with each other and within corporate activity. Indeed, one can say that there has been a trend . . . towards greater corporate social innovation. In other words, there is increasing alignment between social and economic objectives which, among other things, is intended to create greater social value."[9] In addition, in the United States several new corporate legal forms are available that require that the provision of social value be a primary consideration for the firm. These will be considered in Chapter Ten.

A study of twenty social enterprises hosted in private companies provides information on the financing mechanisms of these social ventures.[10] Numerous ventures used more than one source of financing.

- Internal budget allocations were used by ten ventures.

- A percent of corporate income (sales, gross income, or profit) or cause-related marketing was used by nine ventures.

- Donations were used by eight ventures. The majority of these came from employees, but some also came from the corporate foundation, suppliers, partners, government, or community groups or individuals.

The finding that the overwhelming majority of funding comes from internal corporate sources attests to the reliance of social ventures on corporate decision making and strategy. The venture will be one among a number of projects, programs, and initiatives competing for financial support. The strategic role assigned to social initiatives by the firm will determine the availability of funds as well as the design and content of the ensuing social ventures.

FUNDING NONPROFIT SOCIAL ENTREPRENEURSHIP

We now turn to the funding options for social entrepreneurial ventures in non-profit organizations. As we will see, these options include funding from philanthropists, government funders, and earned income.

Nonprofit Revenue Sources

Nonprofits have more income options than government and for-profits. Nonprofits can obtain income from philanthropy, government grants and contracts, and market-based sales. The National Center for Charitable Statistics reported that in 2010 nonprofit organizations of all types earned an estimated $2.2 trillion in revenues.[11] For public charities reporting to the Internal Revenue Service, the two most important streams of financial resources were earned income through fees and philanthropy. These revenues were derived from the following sources:

- Fees for services and goods from private sources: 49.6 percent

- Fees for services and goods from government: 23.9 percent (Medicare, Medicaid, contracts)

- Private contributions: 13.3 percent
- Government grants: 8.3 percent
- Other income: 4.9 percent

There are several ways to interpret these figures. Income from fees is by far the most important source of nonprofit revenue, accounting for 68.5 percent of total income. Philanthropy provides only a modest portion of total revenue. It is also useful to distinguish between public and private funding. Using this approach, private sector fees still provide half of nonprofit revenue. Government becomes the second largest funder, providing 32 percent of income.

Social entrepreneurs will need to decide which funding source(s) will sustain and grow their social ventures. This will be based on the funding that is available in the venture's subsector, or field, and the attraction that the venture has for the funders in that subsector. In terms of the first factor, Figure 6.2 shows that

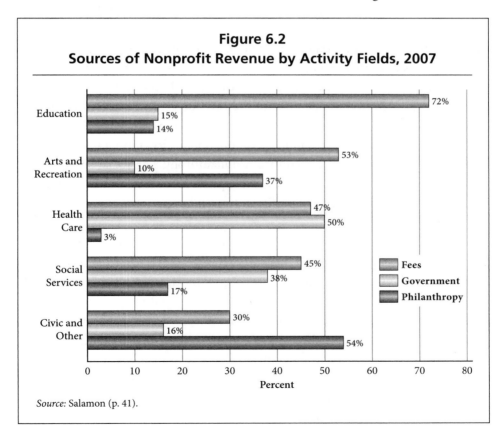

Figure 6.2
Sources of Nonprofit Revenue by Activity Fields, 2007

Source: Salamon (p. 41).

nonprofit income sources vary widely by nonprofit field of activity. Although the breakdown of income also varies within each field, the figure shows that, overall, fees are a very prominent source of funding in each field. They provide 72 percent of revenue in the field of education, 53 percent in arts and recreation, 47 percent in health care, and 45 percent in social services. Government funding is prominent in health care and, to a lesser degree, in social services. Philanthropy provides 54 percent of the revenue in the civic and other field and 37 percent in the arts and recreation field.

In addition, nonprofit revenue has grown. Between 1997 and 2007, the sector grew by 53 percent, for an annual growth rate of 4.3 percent—well over the 3.0 percent annual growth of the U.S. economy in the same time period.[12] Fee revenue grew by 64 percent during this period (adjusted for inflation), accounting for almost 60 percent of the revenue increase of the whole nonprofit sector. Philanthropy also grew by 64 percent. Because it was a small percent of total income in 1997, this increase accounted for only 12 percent of total sector revenue growth. Although government funding increases grew more slowly, they still accounted for an additional 30 percent of sector revenue growth.[13]

Figure 6.3 shows that revenue growth varied widely by subsector. The figure shows that fees again account for much of this growth. For health and for education and research nonprofits, most of the revenue growth came from fees. In addition, a third of the revenue growth for health nonprofits came from government sources. For culture and recreation nonprofits, most of the revenue growth came equally from fees and from philanthropy. For social service nonprofits, most of the revenue growth came equally from fees and from government. Only for environment nonprofits did revenues growth come mostly from philanthropy.

The data we just examined mean that social ventures can obtain income from a number of sources including: grants and donations, government grants or contracts, fees, and investments. The venture's appeal to various types of funders will be the key factor in the likelihood of funding. The social value to be produced for others will be the basis of appeals for philanthropic funding, as givers do not get any direct benefits from their gifts or grants. Government grants and contracts will specify outputs and outcomes. For earned income, the goods or services that paying customers want are critical. These commercial market-driven transactions are based on the match between the wants or needs of buyers and the value of the products or services the venture produces. Finally, investors will

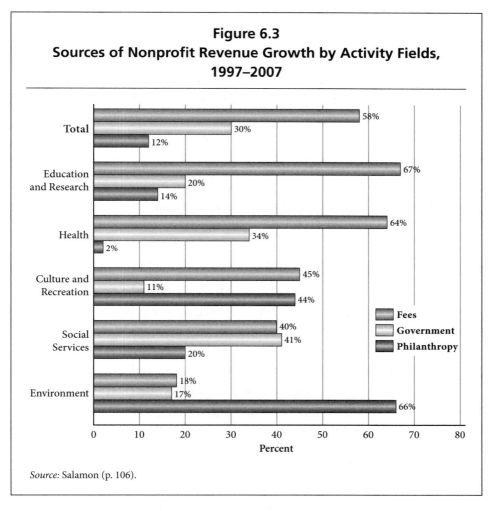

Figure 6.3
Sources of Nonprofit Revenue Growth by Activity Fields, 1997–2007

Source: Salamon (p. 106).

have a mix of self-interest and social concern. In this case, the venture will need to provide both social value and financial returns—so-called "blended value."

Karen Froelich has described the characteristics of the major nonprofit funding types according to a number of criteria.[14] Volatility refers to year-to-year fluctuations of income. Goal displacement occurs when goals and activities are modified to satisfy the wishes of funders. Funding can also have implications for nonprofit processes and structure. Formalization is a measure of the degree to which procedures and positions are explicitly defined. Standardization involves using guidelines, rules, or specifications to assure uniformity of behavior. Professionalization refers to the number of positions that require professional

Table 6.1
Characteristics of Major Nonprofit Funding Types

	Private Contributions	Government Funding	Commercial Activity
Revenue volatility	High	Low	Moderate
Goal displacement effects	Strong	Moderately strong	Weak
Process effects	Formalization	Formalization, standardization	Rationalization
Structure effects	Professionalized administration	Professionalized bureaucracy	Professionalized business forms

Source: Froelich (1999, p. 265).

credentials. Rationalization is evident when activities are guided by objective, rational criteria. Table 6.1 shows how these factors are related to the three major funding types.

The table shows that private contributions are subject to higher revenue volatility compared to the other funding strategies. Goal displacement is also higher, due to the power that donors can wield through either the large size of their gifts or accompanying restrictions. In addition, the formalization and professionalization of foundation and corporate giving creates pressures in nonprofits to adopt formalized processes and professionalized administration in order to accommodate them.

Government funding exhibits low revenue volatility as a result of multi-year funding of grants and contracts and the likelihood of funding renewal. Goal displacement is moderately strong, due to government mandates on both program features and choice of clientele. In addition, if programs are under-funded, the need for internal resource reallocations can result in goal displacement. Government funding also requires detailed performance, monitoring, and reporting, which necessitates highly formalized and standardized procedures and reduced administrative autonomy. The resulting professionalized bureaucracy becomes similar to that of government agencies.

Finally, commercial income entails moderate revenue volatility, depending on organizational and industry factors. Commercial activities can be strongly to weakly related to the nonprofit's mission. The possibility of mission drift is discussed later in this chapter. The effects of commercial strategies on processes and structures include greater use of for-profit business techniques, which could entail more rationalization (such as cost-benefit analysis), expanded roles for business professionals, or use of business structural forms such as subsidiaries.

As our discussion has shown, each of the funding types has advantages and disadvantages that entail particular opportunities and constraints and require different managerial tasks. In addition, it is usual for nonprofits to have a mix of funding types, as we saw for FareStart. This will complicate the overall funding process. We discuss the implications in the following section.

Income Portfolios

Some have advocated that social enterprises should strive for 100-percent fee income.[15] However, research has shown that this level of fee income is unrealistic for social enterprises working with disadvantaged groups, and that long-term sustainability is built through a strategy of diversification.[16] A good starting point for a funding strategy is the nature of the social value produced and the incentives and ability for beneficiaries to pay. To determine the prospects for funding, Dennis Young advocates a "benefits approach" to funding that entails answering these two questions to assure adequate funding:[17]

- Are the benefits accruing to beneficiaries being captured through appropriate income sources?

- What adjustments to outputs might yield a stronger mix of beneficiaries and associated income and thereby improve the financial position of the organization?

It is useful to think of multiple funders as constituting a portfolio of income-generating sources. FareStart built an impressive portfolio of public and private funding sources. A number of portfolio considerations are important, including funding alignment, balance, roles, and interaction.[18] A primary consideration is ensuring that all funding sources are aligned with the mission, the core assets, and the organization's structure and capacity. If this is not the case, internal stresses and strains will develop.

The portfolio's balance is determined by factors such as the number, magnitude, stability, and growth potential of the funding sources. Another important factor is the resulting diversification and dependence. This is determined by how many of the different funding types (philanthropy, fees, government, and loans) are represented in the portfolio and the number of sources (funders) of each type. Moderate diversification entails having multiple types, but few sources, whereas significant diversification entails having a multitude of both.[19] FareStart has high diversification, obtaining funding from a number of different funder types and multiple funders in each type. Moderate dependence entails having few types but multiple sources, whereas significant dependence entails having few types and few sources. Although diversification can mitigate the risk of serious consequences due to the loss of a funding source, it should not be assumed that maximum diversification is ideal. Each income type and each source comes with transaction costs, and the venture needs to consider the trade-off between the increased transaction cost of obtaining a new income source and the benefits of that source.[20]

It is also important to consider the economic role that funding plays and the interaction between funding types. Funding could be designed to cover the operating cost of programs or to generate a surplus, which could then be used to initiate or fund other programs. If funds do not cover or exceed operating costs, the funding would still reduce program reliance on other funding types. If the income is unrelated to the mission, it could be used to subsidize mission-related activity or to cover fixed costs. In addition, funding incompatibilities should be avoided. Obtaining income from fees might signify to some donors that philanthropy is no longer needed. Obtaining funding from a particular source might be seen as contrary to the mission; for example, obtaining funds from the alcohol industry might hurt the image of a drug rehabilitation program.

In the remaining sections of this chapter we consider the major funding sources for social entrepreneurship in detail.

PHILANTHROPY AND SOCIAL ENTREPRENEURSHIP

Philanthropy has historically been a significant source of support for nonprofits, and although fee income has seen the largest increases recently, philanthropy continues to be important. As shown previously, in 2010 donations and grants provided about 13 percent of overall revenue of the nonprofit sector. As shown in Figure 6.2, nonprofit fields differ widely in their reliance on philanthropy. For example, in 2007, arts and culture nonprofits got 37 percent of their revenue from philanthropy, whereas social service nonprofits got 17 percent and health nonprofits got only 3 percent.[21] Giving USA reports that in 2011, contributions totaled $298.4 billion.[22] Most of this came from individual donors. Individuals contributed 73 percent of the total, foundations contributed 14 percent, bequests accounted for 8 percent, and corporations contributed 5 percent. In terms of the distribution of this philanthropy, Giving USA reports the following:[23]

- Religion: 32 percent
- Education: 13 percent
- Human services: 12 percent
- Health: 8 percent
- International affairs: 8 percent
- Public-society benefit: 7 percent
- Arts, culture, and humanities: 4 percent

In addition, nonprofits derive tremendous benefits from people who *volunteer* their time to the organization. National Center for Charitable Statistics reports that in 2011, 64.3 million people volunteered at least once during the year. Americans volunteered an estimated 15.2 billion hours that year.[24] Besides the contributions they make to the operation of nonprofit programs, their labor also saves nonprofits from having to hire paid employees to do this work. In this way, they are a valuable financial resource for nonprofits. The hours contributed by volunteers in 2011 equates to 8.9 million full-time equivalent workers. If nonprofits had to pay for this work, it would have cost them $296.2 billion (assuming a full-time employee works 1,700 hours a year at a $19.50 hourly wage).

Philanthropy can play different roles in nonprofits. Fogal distinguishes three stages of fundraising development.[25] In the *formative* stage, fundraising has a secondary role in the organization and is focused on techniques to raise needed income, such as mass appeals through direct mail solicitation. The idea is to sell the organization to donors; this is commonly carried out by hired fund-raising firms. In the *normative* stage, donors have a closer and longer-lasting relationship to the organization; for example, as members or clients. Thus they identify more with the organization. Fundraising is done by organizational staff, and maintaining the relationship becomes an important goal. In the *integrative* stage, philanthropy is at the center of the organization, and donors are regarded as key participants in the organization's work and life. For example, they are advocates of the organization and participate in fundraising. They become major donors whose generosity can be an example for others.

Donors tend to be conservative, which means that they will contribute to established nonprofits and successful programs.[26] Consequently, new social ventures or those in areas not traditionally supported by philanthropy may encounter difficulty getting philanthropic support. There are, however, several new approaches that a social venture could adopt to appeal to donors. In recent years, donors are increasingly apt to think of their donations as investments. *Donor-investors* are committed to social change, strongly share the values of the nonprofits they support, see themselves as partners in the creation of social value, and want their donations to achieve demonstrated social results. This is likely to make well-designed entrepreneurial social ventures particularly appealing to them. The characteristics of donor-investors influence the manner in which they should be approached, including:[27]

- *Cultivation*: focus on investor's needs, values, and interests
- *Solicitation*: emphasize social outcomes and how the donation is really an investment in the social outcome through the organization
- *Stewardship*: provide ongoing feedback about the impact of the investment on social outcomes and the way(s) they advance the donor-investor's values

Cultivating the needed sense of partnership means that a normative fundraising strategy is required. As a successful relationship is extended and deepened over time, an integrative funding relationship becomes more likely.

Venture Philanthropy

Venture philanthropy is an outgrowth of the investor approach and uses a venture capital model for funding. Of most importance to social ventures, the venture capital model entails multiyear funding, funding for overhead and capacity building, and organizational assistance. For example, Social Venture Partners (SVP) was launched in Seattle in 1997 by a group of philanthropists who wanted to do more than just write checks. This entailed getting more engaged with the nonprofits they funded. There are now over 2,600 members in SVP organizations in thirty cities in North American, Japan, and India. In each SVP organization, members pool their money and make investments in vetted nonprofits. Nonprofits get three to five years of unrestricted funding and assistance in capacity building from volunteers and paid consultants. SVP members volunteer their time and talents to assist the nonprofits or SVP and engage in shared learning about issues and solutions.

In addition, in April 2009 the federal government established the *Social Innovation Fund* (SIF) as a program of the Corporation for National and Community Service (CNCS).[28] The SIF combines public and private funds to assist community-based solutions with evidence of results in any of three priority areas: economic opportunity, healthy futures, and youth development. The SIF makes grants to intermediaries that are well-positioned in communities to identify promising programs. Grants typically range from $1 million to $5 million annually for up to five years. Intermediaries match the federal funds dollar-for-dollar and hold open evidence-based competitions to identify the most promising innovating nonprofit organizations. Nonprofits must provide evidence of effectiveness and, if selected, must also match the funds they receive. Grantees also receive significant technical assistance from CNCS to support implementation of their programs. In addition, they must participate in evaluations of program impact.

The SIF model is distinguished by three notable outcomes:

- The reliance on outstanding existing grantmaking "intermediaries" to select high-impact community organizations substitutes for building new government infrastructures.

- The requirement that each federal dollar granted be matched 1:1 by the grantees and again by their subgrantees with money from private and other nonfederal sources, which increases the return on taxpayer dollars and strengthens local support.

- The emphasis on rigorous evaluations of program, which not only improves accountability but also builds a stronger marketplace of organizations with evidence of impact.

The SIF launched its first competition in 2010 and selected eleven intermediary grantees. These 2010 grantees have made awards to more than 150 subgrantees serving low-income communities across the country. The 2011 competition selected five additional grantees; the third, in 2012, was planned to engage between three and five new grantees. As of February 2012, $95 million in federal funds had been awarded, which leveraged an additional $250 million in private funds. Over 150 private philanthropic funders partnered with the SIF, including private foundations, community foundations, corporations, and individual donors. Finally, more than one hundred cities in thirty-three states and the District of Columbia are being directly affected by the SIF.

GOVERNMENT FUNDING

In 2009, federal, state, and local government in the United States spent a total of $3.1 trillion on social welfare services, which includes health, education, welfare and social services, social insurance, and housing and community services.[29] As we noted earlier, nonprofit organizations received roughly 32 percent of this. Government funding can come to nonprofits through a variety of paths. Funds may be provided directly by one government agency of one level of government or funneled through other government agencies or levels. For example, a nonprofit may get funding directly from the federal Department of Housing and Urban Development (HUD). Alternatively, HUD money may be allocated to state or local government agencies, which in turn provide it to local nonprofits. States and local governments can also augment this federal money with their own funds. Additional funding can originate at the state and local levels. Nonprofits can also obtain government funds indirectly through government programs that provide assistance to individuals, who then purchase services from nonprofits; this assistance may be in the form of vouchers, tax credits, or per-capita subsidies.[30] Examples include Medicare payments, college loans, and housing vouchers.

Government funding has advantages and challenges. Government can be charged to provide services to constituencies for whom private or market support is lacking. For example, nonprofits seeking to provide reproductive health services for the poor may have difficulties obtaining philanthropic funding. Government funding could provide a steady source of income. However, government funding imposes requirements on nonprofits. These are more substantial for contracts than for grants or indirect sources, which come with fewer strings attached. For contracts: "Substantial transaction costs are often associated with building and maintaining the necessary capacity, skills, and political acumen to navigate governmental systems for funding eligibility and maintaining mandated reporting and evaluation procedures. Governments also have a reputation for slow payment of their bills, requiring nonprofits to set aside working capital to manage cash flows."[31]

Nonprofits can take a number of steps to manage the challenges of government contracting:[32]

- Enhance the board's role in contracting through board membership, increased board advocacy, and increase community presence on the board.

- Ensure that executive leadership is knowledgeable about government contracting and contract management.

- Broaden the agency's constituency in order to counteract the narrow focus of the government contract. This can be done by expanding the composition of the board, joining with other organizations, altering the rules of membership, or creating advisory committees.
- Engage in the policy process by representing the needs of clients and the community, enlisting key community leaders, and making leaders aware of the organization's activities.

EARNED INCOME, LOANS, AND EQUITY

Social entrepreneurs can obtain funding from a variety of market-related sources, including funds they earn in the marketplace, loans from a variety of sources, and a new breed of private investors.

Earned Income   Although nonprofit earned income is not a new phenomenon, as the figures cited earlier show, it has become much more important recently. This stems from increased needs and cutbacks in government funding, limitations on philanthropy, increased competition, and a conservative ideological emphasis on market-based solutions in public and nonprofit sectors.[33]

It is important to consider the degree to which the activities undertaken to generate income contribute to the mission on the one hand and generate financial surpluses on the other. Figure 6.4 shows four possibilities.[34] If the level of income is low and the activity generating it is only tenuously related to the mission, the income may be seen as *disposable*, and the organization should assess whether it is worth pursuing. It may be advisable to continue the activity if the level of income it generates is expected to grow. In addition, there may be non-financial objectives, such as community expectations that services are offered to particular beneficiaries. Low income will play a *supplementary* role if the activity that generates it contributes to the mission. The organization should evaluate whether the level of income could be increased with the same mission impact or mission impact could be increased by nonearned activities.

Earned income activities that are unrelated to the mission but generate significant revenue play a *sustaining* role. For example, a museum may publish a magazine that carries advertising that has nothing to do with its mission of art education and preservation. Or a university may operate a cafeteria open to the public. It is important to note that nonprofits are required to pay tax on business income which is unrelated to their missions. This is called UBIT (unrelated

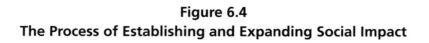

Figure 6.4
The Process of Establishing and Expanding Social Impact

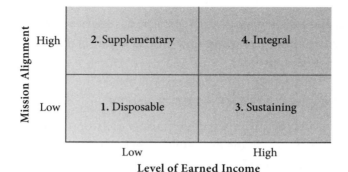

Source: Wei-Skillern, Austin, Leonard, and Stevenson (2007, p. 14).

business income tax). In addition, although there is no fixed guideline, if a nonprofit's level of unrelated income is high, it may encounter legal problems. One legal counsel advises, "If an organization's unrelated business income exceeds 20 percent of gross income, then the legal risks and options available to the organization should be carefully evaluated and monitored. Once an organization's unrelated business income exceeds 50 percent, it may be difficult to continue to demonstrate to the IRS that the organization primarily furthers exempt purposes."[35] In these cases, the nonprofit should assess whether too much activity is being diverted from the mission. One option is to establish this activity as a for-profit subsidiary. Finally, earned income activity may be *integral* to the organization. In this case the activity is highly aligned with the mission and generates substantial revenue. For example, Goodwill Industries obtains the majority of its revenue from the sale of used goods. We also saw that FareStart receives 44 percent of its income from mission-related commercial activity. Given the mission alignment, the nonprofit is not taxed on this income. Although this arrangement overcomes the limitations of the others, there may be tensions between mission and market activity. For example, in order to increase revenues, an organization may be tempted to serve higher-paying clients to the detriment of those who are unable to pay as much but also need the services. Social enterprises should be aware of and guard against mission drift.

Several other considerations come into play in deciding whether an income-producing program should be provided by the organization or be separately incorporated.[36] Programs with the following characteristics are more appropriate for separate incorporation:

- Buyers are motivated entirely by self-interest.
- The primary motive for production is revenues.
- Sales generate a positive profit stream.
- Employees are paid.
- Suppliers charge normal rates.

On the other hand, programs with these characteristics are more appropriate for direct provision:

- Outputs appeal to purchasers' goodwill and sense of charity.
- The primary motive for production is the mission.
- Sales do not cover program costs.
- Volunteers are available to contribute to the program.
- Suppliers subsidize operations with lower rates or donations.

Anderson, Dees, and Emerson outline three strategies that social ventures can use to obtain earned income. These include getting paid for what they already do, launching a new business venture, or building revenue relationships.[37] To summarize their discussion: getting paid for what you already do assumes that an ongoing venture makes a decision to start charging primary beneficiaries, charging an interested third party, or both. There are a number of potential benefits. Charging for a service will screen out those who get less value, encourage efficient use of resources, and signal program quality. Paying clients will not see themselves as recipients of charity, will have more commitment to the program, and will let the organization know if they are not getting the value they expect. Finally, this strategy can generate resources for other programs that need additional funding. On the downside, clients may resist the imposition of fees for what formerly was provided free of charge. Additionally, staff and board members may have moral concerns about shifting a charity-based program to a fee-based program.

New business ventures are formed on the basis of things the organization owns or can produce that are of value to others. Mission-based ventures are probably the most common. This entails the production and sale of goods or services that advance the mission; for example, training and employing the disadvantaged. Other ventures, however, could be based on the competencies, skills, and knowledge of staff; tangible or intangible assets that the organization owns; or relationships that the organization has with donors, clients, staff, alumni, board members and others. Benefits include positive effects on the mission, enhancement of the business and strategic skills of staff, an entrepreneurial organizational culture, and improved market discipline.

Business ventures face a number of challenges. The organization's management, staff, culture, and infrastructure must be adequate to support the venture. Initial and ongoing funding must be obtained and changes in markets and environmental factors must be weathered.

Finally, revenue relationships can be formed through partnerships with corporations to generate income that is shared by the partners. This includes cause-related marketing, joint ventures, licensing, and sponsorship agreements. Each of these strategies has potential benefits, risks and challenges, and key success factors that should be carefully considered.

In *cause-related marketing*, a company's marketing is associated with a nonprofit. The nonprofit contributes its name and commitment to a cause and receives a portion of the company's sales. For example, KaBOOM!, a producer of playgrounds, partnered with Ben & Jerry's to develop and promote a new ice cream flavor, KaBerry KaBOOM! Ben & Jerry's provided KaBOOM! with a portion of the sales of the ice cream. In addition to revenue, the nonprofit could also gain increased visibility. Promotions of the relationship often link the logos of the two organizations in advertising, displays, and media campaigns. In all linkages between a nonprofit and a company, it is important for the nonprofit that the company's products do not conflict with the nonprofit's mission.

Joint ventures are new initiatives undertaken by nonprofits and companies to produce a program, product, or service. They take advantage of unique assets, strengths, or capabilities of the partners. The nonprofit can gain access to new capital, management, or technical skills. Risks include distraction from the nonprofit's mission, potential financial losses, damage to the nonprofit's reputation through the actions of the company, and possible negative legal sanctions [38]

A *licensing agreement* is a contract that permits a company to use the nonprofit's name or logo on its products in return for a royalty payment to the nonprofit.[39] The company hopes to both attract customers who identify with the nonprofit's cause and appear more caring. In this case, the nonprofit will be seen as endorsing the company, making consistency between the company's products and the nonprofit's mission especially important.

In a *sponsorship*, company pays for the use of its name or logo in connection with the nonprofit's products or services.[40] Sponsorship is evident at many nonprofit events, such as the T-shirts worn by participants in a cause-related sporting event or race. The Race for the Cure is a well-known example.[41]

Loans and Equity Finance Investors also have options for making social impacts. Investing in social ventures is not new. For more than four decades, foundations in the United States have used program-related investments (PRIs) to address social needs. Investments have been made to meet needs ranging from housing, education, and health to community development, the environment, and arts and culture. PRIs are investments made by foundations to support charitable activities, and, unlike grants, PRIs give foundations a return on their investment through repayment or return on equity. According to the Ford Foundation, since their initial use in the 1960s, PRIs have helped organizations establish a loan repayment history, generate earned income, gain access to new funding, and develop a financial management history.[42] Foundations have generally been slow to adopt PRIs as vehicles for charitable purposes. A study by the Center on Philanthropy at Indiana University showed that during the past two decades, less than 1 percent of U.S. foundations made PRIs each year. In 2004, a peak year of PRI activity in terms of the total number of PRIs, only 137 foundations made PRIs, totaling $312.6 million, which accounts for only a small portion of the country's foundations and grants. Foundation grants that year totaled $31.8 billion.[43] The study concluded, however, that currently a growing number of funders are actively seeking to learn about the use of PRIs and how they can achieve positive social impact. Help in providing PRI is also available. For example, RSF Social Finance (RSF), a nonprofit financial services organization, assists foundations who seek to participate in PRI but do not have the in-house capacity to do so.[44] With a minimum investment of $100,000 and a five-year term, foundations participating in a RSF PRI Fund receive a 1-percent annual return. Because the RSF PRI Funds are a pooled investment vehicle, foundations also support a wider range of projects than would otherwise be possible, which both mitigates risk and maximizes social impact.

Compared to for-profits, nonprofits lack well-developed mechanisms to fund growth. This is due in large part to a lack of intermediaries that channel information among donors, investors, and nonprofits. This is changing, however, and a nascent capital marketplace for nonprofits is emerging.[45] Some new intermediaries play a role analogous to that of mutual funds, soliciting money from individuals and foundations, conducting due diligence to find effective nonprofits, and monitoring performance. Others function like venture capital funds and partner with fund recipients to formulate and execute a strategy for delivering social impact. For example, the Robin Hood Foundation and New Profit serve as information and financial intermediaries between donors and nonprofits, a classic combined model that's prevalent in the for-profit sector.[46]

A variety of newer financial vehicles have recently been deployed to support social ventures, and their use has given rise to speculation that we are witnessing the birth of new capital markets that could unleash significant new resources for social ventures. For example, *impact investors*: "intend to create positive impact alongside various levels of financial return, both managing and measuring the blended value they create."[47] These investors use return, risk, and impact to evaluate investment options. Investors can be private sector firms (for example pension funds or development banks), nonprofits (such as RSF), or individuals. This capital may be in the form of equity, debt, working capital lines of credit, and loan guarantees. Examples include investments in microfinance, community development finance, and clean technology. A 2009 report from the Monitor Group, a research firm, estimated the impact investing industry could grow from an estimated $50 billion or so in current assets to $500 billion in assets within the next decade.[48] If so, this would approach the collective assets of foundations and constitute a significant source of funding.

Impact investors will differ in the degree to which they favor financial returns or social impact:[49]

- Finance-first investors seek to optimize financial returns, with a floor for social impact. They are mostly commercial investors looking for market-rate returns while providing some social or environmental good.

- Impact-first investors seek to optimize social or environmental returns, with a financial floor. They will accept a range of returns, from principal preservation to market rates.

An example of an impact-first investor is RSF's Social Investment Fund.[50] This is a diversified, direct loan fund comprising over eighty leading nonprofit organizations and for-profit social enterprises. The fund supports mortgage loans, working capital lines of credit, and inventory financing to nonprofit and for-profit organizations dedicated to improving the well-being of society and the environment. Besides these social and environmental returns, fund investors get a financial return similar to that of a bank CD.

Other impact investors intend to create meaningful social and environmental impact but also require evidence of such impacts.[51] Social impact bonds (SIBs), also known as pay-for-success bonds, are a good example. They align the interests of nonprofit service providers, private investors, and governments.[52] An intermediary issues the SIB and raises capital from private investors. The intermediary transfers the SIB proceeds to nonprofit service providers, which use the funds as working capital to scale evidence-based prevention programs. By providing effective prevention programs, the nonprofits improve social outcomes and reduce demand for more expensive safety-net services. Throughout the life of the instrument, the intermediary coordinates all SIB parties, provides operating oversight, directs cash flows, and monitors the investment. An independent evaluator determines whether the target outcomes have been achieved according to the terms of the government contract. If they have, the government pays the intermediary a percentage of its savings and retains the rest. If outcomes have not been achieved, the government owes nothing. If the outcomes have been achieved, investors are repaid their principal and a rate of return.

All stakeholders benefit. Nonprofits gain access to growth capital to scale up operations as well as access to a stable and predictable revenue stream without labor-intensive fundraising. Investors gain both financial returns and social impact and participate in a new asset class with portfolio diversification benefits. Government gains accountability for taxpayer funds, reduces its need for costly downstream remediation, and increases its supply of effective services for citizens, without financial risk. Community gains access to an increased supply of effective social services and reduces its need for crisis-driven interventions.

CONCLUDING THOUGHTS

In this chapter we have examined the funding options for social entrepreneurship. Although social ventures' primary purpose is not to maximize funding, funding is critical for their existence. The type of funding that is available depends on the institutional nature of the social venture (public or private, nonprofit or for-profit) and the venture's mission. In some cases, numerous funding options may be available; in others, the options are limited. In each case, social entrepreneurs need to be aware of the opportunities and challenges of different funding sources as well as the management challenges they entail.

In the next chapter we move to the consideration of social entrepreneurship in existing organizations. This setting has a number of consequences for social entrepreneurship, including how it gets initiated and how it fits with the other programs in the organization.

EXERCISES

Exercise 6.1

In general, would public agencies, for-profits, or nonprofits have more different sources for funding their social ventures? How might this impact their social entrepreneurship? Illustrate your points with real or hypothetical examples of ventures in each of the sectors.

Exercise 6.2

For nonprofits, how might venture philanthropy funding for social entrepreneurship differ from routine funding for ongoing social programs in established social service providers? Illustrate your points with an entrepreneurial venture on the one hand and an established ongoing social program on the other.

Exercise 6.3

What are the benefits for social entrepreneurship of funding from earned income? Suggest a social venture that could be funded with earned income. What might some of the challenges of attaining and using earned income sources be? Would the venture you suggested also have these challenges? If so, how might the venture deal with them?

PART THREE

Understanding and Managing the Social Intrapreneurial Process

chapter SEVEN

Social Intrapreneurship: Innovation from Within

Founded in 1986, Partners in Christ International (PICI) is an international, nondenominational Christian-mission organization headquartered in Tempe, Arizona. The mission of PICI is to "[serve] evangelical churches on both sides of the Mexican-American border by linking them together in partnering relationships." It strives to implement this mission by partnering with indigenous churches and ministries to meet needs and opportunities that enhance or complement their work.

A key strategy in PICI operations is to develop alliances among indigenous Protestant churches in order to train and empower local pastors and church leaders. PICI has done so in Hermosillo and Guaymas, cities in the Mexican state of Sonora. Pastors meet together to offer each other advice and encouragement as well as to develop a strategy for ministry throughout the entire city. Furthermore, they collaboratively teach seminary courses for church members: each pastor teaches a course, and community members can enroll and receive systematic, in-depth instruction that would otherwise be unavailable to them. These church alliances also lead to events and regional conferences, and they offer the opportunity to mobilize the Christian community toward the vision or message the churches have collaboratively agreed upon.

During its early years, PICI provided financial and advisory support to Casa Elizabet, a children's home in the town of Imuris, Sonora, and assisted local churches in Sonora with their church

143

planting efforts. As opportunities to serve in Sonoran communities increased, PICI began organizing short-term trips in which teams from Arizona and various other parts of the United States could support and work alongside Mexican churches. PICI coordinates approximately five to ten mission trips every year—teams from the United States travel to Mexico or Nicaragua for a week and work alongside local churches. Trips may vary in detail, but nearly all of them focus on construction projects, evangelism, or medical care. Additionally, PICI raises funds to support two orphanages in Nicaragua and coordinates medical care trips to Mexico, Nicaragua, Kenya, and India as well as to English camps in Slovenia. In the United States, its volunteer-run "Wheels from Above" program provides disabled people with motorized wheel chairs.

Finally, PICI supports Hispanic ministries by selling Bible-study and discipleship materials in Spanish. Hispanic church leaders in both Mexico and the United States order books from PICI's Arizona headquarters.[1]

In an article titled "Have a Real Impact; Keep Your Day Job," Nancy McGaw suggests that social intrapreneurship is a promising approach to solving pressing social and environmental problems. Social entrepreneurs no longer have to create their own organizations to tackle societal problems; rather, they can do this from their current job. Nancy shares a few examples from her experience as the director of the First Mover Fellowship Program at the Aspen Institute Business & Society Program, where she has worked with exceptional social intrapreneurs in businesses around the world and studied the innovations they are piloting in their organizations:

> Take James Inglesby at Unilever, for example. James is using his expertise as a chemical engineer to develop new business models for base-of-the-pyramid consumers. Suzanne Ackerman-Berman at Pick n' Pay in South Africa is leading an innovation lab to help small-scale farmers and entrepreneurs become reliable suppliers to the retail industry. Dawn Baker at Dow is revamping leadership development offerings to ensure they mesh with their company's sustainability objectives. Matt Ellis at CBRE, a global leader in real estate services, is designing financing structures that will

provide capital for clients' energy efficiency initiatives. At the cloud-computing company VMware, Nicola Acutt is running technical service projects to tap into the creative energy of talented employees to solve social problems and uncover business opportunities.[2]

So far in this book, our discussion has focused on social entrepreneurship start-ups; that is, a social entrepreneur recognizes an innovative opportunity to address a social need and gathers all the necessary resources to develop that opportunity into a new organization. However, all social entrepreneurial activities do not fit this mold: as the aforementioned examples show, social entrepreneurship often originates out of existing organizations, be they public, nonprofit, or for-profit entities. Some individuals might be attracted to the mission of an existing organization and thus decide to devote their entrepreneurial energy to working with the organization; others might be attracted to the idea of turning a failing organization around.[3] In fact, suggests Peter Frumkin, the entrepreneurial activities of individuals who join existing nonprofit organizations may be part of the reason for the low rate of nonprofit failure.[4]

In this chapter, we consider "social intrapreneurship" as a subset of social entrepreneurship. Defined as social entrepreneurship within an established organization, social intrapreneurship can refer to either new venture creation or entrepreneurial process innovation. We begin by discussing the concept of social intrapreneurship and its various dimensions (new business venturing, product and service innovation, and self-renewal). We then present a conceptual framework for understanding the antecedents and consequences of social intrapreneurship. We then look into the social intrapreneurial process and address the following questions: How do entrepreneurial opportunities come into existence in an established organization? Which people in the organization pursue these opportunities? Why does the organization choose to implement some social entrepreneurial opportunities but ignore others? We conclude the chapter with a discussion of the unique challenges and opportunities of promoting social intrapreneurship.

CLARIFYING THE SOCIAL INTRAPRENEURSHIP CONCEPT

Unlike social entrepreneurship start-ups, social intrapreneurship has received almost no scholarly attention until very recently. To better understand this concept, we first briefly discuss its cousin concept in commercial entrepreneurship: intrapreneurship.

The notion of intrapreneurship first appeared in an article written in 1978 by Gifford and Elizabeth Pinchot.[5] Variously labeled as "corporate entrepreneurship," "corporate venture," and "internal corporate venture," intrapreneurship can be broadly defined as entrepreneurship with an existing organization. Beyond this point, however, it has been defined in various ways. For example, one definition views intrapreneurship as a process by which individuals inside organizations pursue opportunities independent of the resources they currently control.[6] Another definition views it as "emergent behavioral intentions and behaviors of an organization that are related to departures from the customary" (p. 9).[7] Still another defines it as "the process of creating new business within established firms to improve organizational profitability and enhance a company's competitive position" (pp. 260–261).[8] A fourth definition describes it as "the process whereby firms engage in diversification through internal development" that involves "new resources combinations to extend the firm's activities in areas unrelated, or marginally related, to its current domain of competence and corresponding opportunity set" (p. 1349).[9]

Despite the lack of consensus on the definition of intrapreneurship, most authors seem to agree that intrapreneurship covers not only new business ventures but also other innovative activities and orientations, such as development of new products, services, technologies, administrative techniques, strategies, and competitive postures.[10] Intrapreneurial activities can be formal or informal: some are formal activities with a designated unit (such as the New Venture Division) leading the efforts; others are informal initiatives led by individuals or ad hoc teams within existing divisions. Corporate entrepreneurship activities can be internally or externally oriented. Internal activities may cover product, process, and administrative innovations at various levels of the organization; external activities may include mergers, joint ventures, or acquisitions.[11]

Table 7.1 presents a sample of definitions of social intrapreneurship from this small and emerging body of literature.

As we can see from this small sample of definitions, scholars define social intrapreneurship in a way that is very similar to the way intrapreneurship is defined in the existing literature: it can be the creation of a new venture by an existing organization, but it can also be a program or process innovation in the existing organization. It is not limited to nonprofit organizations but includes government and for-profit businesses as well.

Table 7.1

A Sample of Definitions of Social Intrapreneurship

Author(s), Year	Definition
Brooks (2008)[12]	Social entrepreneurial behavior that occurs within established ventures (p. 161).
Grayson, McLaren, & Spitzeck (2011)[13]	Social intrapreneurs are people within a large corporation who take direct initiative for innovations which address social or environmental challenges profitably (p. 3).
Kistruck & Beamish (2010)[14]	Social entrepreneurship that originates out of existing nonprofit and for-profit organizations (p. 736).
Mair & Marti (2006)[15]	Social entrepreneurship in an established organization. Like intrapreneurship in the business sector, social intrapreneurship can refer to either new venture creation or entrepreneurial process innovation (p. 37).
Schmitz & Scheuerle (2012)[16]	Social entrepreneurship in entrenched organizations, often referring to not-for-profit initiatives that aim at searching for alternative funding strategies (p. 18).
Yusuf (2005)[17]	Social intrapreneurship encompasses entrepreneurial activity that generates social value undertaken within the confines of an organization, either in the private, public, or nonprofit sectors (p. 121).

SOCIAL INTRAPRENEURSHIP DIMENSIONS

A variety of social intrapreneurial activities are observed in organizations across all three sectors and found in large as well as medium- and small-sized organizations. Drawing on insights from prior research on intrapreneurship,[18] we can understand social intrapreneurial activities in terms of three dimensions: new business venturing, product and service innovation, and self-renewal.

New Business Venturing

New business venturing refers to the creation of a new business within an existing organization by redefining the company's products (or services) and/or by developing new markets. For example, Panera Bread recently opened its first Panera Cares Café in Clayton, MO. What distinguishes Panera Cares Café from the other Panera branches is its "pay what you can" menu: no prices or cash registers, only suggested donation levels and donation bins.[19] Examples of similar new business venturing include Mozilla Corporation, which is the for-profit subsidiary of Mozilla Foundation, a nonprofit organization best known for its Firefox browser; and Google Foundation, a nonprofit subsidiary of Google, Inc.[20]

Product and Service Innovation

This dimension includes new product or service development, product or service improvements, and new production or service methods and procedures. One example is the Text 2Help Program—a mobile giving program—created by the American Red Cross. When the American Red Cross debuted this program in collaboration with the Wireless Foundation in the 2008 Text 2HELP campaign, it successfully raised over $190,000 through 38,091 text messages to provide relief for victims of such natural disasters as Hurricane Gustav and Hurricane Ike.[21] Another example can be found in a new product item— "suspended coffee"—on the menu of your local coffee shop. A "suspended coffee" is a cup of coffee paid for in advance by some customers meant for someone who cannot afford a warm beverage (such as a homeless person). The idea of "suspended coffees" originated in Naples, Italy, about a century ago and became popular in coffee shops all over the world in the past few years.[22]

Self-Renewal

The self-renewal dimension reflects the transformation of an organization through the renewal of its mission and strategic focus. It includes the redefinition of the business concept, reorganization, and the introduction of system-wide changes for innovation. For example, in recent years the American Lung Association of Los Angeles County went through a self-renewal process, revisited its organizational mission and strategy, and in 2006 changed its name to BREATHE California of Los Angeles County ("BREATHE LA") to better reflect its renewed focus as "an independent lung health organization to address Los Angeles County's specific air quality and health needs."[23]

The three dimensions collectively form the basis of social intrapreneurship, but they differ in focus. The new business venturing dimension emphasizes developing, within the existing organization, new ventures that may or may not be related to the organization's current mission and strategic focus. The product and service innovation dimension looks at creation of new products, services, and programs as well as some incremental innovation that improves over its current products, services, and programs. The self-renewal dimension focuses on strategy reformulation, reorganization, and organizational change. Although self-renewal may eventually be reflected in new business creation, new product (service) offerings, and/or new market entry, it captures the entrepreneurial orientation and spirit of an organization at a more macro level.

Despite their differences in focus, the three types of social Intrapreneurial activities described above share common characteristics with each other. These common elements are as follows:[24]

- The creation of something new, which could be a new product, service, program, or process, or a new business venture.
- The new product, service, program, process, or venture is intended to create economic and/or social value.
- The new product, service, program, process, or venture requires additional resources and/or changes in how resources are deployed within the organization.
- The new product, service, program, process, or venture involves a higher level of risk for the organization, as it is unproven. Even if the organization is creating something new for itself, but not new to the market, the organization's ability to implement it is still unproven and has a higher chance of failure.
- Through organizational learning during the process of creating and implementing the new product, service, program, process, or venture, the organization develops new organizational competencies and capabilities.

Note that the intrapreneurship literature actually includes a fourth dimension of intrapreneurship: proactiveness. As we discussed in Chapter Two, proactiveness refers to "processes aimed at anticipating and acting on future needs" by pursuing new opportunities and strategically introducing new products and eliminating old operations.[25] We decide to exclude it from the intrapreneurship dimensions, based on the understanding that, as a key aspect of an organization's entrepreneurial orientation, proactiveness is embodied in the practices of new business venturing, new product and service innovation, and self-renewal in an existing organization.

ANTECEDENTS AND CONSEQUENCES OF SOCIAL INTRAPRENEURSHIP

Scholars have identified two main sets of antecedents of social intrapreneurship: internal antecedents pertain to a set of organizational characteristics, and external antecedents pertain to the external environment. These antecedents and their corresponding dimensions are discussed in terms of the interrelationship among these dimensions. Discussion of the consequence of intrapreneurship is focused on organizational performance.[26] In Figure 7.1, we present a conceptual framework of social intrapreneurship, based on models developed by Walker[27] and by Kearney, Hisrich, and Roche.[28] The framework depicts the main antecedents that relate to social intrapreneurship and the impact of social intrapreneurship on organizational performance.[29]

Internal Antecedents: Organizational Characteristics

Internal antecedents refer to certain characteristics of an organization that are critical for any social intrapreneurship to occur. There are many characteristics

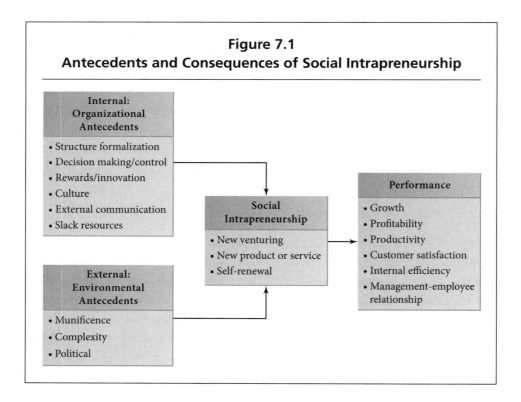

Figure 7.1
Antecedents and Consequences of Social Intrapreneurship

Internal: Organizational Antecedents
- Structure formalization
- Decision making/control
- Rewards/innovation
- Culture
- External communication
- Slack resources

External: Environmental Antecedents
- Munificence
- Complexity
- Political

Social Intrapreneurship
- New venturing
- New product or service
- Self-renewal

Performance
- Growth
- Profitability
- Productivity
- Customer satisfaction
- Internal efficiency
- Management-employee relationship

that make up an organization's internal environment, including: structure or formalization, communication, goals, decision making or control, rewards or motivations, culture, management support, risk taking, and proactiveness. In this section we highlight a few particularly important ones.

Structure Formalization Social intrapreneurship is more likely to occur among organizations with organic structures and low formalization than among organizations with mechanistic structures and high formalization. The birth and development of intrapreneurship demands for greater flexibility and adaptability within an organization because high levels of rigidity and red tape are in conflict with the development of an entrepreneurial culture. As put by Sadler, "Organic structures are more adaptable, more openly communicating, more consensual and more loosely controlled than mechanistic structures" (p. 30).[30]

Decision Making/Control Social intrapreneurship is more likely to occur among organizations with more flexible, decentralized decision making and less formal control systems than among organizations with more rigid, centralized decision making and highly formal control systems. Decision-making structures and systems are necessary for the management and control of an enterprise, but they should not destroy flexibility, intuition, flair, and creativity. Confronted with excessive formal controls, social intrapreneurs may find themselves encumbered and frustrated, and thus less motivated to engage in social intrapreneurial activities.[31]

Rewards and Motivation Social intrapreneurship is more likely to be seen among organizations with high rewards and motivation than among organizations with low rewards and motivation. Entrepreneurial managers will likely find an organization more favorable as a working environment if the organization encourages calculated risk taking and tends not to penalize managers if risky projects fail.[32] Moreover, good performance should be recognized and rewarded; without this, there is no incentive for employees to take risks. An effective reward system that spurs entrepreneurial activity "must consider goals, feedback, emphasis on individual responsibility, and results-based incentives."[33]

Culture Organizational culture refers to a set of shared values, beliefs, and assumptions that help organizational members understand organizational functioning and thus guide their attitudes and behavior in the organizations.[34] Organizational culture is an influential factor in the promotion of entrepreneurial activities within the organization. An organizational culture that gives employees enough leeway to express their creativity and allows them to take risks to pursue new opportunities will facilitate social intrapreneurship. By contrast, an organizational culture that emphasizes cohesion, teamwork, stability, security, cooperation, and conflict avoidance will hinder social intrapreneurship.[35] Put succinctly, social intrapreneurship is more positively related to an organizational culture that is flexible and supportive than to a culture that is rigid and restrictive.

External Communication   External communication refers to the processes and intensity of environmental scanning that allow organizations to retrieve information from and exchange information with their external environments. Social intrapreneurship is more likely to happen in organizations characterized by a higher level of external communication. Research shows that external communication contributes to the adoption of organization innovation in local governments; it helps managers develop knowledge about the external environment, thereby leading to proposals for new ideas or projects.[36]

Slack Resources   Slack resources constitute the difference between total resources and total necessary payments.[37] This slack acts as a resource cushion that firms can use in a discretionary manner, both to counter threats and to exploit opportunities.[38] With slack resources, organizations may have the capacity to innovate, bear the costs of innovation, and experiment liberally. Therefore organizations with more slack resources may experience more activities of social intrapreneurship.

Mission   An organization's mission guides its entire strategic plan at a macro level. This organizational characteristic is particularly relevant for nonprofit organizations, which are often referred to as "mission-driven" organizations. Research finds that nonprofit organizations with a clear, motivating mission tend to be more innovative. Specifically, a clear, motivating organizational mission helps an organization to focus its attention on those innovations that will most likely support the accomplishment of that mission; such a mission also creates a climate in which innovations are given a fair chance to succeed.[39]

External Antecedents: Environmental Characteristics

The external environment is a fundamental determinant of social intrapreneurship. Elements in the external environment that are related to social intrapreneurship may include technological opportunities, industry growth, and demand for new products—which are viewed as favorable for intrapreneurship—and threatening changes and increased competitive rivalry, which are viewed as unfavorable for intrapreneurship. Scholars have organized these elements into three categories: munificence, complexity, and political.

Munificence Munificence refers to the environment's support for organizational growth. It is a multidimensional concept manifested in high industry sales growth, technological opportunities, and the demand for new products and services.[40] The perceived decline of an industry would push organizations into increased renewal activities. Demand for new products (or services) also presents an important demand pull that encourages intrapreneurship. It is therefore expected that technological opportunities, industry growth, and new product (or service) demand will be positively related to social intrapreneurship. Munificent environments help firms build slack resources, which in turn contributes to social intrapreneurship.[41] Furthermore, munificent environments enable organizations to access external resources for support during periods of internal and external problems.[42] It is therefore expected that social intrapreneurship is more likely to occur in more munificent environments than in more stagnant environments.

Complexity A highly turbulent external environment implies a dynamic, hostile, and complex set of environmental conditions.[43] The environment faced by managers, especially public sector managers, is now more complex, dynamic, and threatening than it was in the past. The ability of an organization to respond to changing circumstances is significantly limited, not only by resources but also by the management philosophies and structures that characterize organizations.[44] Social intrapreneurship is more likely to be seen in more complex environments than in more simple and benign environments.

Political This environmental characteristic is particularly relevant for public sector and nonprofit organizations. The prevalence of political constraints leads to frequent changes in public policy and the imposition of short-term budgets and planning horizons on public and nonprofit managers. While business organizations view economic issues as crucial, public and nonprofit organizations are constantly affected by such political issues as the views of opinion leaders, outright manipulation by legislators and interest groups, and opposition to an agency's prerogatives.[45] It is thus expected that social intrapreneurship will be more positively related to organizational performance among organizations that can adapt to and change with the political environment than those that cannot.

Organizational Performance

As put by Covin and Slevin, "the growing interest in the study of entrepreneurship is a response not only to the belief that entrepreneurial activity will result in positive macroeconomic outcomes but to the belief that such activity can lead to improved performance in established organizations" (p. 19).[46] In other words, improved organizational performance is thought to be a result of intrapreneurship. Scholars suggest that organizations that develop organizational environments conducive to intrapreneurship and actually engage in intrapreneurship in terms of entrepreneurial orientations and behaviors may have higher levels of growth, profitability, productivity, or newly created wealth than firms that do not.[47]

For public sector organizations and nonprofits, although they may not yet fully integrate intrapreneurship as business organizations have done, it is apparent that these organizations could derive huge benefits from having an entrepreneurial and innovative culture. These benefits include improved customer service and satisfaction, better internal processes, more appropriate reward systems, improved communication, and better management-employee relationships. Therefore engendering intrapreneurship and innovation in public sector and nonprofit organizations would also enhance the overall performance of these organizations.[48]

MANAGEMENT CHALLENGES OF SOCIAL INTRAPRENEURSHIP

As management experts Tom Peters and Robert Waterman point out in their widely read business book *In Search of Excellence*, one of the most important problems for big organizations is that they have stopped doing something that got them big in the first place: innovation. Peters and Waterman identify eight common themes that determine the success of the corporations that they choose to study, one of which is "autonomy and entrepreneurship—fostering innovation and nurturing 'champions.'"[49]

Ahuja and Morris Lampert identify three organizational pathologies that inhibit breakthrough inventions in established firms: the familiarity trap—favoring the familiar; the maturity trap—favoring the mature; and the propinquity trap—favoring search for solutions near to existing solutions. They argue that by experimenting with novel technologies (that is, technologies in which the firm lacks prior experience), emerging technologies (those that are recent or newly developed in the industry), and pioneering technologies (those that do not build on any existing technologies), firms can overcome these traps and create breakthrough inventions.[50] Although their study is written from a business perspective, their insights can nevertheless be used to improve our understanding of the challenges of social intrapreneurship in public and nonprofit sector settings.

These common challenges aside, the pursuit of social intrapreneurship in public and nonprofit organizations confronts some unique difficulties. Mulgan and Albury identify a number of key barriers to innovation that are particularly prevalent in the public sector:[51]

- *Pressures and burdens:* Managers are so preoccupied with the service delivery pressures and administrative burdens that they barely have time to pause and think about doing things differently.

- *Short-termism:* Short-term budgets and planning horizons prohibit innovations that incur short-term costs, because few innovative businesses would survive an obligation to break even every year.

- *Lack of rewards and incentives to innovate:* The public sector traditionally has higher penalties for failed innovations than rewards for successful ones.

- *Culture of risk aversion:* The obligation to maintain continuity and the accountability to the public, along with poor rewards and incentives, might lead to a risk-averse organizational culture that inhibits innovation.

- *Lack of skills:* Even those managers who have the opportunity and motivation to innovate may not have the skill sets to improve management.

- *Dealing with failure:* Managers are reluctant to close down failing programs or organizations.

Borins provides empirical findings about obstacles in implementing innovation in the public sector from his study of over three hundred government reformers around the world. He categorizes the obstacles to implementing innovation into three groups. The first group consists of barriers that arise from within the bureaucracy/organization, such as hostile attitudes, turf fights, difficulty in coordinating organizations, logistical problems, difficulty in maintaining the enthusiasm of program staff, difficulty in introducing new technology, union opposition, middle management resistance, and public sector opposition to entrepreneurial action. The second group of obstacles arises primarily in the political environment; these include inadequate funding or resources, legislative or regulatory constraints, and political opposition. One obstacle that frequently arises in both the bureaucratic and the political arena is inadequate resources, a result of funding decisions made at either the bureaucratic or political level. The third group of obstacles exists in the external environment: public doubts about the effectiveness of the program, difficulty reaching the program's target group, opposition by those affected in the private sector—including entities that would experience increased competition—and general public opposition or skepticism.[52]

In a comparative study of ten cases in Africa and Latin America, Kistruck and Beamish examine social intrapreneurship in light of the social context and the local environment. They argue that, because an organization is embedded in its social context, its existing cognitive schema, patterns of relationships and cultural norms serve as a double-edged sword: they provide a source of opportunities as well as constraints to the organization's social intrapreneurial efforts. Their findings show that nonprofit organizations differ significantly from their for-profit counterparts in their ability to successfully engage in social intrapreneurship. More specifically, attempts to shift nonprofit forms toward a more financially or market-oriented approach were much less effective than shifting for-profit forms toward a more social orientation. The researchers identify three types of embeddedness that resulted in this difference: cognitive embeddedness, network embeddedness, and cultural embeddedness.[53]

In terms of cognitive embeddedness, although either a nonprofit or for-profit organization needs to go through a cognitive shift in the minds of its internal stakeholders (that is, employees) when transitioning to be more social entrepreneurial, the employees in the nonprofit cases experienced a much higher degree of cognitive overload with the introduction of more market-based activities. In particular, the employees in the nonprofit cases tend to view social and financial objectives as contradictory, whereas the employees in the for-profit cases tend to view them as complementary. As a result, nonprofit employees are less able to reconcile financial with social goals and communicate these goals to other stakeholders than are their for-profit counterparts.[54]

In terms of network embeddedness, the nonprofit organizations in this study interacted with stakeholders in developing countries for decades; this developed an extensive social network that facilitated their work in those countries. When the nonprofits attempted to change the nature of the relationship with their stakeholders from unidirectional and donative to bidirectional and transactional, the local residents responded negatively to this change: in many cases, despite having long-term agreements in place to offset high initial investments, the locals would opportunistically engage in side-selling of their products, often leaving the nonprofit social venture unable to fill orders and quantities. In contrast, the for-profit forms were able to leverage their embeddedness in the current marketplace when broadening their networks to pursue socially focused goals.[55]

In terms of cultural embeddedness, members of the nonprofit sector in developing countries were not necessarily seen as altruistic or driven by intrinsic rather than extrinsic value. The perception that fraud often occurs in nonprofit organizations in developing countries and that many nonprofit employees there have high-paying jobs and live a fancy lifestyle has led to a lack of public trust in the nonprofit form.[56]

Taken together, cognitive, network, and cultural embeddedness play an important constraining role as an organization begins to engage in social intrapreneurial activities. This constraining role is found to be more salient in nonprofit organizations than in their for-profit counterparts.

Research has also proposed various ways of overcoming challenges to social intrapreneurship with various levels of success. Borins identifies three main classes of tactical approaches to overcoming barriers in public sector innovations:[57]

1. *Persuasion*—highlighting the benefits of an innovation, establishing demonstration projects and social marketing

2. *Accommodation*—consulting with affected parties, co-opting affected parties by engaging them in the governance of the innovation, training those whose work would be affected, compensating losers, and ensuring the program is culturally and linguistically sensitive

3. *Others*—finding additional resources, resolving logistical problems, preserving and exerting continuous effort, gaining political support and building alliances, having a clear vision and focusing on the most important aspects of the innovation, modifying technology, changing legislation or regulations, providing recognition for program participants or supporters.

The study clearly illustrates that the successful innovators are those who take objectives seriously and seek to systematically address concerns.

CONCLUDING THOUGHTS

In this chapter we have discussed various aspects of social intrapreneurship, such as the nature and dimensions of social intrapreneurship, the antecedent factors and intended outcomes, and the various challenges that an organization confronts as it engages in social intrapreneurship. Yet some important questions remain unanswered: What is the process through which established organizations engage in social intrapreneurial activities? How can they manage the conflict between the new and the old? Organizations must take on the challenge of managing the social intrapreneurial process in a way that allows for enough exploitation to ensure current viability but also enough exploration to ensure future viability. However, it is not easy to achieve an appropriate balance between these two efforts. In particular, large, established organizations tend to be more competent at exploiting opportunities closer to their existing businesses and competencies, but less effective in developing exploratory or breakthrough innovations. They also oscillate between "creating the future" by pursuing exploratory opportunities and "protecting the core" by pursuing exploitative opportunities.[58]

In the next chapter, we further explore this fundamental challenge through an in-depth discussion of how to effectively manage the social intrapreneurial process.

EXERCISES

Exercise 7.1

What are the three dimensions of social intrapreneurship? Use examples to contrast and compare the three dimensions.

Exercise 7.2

Identify an organization that engages in social entrepreneurial activities and describe in detail the internal and external antecedents of social intrapreneurship. In the context of the organization, what are the performance implications of social intrapreneurship?

Exercise 7.3

What are the challenges of social intrapreneurship? Do the challenges vary with the age, size, or type of the organization, or the sector in which the organization operates? Propose several ways to overcome the challenges. Illustrate your points with examples.

Managing the Social Intrapreneurial Process

At the turn of the first decade of the twenty-first century, nearly 40 percent of adults in Kenya were still "unbanked"; that is, they had no access to financial services. When they needed to transfer cash across the country, they had to send it through friends, family, or someone like a bus driver who would transfer the money for a fee. On the other hand, most adults had mobile phones.

These facts were seemingly unrelated to each other, and yet two social intrapreneurs at Vodafone, an England-based global telecom giant that owned 40 percent of Kenya's leading mobile communication provider, Safaricom, took notice and recognized an exciting business opportunity: leveraging Vodafone's mobile infrastructure to deliver financial services to people in Kenya. Nick Hughes, then head of Social Enterprise at Vodafone, came up with the idea of using mobile phones to make the distribution of microfinance loans in Africa more efficient. Nick submitted a proposal to the U.K. Department for International Development (DFID) for matching funding, and received a £960,000 grant in May 2004 to kick off the project. The company more than matched the pledge, with funding of £990,000. While Nick was selling the idea to Vodafone executives, Susie Lonie, a senior product manager at Vodafone, conducted pilot work on the ground to determine how and why Kenyans might use mobile technology to transfer money. Susie and her team found that receiving money from family and friends was one of the primary means of support for the poorer segment of Kenya's population. As is common in many developing

161

countries, people with marketable skills often move to a city to work and send part of their income back to their families in rural villages.

After over eighteen months of needs assessment and a pilot project, in April 2007 Safaricom launched a new mobile phone–based payment and money transfer service, known as M-Pesa (M stands for "mobile" and *pesa* is Swahili for "money"). The target population of the M-Pesa service is mobile customers who either have no access to a bank or are not qualified to have a bank account due to insufficient income. For a small fee, the service allows these mobile customers to deposit money into an account stored on their mobile phones, to send balances using SMS technology to other users (including sellers of goods and services), and to redeem deposits for cash. Within a year, M-Pesa had gained 1.6 million customers in Kenya. By 2011 there were fourteen million M-Pesa accounts, which held 40 percent of the country's savings. Following M-Pesa's success in Kenya, Vodafone has extended the service to many other African and Asian countries. Today, M-Pesa is the most successful mobile phone–based financial service in the developing world. It is also worth noting that, in 2010, Nick and Susie jointly received the Social and Economic Innovation Award from the *Economist* magazine.[1]

While being interviewed by his colleague Laura Weiss on Taprootfoundation .org, Aaron Hurst—social entrepreneur and founder of Taproot Foundation, a nonprofit intermediary that engages professionals in pro bono work to build the infrastructure of other nonprofits—raised an interesting question: Why does an organization that was innovative during its early years eventually lose its touch of creativity, and how can the organization manage to remain creative and innovative as it continues to grow? Aaron Hurst went on to explain that

> Early stage organizations, for profit or nonprofit . . . [are] doing a lot of experimentation and they also don't have a large infrastructure so changes are not that difficult to make and failure is not so devastating— you don't have people's jobs on the line, you don't have expectations out there, it's just a much easier environment in which to tinker and experiment and try new things. As you get bigger and bigger two different things happen—one is that you have more and more at stake every time you want to make a change and you have people's livelihoods and

expectations riding on your success. The other is the limits of nonprofit capitalization. They're often staffed so thinly that not only do they not have the resources to implement a brave new wonderful innovation but their staff is working so tirelessly and so hard to keep things going that they don't have the bandwidth to even pause and ask questions.[2]

In this chapter, we focus on the challenges and strategies of managing the social intrapreneurial process. Recent research on intrapreneurship has shifted its focus from "the characteristics and functions of the entrepreneur" to the nature and characteristics of the "entrepreneurial process."[3] Entrepreneurship scholars describe entrepreneurial processes as the sequences of functions, activities, or behaviors associated with perceiving of opportunities, leading to an entrepreneurial event—creation of a new organization.[4] In a similar vein, we define the social intrapreneurial process as *the sequences of functions, activities, or behaviors associated with perception of social entrepreneurial opportunities, leading to the creation of a new good, service, and venture in an existing organization.*[4]

As briefly mentioned at the end of Chapter Seven, in order to effectively manage the social intrapreneurial process, established organizations must be able to overcome a fundamental challenge: How can they manage the conflict between the new and the old? How can they achieve an appropriate balance between exploration and exploitation? Understanding and resolving the important challenge of balancing the new and the old requires a more careful examination of the key role of management in the social intrapreneurial process.

This chapter delineates the distinctive roles of three levels of management: frontline, middle, and top management. It begins with a discussion of the role of middle managers and frontline managers. Frontline managers are those who are directly responsible for the people who physically produce the organization's products or provide its services. We describe frontline managers as champions who create, define, or adopt an idea for a social innovation and are willing to assume significant risk to implement the innovation. Occupying positions between the strategic apex and the operating core of an organization, middle managers play two distinctive roles that provide impetus for social entrepreneurial initiatives: evaluating and selling. First, they evaluate the strategic merits of social entrepreneurial initiatives emerging from lower organizational levels and assess their potential for future organizational growth. Second, they gain top management's attention and support for an entrepreneurial initiative that may fall outside the organizational agenda. Next, we discuss the role of top managers. Top managers are responsible for setting goals for the organization, deciding what actions are necessary to meet them, and determining how best to use resources. The willingness and capacity of top management to facilitate and promote innovation in the organization is crucial to the success of social intrapreneurship.

THE NATURE OF INNOVATION IN ESTABLISHED ORGANIZATIONS

Before we continue to discuss the social intrapreneurial process, it is useful to make a distinction between exploratory and exploitative opportunities or initiatives. We focus on relatedness to an organization's core competence as an important distinguishing feature of social intrapreneurial opportunities. Accordingly, "exploratory opportunities" refer to those that are unrelated or marginally related to an organization's core competence, whereas "exploitative initiatives" indicate related ones. This distinction is consistent with Robert Burgelman's notion of autonomous and induced strategic initiatives in an established firm. According to Burgelman, most strategic activities are induced by the firm's current concept of strategy (for example, new product development projects for existing business), but autonomous strategic activities that lie outside the scope of the current concept of strategy also emerge. Thus autonomous strategic initiatives provide the basis for exploratory innovations, whereas induced strategic initiatives lead to exploitative innovations.[5]

Note that we conceptualize exploratory and exploitative opportunities in a manner corresponding to some definitions of exploratory and exploitative innovations. Prior research, for example, defines exploratory innovations as radical innovations that are designed to meet the needs of emerging customers or markets and that require new knowledge or departure from existing knowledge.[6] Following such definitions, exploratory and exploitative opportunities can be understood as opportunities that, if pursued, may lead to explorative and exploitative innovations. However, all of the opportunities may not eventually translate into actual innovations.[7]

A TWO-PHASE MODEL OF THE SOCIAL INTRAPRENEURIAL PROCESS

Robert Burgelman presents a model of the strategic process concerning entrepreneurial activity in large, complex organizations (see Figure 8.1). Here, the

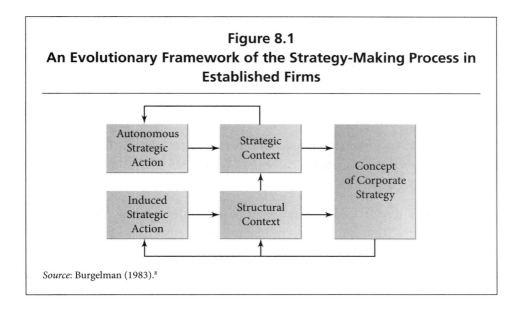

Figure 8.1
An Evolutionary Framework of the Strategy-Making Process in Established Firms

Source: Burgelman (1983).[8]

structural context refers to the administrative mechanisms used to implement corporate strategy, whereas the strategic context refers to the political process by which middle managers convince top management to redefine the corporate strategy in order to accommodate autonomous strategic initiatives that fall outside the current concept of strategy.

Burgelman makes the following key points:

• First, firms need both diversity and order in their strategic activities to maintain their viability. Diversity results primarily from autonomous strategic initiatives of participants at the operational level. Order results from imposing a concept of strategy on the organization.

• Second, managing diversity requires an experimentation-and-selection approach. Middle-level managers play a crucial role in this through their support for autonomous strategic initiatives early on, by combining these with various capabilities dispersed in the firm's operating system, and by conceptualizing strategies for new areas of business.

• Third, top management's critical contribution consists in strategic recognition rather than planning. By allowing middle-level managers to redefine the strategic context, and by being fast learners, top management can make sure that entrepreneurial activities will correspond to their strategic vision, retroactively.

- Fourth, strategic management at the top should be to a large extent concerned with balancing the emphasis on diversity and order over time. Top management should control the level and the rate of change rather than the specific content of entrepreneurial activity.

- Finally, new managerial approaches and innovative administrative arrangements are required to facilitate the collaboration between entrepreneurial participants and the organizations in which they are active (p. 1349).[9]

Burgelman's model is a useful step toward understanding the processes and mechanisms through which intrapreneurial opportunities emerge and develop into new products, services, technologies, and ventures in an existing organization. Yet many questions remain unanswered. For example, how do intrapreneurial opportunities come into existence in an organization? In particular, how do exploratory initiatives (or autonomous strategic initiatives, to use Burgelman's term) emerge in the organization? How is it that some people pursue these opportunities and others do not? How does the organization choose to implement some intrapreneurial opportunities but ignore others?

In an effort to answer these questions, Ren and Guo introduce a two-phase model of the intrapreneurial process.[10] They argue that the process of discovering, evaluating, and choosing intrapreneurial opportunities in an existing organization goes through two phases: the prescreening phase, in which many opportunities are discovered, and the screening phase, in which opportunities are evaluated and a few of them are chosen for further exploitation. With a focus on the screening phase, they then argue that the organization's selective attention to some opportunities (and not others) is jointly influenced by organizational attention structures[11]—the social, economic, and cultural structures that govern the allocation of attentional focus of managers—and "policy windows"[12]—situations in which firm managers are prompted to make a choice among multiple, competing opportunities existing in the organizational boundary. Organizational attention structures tend to favor exploitative opportunities over exploratory opportunities. "Policy windows" provide opportunities for intrapreneurs to "sell" their opportunities to management, but their effects on particular opportunities differ.

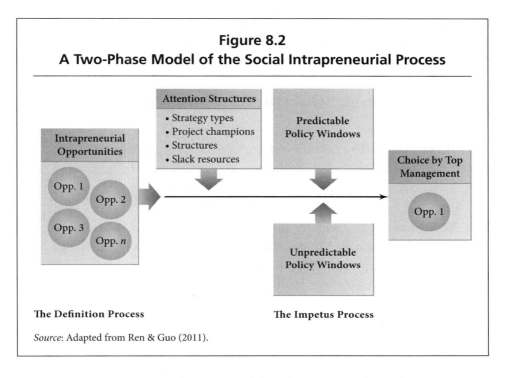

Figure 8.2
A Two-Phase Model of the Social Intrapreneurial Process

Attention Structures
• Strategy types
• Project champions
• Structures
• Slack resources

Intrapreneurial Opportunities

Opp. 1
Opp. 2
Opp. 3
Opp. *n*

Predictable Policy Windows

Choice by Top Management

Opp. 1

Unpredictable Policy Windows

The Definition Process

The Impetus Process

Source: Adapted from Ren & Guo (2011).

Now, we extend Ren and Guo's model to the context of social intrapreneurship. We highlight two phases of the social intrapreneurial process: the *definition* process, that is, the process of defining new opportunities; and the *impetus* process, that is, the process by which the new opportunities gain and maintain support in the organization. Figure 8.2 provides an illustration of a simplified version of the model.

THE DEFINITION PROCESS

The definition process refers to the process through which social intrapreneurial opportunities are discovered by participants of the organization (employees, volunteers, consultants, and so on). Carrying with them different backgrounds, expertise, and perceptions of problems and solutions, participants—prospective intrapreneurs—exchange ideas and concerns with the organization and with each other. Through communication, various innovative opportunities emerge as certain problems are coupled with solutions by some participants; as a result of the ongoing communication, a pool of opportunities is developed.

Communication can take such forms as project meetings, emails, and intranet, as well as other types of dialogue. Research has provided evidence that the quality and amount of communication are key to the successful initiation of intrapreneurial opportunities.[13]

Floyd and Wooldridge provide a nice description of what is happening during this phase:[14]

> [Intrapreneurial opportunities] are perceived within organizations because individuals have access to unique information through weak social ties and because they are willing to accept ideas based on subjective criteria. Either these individuals or other central actors then become associated with an idea, and as they successfully articulate and demonstrate the idea to others, it becomes the focus of an initiative. Shared experience then becomes the basis for further development of the idea (trials, prototypes, etc.), and this leads to increased acceptance and skill-building across the organization [p. 138].

Communication is central to the development of a pool of ideas and initiatives in the definition phase. A case study of a community-based organization in South Central Los Angeles provides evidence that an innovative project often emerges through informal communications between the organization and its stakeholders. For example, in its early years, the founding executive director of the studied organization and his staff used to walk through the neighborhood, paying door-to-door visits to residents. The organization also provided office space for block clubs in the local neighborhood and to several other community groups. The conversations between the founding executive director and block club members led to the recruitment of the block captain as the organization's very first program director. The block captain volunteered for this position and implemented the snow trip project—an annual recreational event designed for kids in the neighborhood. The project was funded through the block captain's personal network, some internal resources, and some corporate sponsors, but was mainly administered by block club members.[15]

Burgelman discusses the vicious circles in the definition process.[16] When an intrapreneurial project is initiated by a frontline manager at the operational level, it often encounters resistance from higher-level managers, who are reluctant to provide resources unless the project initiator can demonstrate the feasibility of the project. Hence the emergence of vicious circles: resources cannot be obtained unless project feasibility is demonstrated, but such a demonstration requires resources. Burgelman notes that project championing activities serve to break through these vicious circles. Using bootlegging and scavenging tactics, the successful project champion can provide positive information, which reassures higher-level management and gains their support.

In this phase, middle managers play a crucial role: they prescreen the entrepreneurial opportunities that exist in the organization and determine which opportunities to give impetus to. With limited time and attentional capacities, they notice only a subset of the entrepreneurial opportunities. Selective attention to entrepreneurial opportunities is shaped by several attention regulators: strategy types, project champions, structural positions, and slack resources.[17] These regulators jointly influence the allocation of middle managers' attention among entrepreneurial opportunities, especially exploratory versus exploitative ones.

• *Strategy types*. In a widely cited typology, management experts Miles and Snow identify four strategy types: prospector, analyzer, defender, and reactor. A prospector strategy emphasizes the development of new markets and the provision of new products/services, routinely takes externally rather than internally directed actions. In contrast, a defender strategy focuses on maintaining a stable market, produces a limited set of products/services directed at narrow market segments, and rarely searches outside their domain for new opportunities. An analyzer exhibits characteristics of both a prospector and a defender, taking fewer risks than a prospector, but not as committed to stability as a defender. A reactor does not follow a coherent strategy, reacting only to environmental pressures, and is often seen as lacking direction or focus.

Strategy types regulate the attention of middle managers toward certain entrepreneurial opportunities. In particular, a defender strategy entails a management control system that places a greater emphasis on financial measures such as short-term budgets, whereas a prospector strategy entails a management control system that places more weight on nonfinancial criteria such as product/service innovation and market share. As such, middle managers in prospector organizations are more motivated to pursue exploratory opportunities, whereas middle managers in defender organizations are more motivated to pursue exploitative opportunities.

- *Project champions.* These are organizational members who create, define, or adopt an idea for an innovation and are willing to assume significant risk to implement it.[18] Project championing activities are necessary to turn a new idea into a concrete new project. These activities are usually performed at the level of frontline managers. Because exploratory opportunities usually have longer life cycles and entail higher technological and market uncertainties, it may be more difficult to recognize exploratory opportunities than exploitative ones. In the absence of project champions, therefore, the chance for middle managers to recognize an exploratory opportunity tends to be lower than it is for an exploitative opportunity.

- *Structural positions.* In established organizations, innovative ideas are often introduced as pilot programs, which must be evaluated before they are applied to the entire organization. The implementation of these ideas often entails the development of new structures in a given organization, such as interdepartmental committees or special task forces, even a separate department or division (as in the case of the Social Enterprise Division at Vodafone).[19] These structural arrangements within the organization serve to facilitate the development and implementation of exploratory initiatives.

- *Slack resources.* As discussed earlier, this term refers to "the pool of resources in an organization that is excess of the minimum necessary to produce a given level of organizational output" (p. 1246).[20] Levels of slack resources may affect the ability of managers to focus on exploratory entrepreneurial opportunities: with more slack resources, managers pay more attention to the advantages of greater innovation and experimentation rather than to the dangers and risks.

THE IMPETUS PROCESS

As discussed in the previous section, middle managers play a crucial role in the identification of an innovative opportunity in the definition phase. After surviving the definition phase, an innovative initiative still needs additional impetus before it can receive the necessary resources for further exploitation. During the impetus phase, "policy windows" play an important role in top managers' decision to screen these innovative initiatives and select some for further exploitation. A policy window is a situation in which an internal or external event prompts managers to prioritize initiatives at their disposal and choose to spend limited organizational resources on some of them.[21] There are two types of policy windows. "Predictable policy windows" are more institutionalized and occur more frequently, such that their openings and closings are more predictable to managers. "Unpredictable policy windows" are more random and occur less frequently.[22]

Predictable Policy Windows

This category includes weekly staff meetings, quarterly strategy meetings, board meetings and retreats, and so on. These policy windows are predictable in that they accompany recurrent procedural events.

Because the windows are predictable and usually initiated by the organization, managers can plan for their opening in advance of their actual occurrence. Furthermore, these routine events likely create "business as usual" conditions that motivate managers to rely on their habitual tendencies to guide their interpretation and behavior. Therefore, when facing predictable situations, managers are likely to adopt established rules of the game and restrict the range of opportunities that they consider. In other words, they operate within their comfort zones. In an organization that emphasizes a defender strategy, for example, managers tend to favor exploitative opportunities, as they conform to the strategic orientation of their organizations. Similarly, managers in an organization that adopts a prospector strategy likely favor exploratory opportunities.

Funding opportunities, usually in the form of Requests for Proposals (RFPs) from government as well as foundations and other grant-giving agencies, represent a major form of predictable policy windows in the nonprofit context. Funding opportunities influence the impetus process in several ways. First, funding opportunities come with financial resources. Because nonprofit organizations often lack adequate financial resources and are dependent on a steady stream of revenue, these funding opportunities are very attractive because they represent reliable sources of revenue. Funders (such as government funding agencies, foundations, corporate and major individual donors) are both powerful and legitimate in the eyes of nonprofit managers, as they control financial resources that are critical to the survival of every nonprofit organization. Secondly, recurring funding opportunities help generate rules and routines in an organization. A primary source for the generation of rules is the organization's historical experience. Historical organizational precedent facilitates action by providing decision makers with readily available solutions to a recurring issue. Many funding opportunities occur on a routine basis, and when an organization responds to the same funding opportunity over time it develops routines and competencies. These routines and competencies tend to increase the attention to the same funder (as well as those well-known issues or proposals that are favored by this particular funder). Thirdly, most funding opportunities only stay open for a short period of time, thus creating deadline situations that impose a sense of urgency on funders and their proposals.

The attractiveness of funding opportunities as a predictable source of revenue, and the myriad rules and regulations that come with them, have required organizational decision makers to devote their time and attention and fight hard to gain financial success. Their experiences and achievements, however, might possibly be turned into a "competency trap"[23] or "success trap."[24] Having competence in the delivery of the same type of services in response to the same issue in the community (as reflected in the recurring funding opportunity) leads to success, which leads to more experience with the same issue area, which in turn leads to greater competence. As a result of this positive local feedback, organizational decision makers become focused on well-known alternatives (or issues), underestimating the potential benefits of the unknown.[25]

Unpredictable Policy Windows

Also labeled "triggering events" or "strategic surprises," unpredictable policy windows result from unexpected, nonroutine events, such as technological shocks and environmental jolts. The uncertain and threatening nature of unpredictable policy windows generates a strong sense of urgency, because it delivers the clear message that "business as usual" no longer exists. Managers are therefore motivated to switch their cognitive gears from "habits of minds" to "active thinking."[26] In other words, they step outside of their comfort zones. They begin to reexamine the effectiveness and appropriateness of their established ways of doing things and implement important changes in organizational strategy and structure, if necessary.

These urgent, threatening policy windows may be perceived as "a negative situation in which loss is likely and over which one has relatively little control,"[27] which should evoke some organizational response. For example, when the Obama administration decided in 2011 to drastically cut Community Services

Block Grants, the major funding source for the anti-poverty programs carried out by the nation's 1,100 community action agencies, it created an unpredicted policy window that forced community action agencies to rethink their mission and experiment with new ways of delivering services.[28] They began questioning the idea of "sticking to their knitting" and pursuing new ventures outside of their traditional domains.

The *Nonprofit Quarterly (NPQ)* offers another fascinating example of how the fast-changing technological, financial, and political environments have opened windows of opportunity for an organization to become more innovative in its program design and implementation. *NPQ* is a nonprofit publisher online and in print, with a mission to promote an active and engaged democracy. Founded in 1999 as a print magazine that was research-based and practitioner-oriented, *NPQ* was critically acclaimed and often referred to as the *Harvard Business Review* of the nonprofit world. As the magazine continued to grow in scope and national reputation, the leadership team of *NPQ* began exploring new ways of disseminating information and knowledge and reaching out to a broader reader base. One such effort was to offer a daily on-line news feature, "Nonprofit Newswire," distributed by e-mail as "Nonprofit Headlines." In a personal communication with the authors, Ruth Cambridge, editor-in-chief at *NPQ*, recalls:

> What happened was that as Obama was elected and the [recent economic] downturn happened we recognized that the rate of change in the operating environment of most nonprofits would be intense and that they would need a source to help them track the change in a grounded way that addressed policy, practice, and revenue so it was a mission/impact reason for starting the newswire. It also responded to another issue more on the enterprise side, which was that with the rise of digital publishing, the frequency of publication became an ever greater concern—we needed to establish ourselves as immediately present and responsive.

The economic recession beginning in 2008, however, also posed serious financial challenges that threatened to jeopardize the launching of the new program, as the reduced budget could no longer afford hiring professional journalists to produce the news content on a daily basis. With minimal financial resources at its disposal to hire new people, *NPQ* turned to one resource it did have: its extensive network of readers, contributors, and supporters. In 2011,

NPQ started its collaborative journalism program, which relied on the volunteer work of lay journalists consisting of nonprofit practitioners to report on the critical events and questions of the nonprofit and voluntary sector. Despite the economic downturn, *NPQ*'s "Nonprofit Newswire" and collaborative journalism program has proved to be a huge success. As one of its twenty-three thousand readers nicely puts it, "Like a cup of strong coffee first thing in the morning, the *NPQ* daily e-mail wakes me up, often to new ways of thinking about issues that concern not just nonprofits but society as a whole."[29]

Threatening situations generated by unpredictable policy windows can be further separated into two broad categories of threat perceptions: resource-related threats and control-related threats. The former type of threats relates to a potential loss of tangible resources (such as a likely loss of resources due to a competitor launching a new product), whereas the latter pertains to a potential loss of control (for example, a regulatory body issues a new regulation harmful to the organization, leading to a more controlling environment).[30] Both types of threatening situations may prompt organizational response, but the jury is still out on whether and how they differ in their implications for the kinds of entrepreneurial opportunities that managers will likely pursue.

INITIATORS OF INNOVATIONS IN PUBLIC AND NONPROFIT ORGANIZATIONS

Quinn, Mintzberg, and James emphasize the importance of promoting innovations in a rapidly evolving environment. They note, "In these situations, it is often not the boss, but someone in an odd corner of the organization—a champion for some technology or strategic issue—who takes on the entrepreneurial role" (p. 531).[31] As in the case of the M-Pesa service launched by Safaricom (presented at the beginning of the chapter), the two social intrapreneurs who played the most instrumental role in the development of M-Pesa were not part of the top management: Nick was a department head (middle-level manager), and Susie was a product manager working in the field (frontline manager). Yet they were able to recognize an opportunity and make the connections that allowed Safaricom to leverage its core competency to deliver mobile phone-based financial services to people in Kenya.

Borins has conducted extensive research on innovation in the public sector. His findings from two samples have challenged the conventional wisdom that innovation in the public sector comes from the top; rather, they have shown that

Table 8.1
Initiators of Innovation in the Public Sector

Initiator	USA, 1999–1998 (percent)	Commonwealth, advanced (percent)	Commonwealth, developing (percent)
Politician	21	11	15
Agency head	25	39	37
Middle manager	43[a]	75	44
Front line staff	27[a]	39	7
Middle management or front line staff	51	82	48
Interest group	13	2	11
Citizen	7	0	11
Program client	3	5	0
Other	6	9	11
Total	126	148	133
n	321	56	27

Notes: n = number of innovations. [a] indicates that the breakdown between innovations initiated by middle managers and innovations initiated by frontline staff for the U.S. data was based on 104 cases from 1995 to 1998. In the 217 cases from 1990 to 1994, these groups were coded together.

Source: Borins (2001, p. 28).

middle managers and frontline staff are clearly the driving force behind most innovations.

As shown in Table 8.1., in the United States sample, slightly over 50 percent of the innovations originate from middle managers or frontline staff, 25 percent from agency heads, 21 percent from politicians, 13 percent from interest groups, and 10 percent from individuals outside government (that is, citizens and program clients). In the sample from the economically advanced countries of the Commonwealth (Canada, Australia, New Zealand, Singapore, U.K.), the proportion from middle managers or frontline staff (82 percent) and agency heads (39 percent) is even higher. The developing countries in the sample (Bangladesh, Ghana, India, Jamaica, Malaysia, Seychelles, South Africa, and Zimbabwe) have shown similar results.[32]

Borins also identifies three ideal types of innovation in the public sector, based on the systematic differences in the circumstances of innovations initiated by different levels of management:

• *Politically directed innovation in response to crisis.* Politicians tend to be the initiators of this type of innovation, as they are expected to lead the response when there is a crisis in the public sector. An example is the City of Seattle recycling program: after the City's two landfills reached capacity and ceased operation in the mid-1980s, the mayor and city council responded by establishing a greatly expanded recycling program that became a global leader.

• *Organizational turnarounds led by agency heads.* When a public sector agency is not performing well, the leadership turnover often provides the momentum for the new agency head to lead a turnaround by taking innovative steps.

• *Bottom-up innovation.* Middle managers and frontline staff tend to initiate innovations in response to internal problems or in view of opportunities made available by new technology.

THE ROLE OF FRONTLINE MANAGERS IN THE SOCIAL INTRAPRENEURIAL PROCESS

Frontline staff often function as champions who create, define, or adopt an innovative idea and are willing to assume significant risk to implement the innovation.[33] Project championing activities are necessary to "turn a new idea into a concrete new project in which technical and marketing development could begin to take shape" (p. 232).[34] Project champions, especially influential ones, play a key role in producing entrepreneurial opportunities. PaperSeed Foundation offers several interesting examples of project champions. A recent project that PaperSeed funded was the publication and distribution of *Pepper's Dragons*, written by Dr. Stacia Bjarnason, a licensed therapist who had been working with the children directly affected by the shootings at Sandy Hook Elementary School in December 2012. She collaborated with an illustrator to create this book for children to share with their families during the healing process. The idea of funding this book actually came from one of PaperSeed's volunteers, a CellMark employee whose daughter goes to Sandy Hook School and lost her best friend in the shootings. The author was counseling his daughter when the idea for the book arose. Similarly, the idea of establishing the science laboratories and music program for a girls' orphanage in Mexico also came from a volunteer who was an employee of CellMark's Finance and Risk Team and who knew of the orphanage through a commercial connection from that area. In both cases, it was the frontline volunteer staff who first identified the opportunity and then convinced the top management to adopt it.[35]

Some scholars note that champions are more likely to be involved with exploratory opportunities; others find that champions are involved equally with exploratory and exploitative ideas. Because exploratory opportunities usually have longer life cycles and entail higher technological and market uncertainties, it may be more difficult to recognize exploratory opportunities than exploitative ones.

THE ROLE OF MIDDLE MANAGERS IN THE SOCIAL INTRAPRENEURIAL PROCESS

Middle managers occupy positions between the strategic apex and the operating core of an organization.[36] Their job titles may include general manager, regional manager, divisional manager, and program director, among others. There are two complementary views about the contribution of middle managers. The first posits that middle managers make their contribution primarily through implementing strategic decisions by facilitating information flows between top managers and operating-level managers. Within this context, middle managers' entrepreneurial behavior is mainly top-down—induced by top management—and focused on developing innovations based on existing business and competence.

In the second view, middle managers also contribute to corporate strategy formation. The unique contribution of middle managers to corporate strategy formation results from their key role in autonomous strategic activities. Whereas frontline managers are deeply involved in the process of defining new business opportunities, middle managers are particularly important for managing the activities by which the new opportunities gain and maintain support in the organization; that is, the impetus process. This process is bottom-up: middle managers evaluate and sponsor strategic initiatives championed by frontline managers, then "sell" these initiatives to top management through strategic building and organizational championing activities.

Floyd and Wooldridge thus develop a typology of four middle management strategic roles:[37]

- *Championing strategic alternatives.* Middle managers bring entrepreneurial and innovative proposals to top management's attention.

- *Synthesizing information.* Middle managers also supply information to top management concerning internal and external events. As organizational linking pins, middle managers are positioned uniquely to combine strategic with operational information. They infuse information with meaning through evaluation, advice, and subjective interpretation.

- *Facilitating adaptability.* Middle-level managers make organizations more flexible and stimulate behavior that diverges from official expectations. Matrix structures, task forces, and simple informality increase information sharing and facilitate learning by encouraging organization members to sense changing conditions, experiment with new approaches, and implement deliberate strategy.

- *Implementing deliberative strategy.* Middle managers are responsible for implementing top management's intentions.

In particular, the "championing alternatives" role is an upward, divergent form of influence that involves justifying and defining new programs, evaluating the merits of new proposals, searching for new opportunities, and proposing projects to top managers. In line with this role, middle managers contribute to firm capability development through three critical mechanisms or stages in the corporate entrepreneurial process: identifying entrepreneurial opportunities, developing entrepreneurial initiatives, and renewing organizational capabilities. These three stages cover both the definition and impetus processes.[38]

Based on prior research, we divide middle managers' championing role in the impetus process into two parts. First, they evaluate the strategic merits of social intrapreneurial initiatives emerging from lower organizational levels and assess their potential for future corporate growth. This *evaluator* role involves the decision to endorse an initiative or not, as well as how much support to offer. It also involves bouncing the idea off of others to verify and assess its feasibility. Second, they gain top management's attention and support for a social intrapreneurial initiative that may fall outside the organizational agenda. In this "seller" role, they reshape the strategic thinking of top management and get them to modify existing organizational strategy to accommodate successful new initiatives.[39]

THE ROLE OF TOP MANAGERS IN THE SOCIAL INTRAPRENEURIAL PROCESS

The crucial role of top managers in the social intrapreneurial process is reflected in four important aspects: (1) transformational leadership, (2) the development of effective management control systems that spur social intrapreneurial activity, (3) the design and implementation of appropriate recruiting strategies, and (4) the development of an organizational culture that values innovation and social intrapreneurship.

• *Transformational leadership.* According to Kouzes and Posner, transformational leadership includes five observable, learnable practices:[40]

- Challenge familiar organizational processes, which entails such activities as searching for new opportunities, experimenting, and taking risks.

- Inspire a shared vision among employees by envisioning and articulating the future and enlisting support from others to join the effort.

- Enable employees to act in accordance with their vision.

- Model the way for employees to perform, with a focus on setting an example and planning small wins.

- Encourage employees to innovate, recognize their contributions, and celebrate their accomplishments.

• *Management control systems.* Management control systems include formalized information-based processes for planning, budgeting, cost control, environmental scanning, competitor analysis, performance evaluation, resource allocation, and employee rewards.[41] To pursue exploratory opportunities, top management should design effective management control systems that encourage prudent risk taking and reward innovation.

• *Recruiting strategies.* Top management is responsible for designing and implementing recruiting strategies that attract, develop, and retain managers with the appropriate skill mix. To pursue exploratory opportunities, appropriate recruiting strategies must be in place to focus on managers who are externally oriented and who have experience in pioneering new products and technologies and developing new markets.

• *Organizational culture.* Top management has a significant role in creating an atmosphere wherein employees are encouraged to experiment. Top managers should create an enabling environment for social intrapreneurship—a culture that is flexible and supportive.[42]

CONCLUDING THOUGHTS

In this chapter we have discussed the distinctive roles of three levels of management: frontline, middle, and top management. In particular, we have examined attention-based effects on the strategic behavior of middle managers in the social intrapreneurial process. We thus offer explanations of how middle managers leverage various types of policy windows and determine whether to turn existing attention structures to their advantage or to dismantle those attention structures in their efforts to sell their chosen initiatives to top management. We hope this framework helps stimulate additional discussion pertaining to the management of the social intrapreneurial process.

EXERCISES

Exercise 8.1

A number of organizational factors affect managerial attention to social intrapreneurial opportunities. Use examples to discuss these attention regulators.

Exercise 8.2

What different roles do top, middle, and frontline managers play in the social intrapreneurial process? How do their roles vary across sectors and/or types of organizations?

Exercise 8.3

How do different types of policy windows affect top managers' decisions to screen innovative initiatives and select some for further exploitation? Use an example to illustrate your points.

PART FOUR

Emerging Trends and Issues

chapter NINE

Social Entrepreneurship in the Public Sector

In January 1987 Diana Gale became director of the Solid Waste Utility for the city of Seattle, with a mandate to establish a new system for waste disposal.[1] Seattle's Solid Waste Utility was located in the city's Engineering Department, reflecting the view that waste disposal was a technical matter. Virtually all city residents used the city's services and ratepayers provided almost all of the utility's revenue. Rates had been low and stable for a number of years, and there was little public concern about waste collection.

Over the years, however, Seattle's trash disposal system had developed capacity problems. In the early 1980s two landfill sites had been filled and were closed. In response, the city began temporarily using a county landfill. But the future use of this landfill was uncertain. In addition, on Thanksgiving Day in 1985 a methane gas leak at a landfill forced the evacuation of a number of families from their homes, creating public concern and highlighting the city's capacity problem. The utility proposed a technical solution—constructing a city-owned incinerator to burn trash. The public, however, was concerned about both the cost of the plant and its environmental impact.

In response, the utility began a more comprehensive study of waste disposal options. This concluded that the city could recycle up to 60 percent of trash and send the rest to a landfill in Oregon. This plan would cost less money and have less of an environmental impact than the incinerator. The plan, however, would require an unprecedented level of recycling, which would in turn require both garbage collectors and citizens to make changes. The plan would be implemented in two phases. Phase one would be a voluntary program of free curbside recycling. Later, phase two would entail a requirement that all residents choose a level of garbage collection from options that varied in features, price, and requirements for how they organized their household trash. Basically, those not sorting recyclables and moving their trash to the curbside would pay more than they did under the old system, while those who took these actions would pay less.

Phase one was to be in place in January of 1989. Gale's major task was to help residents understand and accept the new system and become active participate in trash disposal. Gail laid a foundation for good working relations with the media and, beginning in the fall of 1987, the utility set out to make the campaign for recycling part of media coverage, political discourse, and civic culture. Major education and public relations efforts resulted in over 50-percent participation in voluntary recycling by January 1989.

Anticipating more difficulties in phase two, Gale urged the public to be patient during the implementation stage. Numerous problems did arise, and the implementation of phase two seemed in doubt at times. Problems included political disagreements about the rate structure, difficulties in signing up residents, pick-up delays due to winter storms, households overlooked by trash collectors, and delays in handling complaints. Throughout, the utility responded with as much openness as possible and avoided a defensive posture. It relaxed some of its requirements and improved services. For example, Gale went to contractors to demand more expedient delivery of trash bins, and the utility asked the City Council for emergency funds to help staff its phone system. The utility also used the criticisms as opportunities to provide customers with further information. For example, it ran detailed question and answer format articles in the local newspaper.

Due to these efforts, service improved and complaints declined. Most important, citizens, the media, and local leaders started coming to the utility's defense. This marked the turning point in the implementation of phase two.

The experience of Seattle's Solid Waste Utility illustrates the challenges of undertaking major public sector initiatives. The utility's plan could save the city money and be environmentally responsible. To succeed, however, citizens needed to both buy-in and actively participate. They had to become partners in the creation of social value. The city needed them to view the initiative as legitimate and worthy of support, and the city expended major efforts to achieve this.

In the preceding chapters we described some of the similarities and differences between social entrepreneurship in organizations in different sectors. In this chapter, we examine social entrepreneurship in the public sector in more detail. Specifically, how is entrepreneurship, as practiced in public sector organizations, similar to or different from social entrepreneurship in the private sector? Are there unique challenges and opportunities? What can public agencies do to become more entrepreneurial? We review the characteristics of public sector organizations that influence entrepreneurship and the implications for entrepreneurship of a number of recent public reforms and experiments, and we describe a number of recent trends to promote public sector entrepreneurship.

THE CONTEXT OF PUBLIC SECTOR ENTREPRENEURSHIP

At its core, government (the public sector) is responsible for the direction and control exercised over the actions of the members or citizens of communities, societies, and states.[2] The concern for a public or collectivity means that entrepreneurship in the public sector is social entrepreneurship, akin to the entrepreneurship of nonprofits with social missions. The public sector, however, differs significantly from the nonprofit and for-profit sectors, and these differences must be taken into account to understand the characteristics of public sector entrepreneurship.

The recession, taxpayer revolts, and conservative ideology of the 1980s ushered in an era (which we are still in) of concern about the size and operations of government and calls for new frameworks to guide public sector managers.[3] This includes examining the contributions that entrepreneurship could make to improving government and the coining of the term "public sector entrepreneurship."[4] Public sector entrepreneurship can be defined as the process of creating value for citizens by bringing together unique combinations of public and/or private resources to exploit social opportunities.[5]

Entrepreneurship in the public sector has since been conceptualized in several different ways in the public policy and public administration literature.[6] Public sector entrepreneurship has variously been held to be:

- Exemplary administrators who made dramatic changes in public organizations[7]

- Founders of new and influential political movements, public policies, or public organizations[8]

- Entrepreneurship in the management and operations of public organizations[9]

- Public sector reforms and experiments designed to make public organizations more responsive and efficient[10]

- Privatization and other ways to encourage entrepreneurship in private sector organizations[11]

To be consistent with other chapters, in this chapter we will focus on the last three; that is, entrepreneurship in the operations, outputs, and outcomes of public sector organizations.

We have defined entrepreneurship as a combination of innovation, risk-taking, and proactiveness. The characteristics of government and bureaucracy can present obstacles for these behaviors. A host of factors that can dampen entrepreneurship in public organizations have been suggested.[12] Agencies are likely to have multiple, ambiguous, and hard-to-measure goals and be subject to political interference. Programs need to be equitable, which may hinder efficiency. High-risk projects may be difficult to carry out, because taxpayer money can't easily be subjected to significant risk, and risk/return trade-offs in the public sector are difficult to measure. Limited managerial autonomy, the high visibility of public officials, and the need for consensus in decision making create pressure for incremental change. Short-term budgeting and election cycles make it difficult to allocate or justify the long time periods that may be needed for the results of entrepreneurial ventures to unfold. Bureaucracy and the civil service tend to protect the status quo and put limitations on personnel and reward systems. There may not be enough (or any) competitive incentives for improved performance and accountability among managers for innovation and change. More fundamentally, there is concern that innovative approaches, such as new ways of raising money from private sources, could undermine voter approval and increase the autonomy of public officials. On the other hand, obstacles can also be facilitators of entrepreneurship. For example, would-be entrepreneurs could turn goal ambiguity into managerial discretion, use the media as a source of power, or co-opt outsiders to enable risk taking without personal risk.[13]

A study of public sector managers by Morris and Jones bears out a number of the points just made and calls some others into question.[14] Most managers had positive feelings about entrepreneurship. A large majority (86 percent) felt that fostering entrepreneurship would have a positive impact on organizational performance, primarily by increasing efficiency and productivity, improving service delivery, reducing costs, and improving employee morale. A comparable number (88 percent) agreed that the environment in public sector organizations can be designed in ways that help employees develop entrepreneurial tendencies. Middle managers were twice as likely as top or lower-level managers to be seen by study respondents as the most entrepreneurial. At the same time, the greatest opportunity for entrepreneurship was seen as existing at the top management level. The areas in which entrepreneurship was seen as most critical were planning/organizing/budgeting, service delivery, operations, and human resources.

On the other hand, limitations were also noted. Most managers (77 percent) agreed that the civil service environment discourages entrepreneurial individuals. About the same number (74 percent) felt that public sector organizations become less entrepreneurial as they get larger. Other obstacles to entrepreneurship included

- Policies, procedures, and red tape
- Restrictions on hiring and firing
- Limited size of rewards
- Limited managerial autonomy
- Lack of profit motive
- Interference from politicians
- Pressure to emphasize equity over efficiency
- Ambiguity of goals
- Lack of competition among organizations
- Public sector unions

The authors note that many of these are similar to the obstacles to entrepreneurship cited by corporations.[15] Finally, the study found that some distinct public sector characteristics were not particularly important. These included multiplicity of goals, high visibility, and difficulties in defining one's customer.

In sum, the literature and research shows that in spite of limitations, the public sector is favorable toward entrepreneurship. The sector has been innovative in the past and will need to be so in the future. A more important question is how public organizations can overcome the obstacles just described and more systematically and explicitly use entrepreneurship to address public needs. This question is more important now than ever, in light of the increasing severity and scope of the social issues facing society and increased calls from the public for greater public sector innovation. In response, a number of experiments and reforms have been instituted to make the public sector more entrepreneurial. We describe a number of them in the following section. All of them are still relevant. None of them should be seen as the final answer, nor should they be indiscriminately employed. Rather, they suggest outlooks and methods that could be used to enhance entrepreneurship if the particulars of a given situation warrant it.

NEW PUBLIC MANAGEMENT AND REINVENTING GOVERNMENT

In the late 1980s a new public administration theory was launched that reflected a market-oriented approach to government which was becoming more prevalent at the time.[16] It was designed to correct what was seen as excessively bureaucratic and hierarchical public administration. The approach became known as the new public management (NPM). As articulated by David Osborne and Ted Gaebler in their 1992 book *Reinventing Government: How the Entrepreneurial Spirit Is Transforming the Public Sector*, NPM advocates that public managers serve as entrepreneurs and use business-sector, market-oriented principles for improving efficiency in government agencies.[17] During the Clinton administration, Vice President Al Gore led an initiative (entitled "Reinventing Government") to reform federal agencies using NPM approaches. In the 1990s, NPM became prevalent throughout the bureaucracies of the United States, the U.K., and, to a lesser extent, Canada.

The approach can be summarized in ten principles about how entrepreneurial government should act:[18]

- *Catalytic*: Steer rather than row; move beyond existing policy options and serve as catalysts to generate alternate courses of action.

- *Community-Owned*: Empower rather than serve; promote economic and social independence rather than dependence.

- *Competitive*: Inject competition into service delivery; trying to serve every need overextends government; competition between public, nonprofit, and for-profits will result in greater overall efficiency.

- *Mission-Driven*: Transform rule-driven organizations; excessive rules stifle innovation and limit performance.

- *Results-Oriented*: Fund outcomes instead of inputs; previous evaluation and reward systems focused on fiscal efficiency and control, rarely asking what benefits were gained.

- *Customer-Driven*: Meet the needs of customers, not the bureaucracy; legislative funding has led agencies to function according to their own priorities and those demanded by funders; the private sector has shown the importance of a customer focus.

- *Enterprising*: Earn rather than spend; find innovative ways to do more with less; incorporate the profit motive into government (institute fees, charges, and investments).

- *Anticipatory*: Prevent rather than cure; as problems have gotten more complex, the capacity to respond decreases, and future effectiveness will depend on prevention.

- *Decentralized*: Participation and teamwork rather than hierarchy; use advances in information technology, new communication systems, and participative decision making to create flexible, team-based operations.

- *Market-Oriented*: Leverage change through the market; jurisdictions represent markets of people, interests, and forces (especially economic), and public strategy should be oriented to facilitate markets operating most effectively.

By infusing government operations with entrepreneurial techniques, NPM sought to invigorate how government operates by enhancing its flexibility, responsiveness, efficiency, and innovativeness. It also reconceived government's role in society, seeing it in terms of leading (or steering) in a collaborative setting. NPM remains viable today, and the model is widely accepted at all levels of government and in many nations. A popular example of successful public sector entrepreneurship is garbage collection in the city of Phoenix, as we discussed in Chapter One.

In addition, initiatives consistent with NPM principles are presented and discussed by the IBM Center for the Business of Government. The Center sponsors research, disseminates findings, and creates opportunities for dialogue on a broad range of public management topics (http://www.businessofgovernment .org/). Since 1998 the Center has awarded nearly three hundred research stipends to leading public management researchers in the academic and nonprofit communities, which have resulted in over two hundred reports, all of which are available on the Center's website. Publications focus on current major management issues facing government, including e-government; financial management; human capital management; managing for performance and results; market-based government; and innovation, collaboration, and transformation. The Center also produces *The Business of Government Hour*, a weekly program with government executives speaking about their careers, agency accomplishments and management, and the future of government in the twenty-first century. Another product is *The Business of Government* magazine. Published twice a year, it offers leadership profiles and fresh perspectives on government today. Finally, the Center sponsors a blog that allows academics and practitioners to examine issues facing public managers. Of particular interest on the blog are strategies to cut costs and improve performance. A variety of bloggers at the IBM web site provide specific strategies that federal agencies can undertake to achieve savings in operational functions. A brief description of each cost-saving strategy is presented, along with other helpful references such as case studies (in both the government and private sector), articles, and other web resources.

In spite of its success, a number of issues have been raised with NPM. Some involve operational issues, such as the reconciliation between the decentralization promoted in the model and the public sector's need to coordinate, as well as the relations between the executive and the legislative branches.[19] More central issues are related to the values the model advocates.[20] Critics contend that NPM treats individuals as "customers" or "clients" (in the private sector sense), rather than as citizens.[21] This is seen as an inappropriate borrowing from the private sector model, because businesses see customers as a means to making a profit, whereas citizens are the proprietors, or owners, of government. This issue is central to debates about subsequent frameworks. We will next discuss the framework that was formulated in direct response to NPM.

NEW PUBLIC SERVICE

In reaction to the NPM paradigm, Janet and Robert Denhardt proposed what they termed a new public service model. The new public service (NPS) draws upon work in democratic citizenship, community and civil society, and organizational humanism and discourse theory. NPS does not reject innovation and entrepreneurship in public service, but it "envision(s) a public service based on and fully integrated with citizen discourse and the public interest."[22] We present the major tenets of NPS and the explanations here.[23] According to NPS, the public sector and public administrators should:

- *Serve society rather than steer or control it in new directions.* Citizens should be helped to articulate and meet shared interests.

- *Build the public interest.* Contribute to the creation of a collective, shared notion of the public interest and shared responsibility for its accomplishment.

- *Think strategically and act democratically.* Effective and responsible public action is best achieved through collective and collaborative efforts.

- *Serve citizens, not customers.* The collective interest is not merely the aggregation of individual interests; rather, it is created through a dialogue about shared values, and government should contribute by helping build relationships of trust and collaboration with and among citizens.

- *Accountability isn't simple.* It should include criteria such as statutory and constitutional law, community values, political norms, professional standards, and citizen interests.

- *Value people, not just productivity.* Collaboration and shared leadership based on respect for people will contribute to the long-term success of public organizations and their networks.

- *Value citizenship and public service above entrepreneurship.* Public servants should work with citizens to make meaningful contributions to society rather than act as individual entrepreneurs.

NPS moves away from the market-based aspects of NPM, including using entrepreneurial techniques borrowed from business. That type of entrepreneurship has a relatively narrow profit-driven focus on seeking to maximize productivity, satisfy customers, take risks, and take advantage of opportunities as they arise. The view of NPS is that public administrators do not own public programs and resources. They are instead stewards of public resources, conservators of public organizations, facilitators of citizenship and democratic dialogue, catalysts for community engagement, and street-level leaders.[24] This is not to say that government should not be innovative. It is still just as important to develop new and effective solutions to public problems. Public entrepreneurship, however, should be carried out in a way that respects the role of government and the relationship between government and citizens. This entrepreneurship must be carried out in a shared-power, collaborative, multisector setting. In this way, NPS becomes "a framework *within which* other valuable techniques and values, such as the best ideas of the old public administration and the New Public Management, might be played out."[25] In fostering a dialogue with citizens and community leaders, Seattle's Solid Waste Utility used NPS principles in its recycling initiative, described in the story that opened this chapter.

The need for government innovation and entrepreneurship is widely felt today, and many initiatives are currently under way. These usually have some aspects of NPM and NPS frameworks. We will review a number of them in the remainder of the chapter.

CURRENT PRACTICES AND APPROACHES

In this section of the chapter we describe current practices and approaches to promote public sector involvement with social entrepreneurship. These range from general frameworks to innovative programs and initiatives at a number of levels.

Public Sector Innovation

William Eggers and Shalabh Singh present a guide for public sector innovation.[26] Innovation can come from internal or external sources. Internal sources of innovation include public employees as well as internal partners such as other government agencies. External sources of innovation include citizens as well as external partners such as contractors, nonprofits, and other governments. Each of these can be strategically harnessed to contribute to the following elements of the innovation process:[27]

• *Idea generation*: Create systems to generate and maintain the flow of good ideas. For example, New York and London have created an innovation exchange program in which each shares ideas that have proven effective.

• *Selection*: Filter good ideas by creating an efficient sorting process. For example, the World Bank has established a Development Marketplace, a bazaar in its atrium with booths allocated to 121 teams, each with an idea to propose.

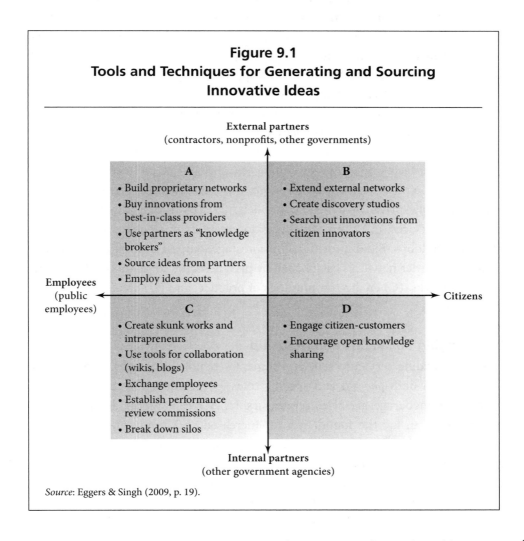

Figure 9.1
Tools and Techniques for Generating and Sourcing Innovative Ideas

External partners
(contractors, nonprofits, other governments)

A
• Build proprietary networks
• Buy innovations from best-in-class providers
• Use partners as "knowledge brokers"
• Source ideas from partners
• Employ idea scouts

B
• Extend external networks
• Create discovery studios
• Search out innovations from citizen innovators

Employees (public employees) — Citizens

C
• Create skunk works and intrapreneurs
• Use tools for collaboration (wikis, blogs)
• Exchange employees
• Establish performance review commissions
• Break down silos

D
• Engage citizen-customers
• Encourage open knowledge sharing

Internal partners
(other government agencies)

Source: Eggers & Singh (2009, p. 19).

- *Implementation*: Convert ideas into products, services, and practices. For example, the Florida 2000 initiative gave teachers handheld devices to record student information.

- *Diffusion*: Manage stakeholders and disseminate ideas. For example, the Florida Department of Children and Families slashed customer wait times, reduced turnover, and saved money. After the department earned several awards and word spread, other state and federal agencies adopted its techniques.

Figure 9.1 shows how in the first stage of the innovation process (*idea generation*) the public organization can use both internal and external participants to generate innovative ideas. The tools and techniques shown in the quadrants include ideas that enhance internal efficiency as well as solicit citizen input. In this way they integrate the NPM and NPS approaches.

The same format can be applied to the other stages of the innovation process. For each stage of the process, we suggest examples for each of the quadrants of the figure. For the *idea selection* stage, our examples are: (A) define mutual benefits and goals, (B) use democratic processes such as online rating tools, (C) use tacit knowledge of employees, and (D) create feedback mechanisms. For the idea *implementation* stage, our examples are: (A) utilize a full range of public-private partnership models, (B) create one-stop portals to a myriad of services, (C) train employees to create competencies, and (D) create feedback loops. Finally, for the *diffusion* stage, our examples are: (A) benefit from transborder networks established by private sector companies, (B) harness social networks, (C) create communities of practice, and (D) create networks of public agencies.

Encouraging Social Entrepreneurship

Besides providing services itself, government sets policies, arenas, and agendas for action. In both general and specific roles, government can take a number of steps to encourage social entrepreneurship. A recent report described how government can lay the foundation for increased social entrepreneurship, set policies to enable and encourage social entrepreneurship, and develop and leverage resources to encourage social entrepreneurship.[28] In this way it can create the same type of environment for social entrepreneurship that it does to encourage commercial entrepreneurship. Government can *lay the foundation* for increased social entrepreneurship by establishing institutions that support and promote social entrepreneurship, such as the Louisiana Office of Social Entrepreneurship, described shortly. In addition, government can grant social problem-solving initiatives more autonomy in how they operate and spend money, set standards that enable them, and publish their positive results. Government also has the unique ability to convene the necessary stakeholders in order to address a particular social issue. By gathering the key players from all sectors, public officials can lead the process of agreeing on the root causes of the social problem, plotting out a course of action for addressing it, and advancing solutions. Further, government can develop awards programs to recognize and reward innovative, effective, and sustainable solutions. These can take the form of publicity, training, networking opportunities, and funding. Finally, as social entrepreneurship can benefit all sectors, government can educate all three sectors on social entrepreneurship's approach to innovation and solving social problems.

Government can *set policy* to enable and encourage social entrepreneurship. Policymakers and leaders of government agencies at all levels can strive to set policies that encourage social entrepreneurial behavior. While it is important to maintain appropriate standards, policies may sometimes present unforeseen challenges for entrepreneurship, and it is important to recognize and evaluate these. It will be helpful for government to explore new tax structures that might enable new organizational forms. Social entrepreneurs are generating solutions that blur the line between the sectors, such as new types of for-profits that have legal requirements to provide social benefits (we discuss these types of organizations in the next chapter). Possible tax benefits for organizations such as these could spur greater philanthropic, private, and public investment in the development of new sustainable organizational models. In addition, reallocating a small percentage of agency budgets to make room for experimentation will yield potentially significant benefits, in effect creating in-house R&D operations, and opening earmarked funds to competitive processes. Rather than providing earmarked funds to the same organizations again and again, a competitive process could use these existing resources to seek out innovative, effective, and sustainable programs that government may not currently be aware of.

Finally, government can *develop and leverage resources* to encourage social entrepreneurship. Government can leverage public dollars by partnering with foundations and corporations to support social entrepreneurship. In this way, government can stretch public dollars while at the same time testing new ideas and giving foundations and corporations increased access to social service systems. Government can create public-private social innovation funds. Public-private social innovation funds take advantage of taxpayer dollars with private funds to make resources available for funding social-entrepreneurial solutions. This enables government to follow a performance-based model for investment, not unlike venture capital funds, to both seed and scale initiatives. (We describe the national-level Social Innovation Fund shortly.) State-level or target-specific funds should also be considered. Government can coordinate volunteer resources to scale innovative solutions. The federal government already leads several programs that direct volunteers toward individual organizations and program sites, such as Senior Corps. These programs and others should be expanded to help scale solutions. Government could establish a National Social Innovation Foundation. A very small percentage of the federal budget could create a sizeable pool of funds for advancing social entrepreneurship and establishing it as a national priority, using the model of the National Science Foundation, for example.

Creating a Culture of Performance Improvement

The Government Performance and Results Act (GPRA) was enacted in 1993 as part of President Bill Clinton and Vice President Al Gore's initiative to reinvent government (introduced earlier in the chapter). The GPRA required agencies to engage in project management tasks such as setting goals, measuring results, and reporting their progress.[29] To comply with the GPRA, agencies produce strategic and performance plans and conduct gap analyses of projects. Agencies are required to develop five-year strategic plans that must contain a mission statement for the agency as well as long-term, results-oriented goals covering each of its major functions. They are required to prepare annual performance plans that establish the performance goals for the applicable fiscal year, a brief description of how these goals are to be met, and a description of how these performance goals can be verified. They must also prepare annual performance reports that review the agency's success or failure in meeting its targeted performance goals. The Office of Management and Budget produces annual report on agency performance. Information is provided with the president's annual budget request.

The focus on performance improvement has continued over subsequent administrations. In 2011, President Obama signed the GPRA Modernization Act of 2010 (GPRAMA) into law. Among other things, GPRAMA establishes new products and processes that focus on goal-setting and performance measurement in policy areas that cut across agencies, brings attention to using goals and measures during policy implementation, increases reporting on the Internet, and requires individuals to be responsible for some goals and management tasks.[30] In addition, the president's fiscal year 2014 budget emphasizes the creation of a culture of performance improvement.[31]

A new report by Donald Moynihan describes the evolution of the federal performance management system since the passage of GPRA in 1993, recent progress in achieving meaningful performance results, and anticipated future changes in light of the requirements of GPRAMA.[32] The report concludes that the culture of performance improvement is more important than compliance with many procedural requirements. The report lays out a number of recommendations, which will both enhance performance and support entrepreneurship in public sector organizations:

• *Connect the performance system to public service motivation.* The goal of any performance management system is to improve performance by creating a culture of performance. The systems, processes, and procedures that commonly accompany any performance management system are intended to help frame it, but they do not produce performance. What is needed is an appeal to public servants' motivation to help others through their work. Leaders need to select clear goals that motivate employees, make goals become the glue that holds networks together, connect each employee's job to program beneficiaries, celebrate success, and link to employee incentive systems.

• *Build a learning culture.* To build an organizational culture that supports performance management requires an environment of continuous learning.

• *Balance top-down targets with bottom-up innovations.* The top-down goal-setting aspect of the performance systems is usually clear, but bottom-up knowledge is also needed. To capture this, agencies should learn from network members who are from multiple levels in the organization; use benchmarking to identify what works and spread it; and disseminate lessons, not just data, on how to improve performance.

• *Integrate program evaluation into the performance management system.* Performance measures can tell leaders *what* is going on, but program evaluation is needed to explain *why* something is occurring. Both are necessary elements in an informed decision-making process. Consequently, agencies should redefine "performance information" to include program evaluation, and evaluation expertise should be incorporated into performance discussions.

• *Ensure that leaders are committed to performance management.* The research reported by Moynihan clearly showed that performance management systems are more likely to succeed when agency leaders are perceived as committed to the performance system and results. Consequently, agency leaders should be selected based on their performance management skills and whether the individuals have experience in using data in management.

To reinforce this, the president's budget for fiscal year 2014 states: "The Obama administration expects agencies to use evidence to set priorities and find increasingly effective and cost-effective practices."[33] It also expects agencies to encourage entrepreneurship by:

• Testing new practices to identify what works

• Adjusting and reallocating resources or changing practices based on evidence of what works

• Constantly asking whether there are lower-cost options for getting the job done

• Sharing information publicly to "enhance accountability and facilitate understanding of the services government provides."

Social Entrepreneurship Incubators

Social entrepreneurship can also be supported by state-level initiatives. Louisiana provides an example. In 2006, it created an Office of Social Entrepreneurship—the first in the nation—to advance social innovation by supporting the creation and growth of the most innovative, measurable, and sustainable solutions to the social problems affecting Louisiana.[34] In 2006, the Office of Social Entrepreneurship partnered with what was then called the Louisiana Serve Commission (now the Volunteer Louisiana Commission) to launch the Changing Louisiana Initiative—a statewide initiative that drew 1,500 participants to city-specific conferences aimed at promoting citizen involvement in social entrepreneurship and volunteerism. In 2007, the Office of Social Entrepreneurship, in partnership with Root Cause, a Boston-based consulting firm, developed a strategic plan for incentivizing innovative and measurable solutions developed by public and private social service providers. As a result, in 2009 the state established the Social Innovators Institute, a program to recognize and support the most promising statewide social innovators. The Social Innovators Institute provided a blend of business and social impact training with individualized consultative support to help social entrepreneurs develop social venture business plans.

In 2009, the Social Innovators Institute named twelve nonprofit organizations statewide as participants, including a new substance abuse rehab facility, a new blood bank, a paint recycling program, and expansions of work activity centers for disabled individuals. During the Institute's program, participants define and study the social problem that their program will address and then develop meaningful measurement systems to track their progress in solving the social problem. Measuring systems involve gathering feedback from external stakeholders and using the information to refine the program's operating model as needed to achieve the social impact desired. Participants conduct extensive market research to build an operating model that will have a high likelihood of success in the market, while also planning for financial sustainability of the social program. In addition, Institute participants meet at monthly peer learning sessions, during which they have the opportunity to learn from each other, to challenge ideas, and to apply critical strategic, financial, managerial, and operational business principles to social problems.

Beyond networking, the Institute provides each participating organization with a dedicated business coach who supports the social entrepreneurs' critical decision making. Business coaches work side by side with the organization's executive and management team to determine critical aspects of the social program—program design, financial strategy and need, marketing strategy, measurement system, and staffing requirements. The coaches also prepare the innovator to successfully implement the program and to seek funding for it. Business coaches will help organizations prepare to compete for three grants awards at a final business competition.

New State-Level Financing: "Pay for Performance" Bonds

States are facing mounting social program costs and lower tax revenues. In response, a plan is being considered by the Minnesota legislature to raise money for state programs by issuing bonds that would offer private investors a 4-percent return on investments they make in needed social services.[35] The state would use the money to pay nonprofit providers that provide job train-ing, help addicts kick their habits, or offer other such services—but only if they produce specific results that would save the state money. The plan has won widespread support among nonprofit groups, think tanks, and legislators in Minnesota.

The idea bears some resemblance to social impact bonds (SIBs), a new finan-cial tool that is attracting interest from foundations and the Obama administra-tion. However, there is a key difference: with social impact bonds, the private investors take all the risk. They contribute money up front and the government repays them, plus a bonus, if the programs they back meet specific goals. If the programs don't meet those goals, they get nothing. Under the Minnesota plan, nonprofits carry the risk. The investors get their return on investment no mat-ter what, but nonprofits get paid only if they succeed. This introduces a measure of risk. The risk may be minimal for high-performing nonprofits or those with endowments or reserves, but may be a barrier for others, who may need a way to raise revenue while they are waiting to get state money. To deal with this, ideas to help these nonprofits are being considered, such as allowing them to borrow money from the state bond pool at a low interest rate or tap into a fund that foundations would create with program-related investments.

CONCLUDING THOUGHTS

This chapter has covered how social entrepreneurship may differ between the sectors. Although we are talking about the same process, the role and charac-teristics of the sectors dictate that the process is carried out in different ways. The public sector in the United States has a number of distinct characteristics, but the most salient is that it exists to serve the citizens of a democratic soci-ety. Consequently, citizens have the final voice in policies and programs. Public demands, however, can be challenging, and in designing innovative social pro-grams, administrators need to balance the potentially competing demands for efficiency and other social objectives.

In the next chapter we continue the focus on how social entrepreneurship is influenced by boundaries. In this case, however, we talk about how social ven-tures span or cross those boundaries. We will consider both the boundaries between organizations and the boundaries between sectors.

Exercise 9.1

How might public sector social entrepreneurship differ from social entrepreneurship in the private sector? In what ways might they be the same? Illustrate your points with examples of public and private sector entrepreneurship.

Exercise 9.2

Consider a service provided by any level of government. Using the goals and ideas from the new public management (NPM) approach, propose a new way to improve this service.

Exercise 9.3

For the same service, use the goals and ideas from the new public service (NPS) approach to propose a different way to improve the service. How does this suggestion differ from the suggestion you proposed in Exercise 9.2? Could these suggestions be combined?

Boundary Spanning and
Social Entrepreneurship

In January 1992, Bethlehem Steel announced plans to close part of its plant in Steelton, Pennsylvania.[1] This would mean a loss of 400 jobs and an uncertain future for 1,600 others. In response, the New Baldwin Corridor Coalition was established to bring together various partners—including business, government, labor, education, and community organizations—to develop conditions that foster the general economic and social development of the Steelton community. The organization was named for a commercial district of nearby Middletown. The impetus for the Coalition came from Ike Gittlen, the local steelworkers' union president, who saw an opportunity to galvanize community support around a vision and proposed a strategy for dealing with basic causes of industrial decline.

At a meeting of the Capital Area Labor Management Council, Gittlen was given an opportunity to present his proposal to the community. As a result, approximately sixty business, labor, political, education, community, and economic development leaders endorsed the idea and cleared the way for the formation of the Coalition. The Coalition's mission was to focus on area business revival, educational integration, human resources, government restructuring, housing and human services, and research and technology. This would entail developing long-term linkages among key groups; for example, in education. Another goal was an enterprise alliance, which would develop new forms of labor-industry cooperation to enhance enterprise competitiveness, job growth, and quality of life.

The Coalition engaged in extensive research, planning, convening, and coordination. Between its founding and 1997, the Coalition reached a membership of over three hundred organizations and produced an impressive array of outcomes. As a result of the Coalition's efforts, two new manufacturing firms and a health clinic were established. The Coalition convened meetings of the enterprise alliance, which engaged labor union and management representatives from five organizations. The Coalition was also instrumental in establishing other cooperative networks. It fostered cooperation among municipal governments by preparing an approach for developing intergovernmental cooperation, sponsoring meetings to explore cooperation, and obtaining resolutions from eight municipal government pledging cooperation. Finally, it supported work to develop collaboration among seven independent school districts and two vocational schools.

The problem of economic decline that this story describes is typical of many communities in the United States today. The task of revitalizing the economic and associated social infrastructure of a community is well beyond the capability of any single organization. So are other complex problems, such as providing health care and improving education. How can organizations make progress against these large problems?

The story of the New Baldwin Corridor Coalition is a striking example of the benefits of organizations working together to innovatively address these problems. Only by a collaborative organizational effort can innovative solutions be developed that attain the scope needed to have an impact. In addition, solutions will involve action in all sectors, and sector boundaries are becoming increasingly blurred as organizations are being called upon to collaborate with those in other sectors. For example, corporations are experimenting with new ways of providing social value, and nonprofits and government are adopting methods from the business world to harness the power of markets. In addition, organizations themselves are incorporating characteristics of those in other sectors, and new hybrid forms of organizations are emerging. In this chapter we examine how social entrepreneurship takes place in collaborative and cross-sector settings. We examine collaboration between organizations as well as within networks of organizations. We also examine how organizations work across sector boundaries to develop innovative solutions.

WORKING ACROSS ORGANIZATIONAL BOUNDARIES

In this section, we consider how social entrepreneurship benefits from organizations working together. We start by describing how solving complex problems requires addressing the ecosystems in which they are embedded. To understand ecosystems, it is important to consider the collaborative relations among the organizations within them. We then examine how social entrepreneurship can

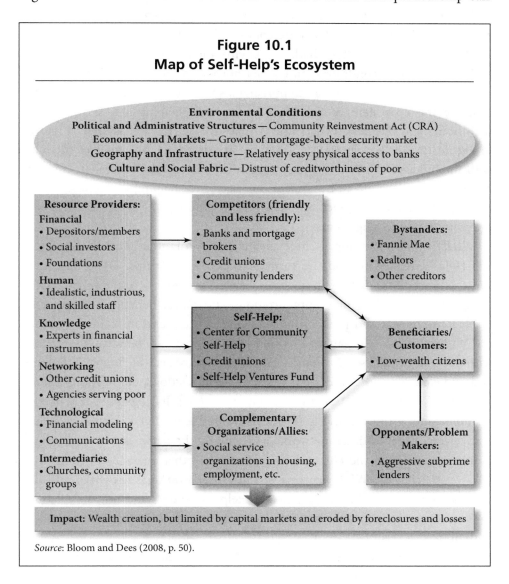

Figure 10.1
Map of Self-Help's Ecosystem

Environmental Conditions
Political and Administrative Structures — Community Reinvestment Act (CRA)
Economics and Markets — Growth of mortgage-backed security market
Geography and Infrastructure — Relatively easy physical access to banks
Culture and Social Fabric — Distrust of creditworthiness of poor

Resource Providers:
Financial
• Depositors/members
• Social investors
• Foundations
Human
• Idealistic, industrious, and skilled staff
Knowledge
• Experts in financial instruments
Networking
• Other credit unions
• Agencies serving poor
Technological
• Financial modeling
• Communications
Intermediaries
• Churches, community groups

Competitors (friendly and less friendly):
• Banks and mortgage brokers
• Credit unions
• Community lenders

Bystanders:
• Fannie Mae
• Realtors
• Other creditors

Self-Help:
• Center for Community Self-Help
• Credit unions
• Self-Help Ventures Fund

Beneficiaries/ Customers:
• Low-wealth citizens

Complementary Organizations/Allies:
• Social service organizations in housing, employment, etc.

Opponents/Problem Makers:
• Aggressive subprime lenders

Impact: Wealth creation, but limited by capital markets and eroded by foreclosures and losses

Source: Bloom and Dees (2008, p. 50).

benefit from collaboration between pairs of organizations and from collaboration within larger sets, or networks, of organizations.

Cooperation in Ecosystems

In order for social entrepreneurs to address complex social problems, such as improving access to health care or urban education, they must understand and often make changes to the larger social systems in which the problems are embedded. These social systems are composed of all the stakeholders involved with the problem as well as the larger environment (such as the relevant laws, policies, economic conditions, and social norms) in which the problem exists. These can be conceptualized as comprising a social ecosystem. Bloom and Dees describe the ecosystem of Self-Help, a nonprofit helping the disadvantaged with home and business ownership.[2] A map of Self-Help's ecosystem is shown in Figure 10.1. Self-Help and its programs are shown at the center of the map, with the linkages to other ecosystem organizations and the ecosystem environment displayed around it. Ecosystems are useful for helping us understand the larger patterns that influence problems—both the range of actors involved and the conditions affecting them.

What is important for us here is the variety of other organizations that Self-Help is related to and the form of these relationships. Other organizations important to Self-Help include service providers, resource providers, competitors, complementary organizations and allies, beneficiaries and customers, opponents and problem makers, and affected and influential bystanders. Within this set of organizations, Self-Help will have cooperative interactions with specific others, such as partnerships with providers of financial, human, and knowledge resources. Besides these one-one relations, connections among larger groups of organization are also important for Self-Help, particularly connections among those working on the same problems. For example, Self-Help is in several organizational networks, particularly the network of social service housing agencies in the city and the network of other agencies working with low-wealth citizens. What happens in these organizational networks can also be of assistance (or a hindrance) to Self-Help. To understand how its relations to other organizations influence Self-Help, we need to consider connections at both of these levels.

In this section we examine what the literature refers to as *interorganizational relationships*. They can be defined as "enduring transactions, flows, and linkages that occur among or between an organization and one or more other organizations in its environment."[3] In practice, these relationships can take a variety of forms and can be referred to by a variety of terms, including cooperation, coordination, collaboration, alliance, joint venture, and partnership. This can be confusing, as these terms are not consistently defined. Unless otherwise noted, we refer to these relationships as *collaboration*. We describe collaboration between organizations at the two levels we described above. We first discuss the development and use of collaborative relations between social entrepreneurial organizations and specific other organizations. We then discuss how social entrepreneurial organizations fit into and use collaborative networks of organizations.

COLLABORATION BETWEEN ORGANIZATIONS

In this section we describe the reasons why organizations may consider collaboration, the types of collaborations that organizations may engage in, and how collaboration is related to innovation.

Reasons for Collaboration

We define collaboration between two organizations as a process in which they "interact through formal and informal negotiation, jointly creating rules and structures governing their relationship and ways to act or decide on the issues that brought them together; it is a process involving shared norms and mutually beneficial interactions."[4]

Why would an organization providing social benefits seek a collaborative relationship with another organization? A variety of internal and external factors that influence the decision to collaborate have been identified. Six perspectives on collaboration involving social-mission organizations have been described, and each of them could be used by social entrepreneurs.[5]

• *Social responsibility*: Emphasis is on the goal and responsibility to solve social problems. Social responsibility is the key basis for the activity of mission-driven organizations. Social missions normally transcend organizational boundaries, and shared interests in social issues can lead to cooperation if collective action will produce more social benefits.

• *Operational efficiency*: Collaboration can be undertaken to produce economies of scale. Such collaboration is often driven by funders or other stakeholders seeking to increase service volume. Funders can be driven by a concern about the duplication of services and the duplication of appeals for resources that results from numerous competing providers. Government agencies, foundations, and federated funders such as the United Way all feel this pressure.

- *Resource interdependence*: Organizations need resources from each other to meet objectives and survive. For example, foundations and nonprofits need each other to meet financial and mission needs. Also, nonprofits may cooperate in service delivery. For example, a nonprofit addressing the needs of the homeless may refer its clients to other providers to address problems related to their homelessness, such as addiction or unemployment. These providers may refer clients in return. In this way, agencies become interdependent as they benefit themselves and their partners.

- *Environmental validity*: Legitimacy is a key resource and organizations will pursue strategies to acquire and bolster it, including collaboration with others. Social benefit organizations are rewarded for living up to social expectations that they cooperate to provide community benefits. A loss of legitimacy in the eyes of key stakeholders will likely be very detrimental for future funding.

- *Domain influence*: Power is a reason for collaboration. An organization can secure resources by enhancing its power or influence in its domain or sphere of activity. Collaboration can be used to increase and control resources, set standards for service, and influence funder priorities. This is a political model whereby organizations seek to align with others who share common interests, to enhance their power to advance their interests over those of other organizations.

- *Strategic enhancement*: Collaboration can be used as a means of increasing competitive advantage. For example, nonprofits must respond to externalities, such as funder or marketplace demands, and these may prove problematic for individual nonprofits. In this case, joint fundraising could produce benefits that two organizations could share but that neither alone could produce. In addition, government or third-party funders may seek more comprehensive services. Several nonprofits, each providing a narrow range of services, could collaborate to provide the continuum of services desired by funders.

Types of Collaborative Relationships

In a collaborative relationship, there is some enduring, mutually beneficial interaction between two organizations. Collaborations vary depending on how loosely or tightly the activities of the two organizations are intertwined. A framework for understanding the range of collaborative relationships organizations engage in is James Austin's *collaboration continuum*. Formulated to describe relationships between nonprofit and for-profit organizations,[6] the continuum is useful in describing the relationship between any two organizations.[7] According to Austin, collaboration intensity varies along seven dimensions. These are shown in the first column of Table 10.1. Each can vary in degree, as shown in the columns of the table as we move horizontally from left to right.

Austin uses these seven dimensions to characterize three types of collaborations. These are, however, only three points on a continuum, and relationships

Table 10.1
The Collaboration Continuum

Nature of Relationship	Simple Collaboration	Transactional Collaboration	Integrative Collaboration
Level of Engagement	Low	————————>	High
Importance to Mission	Peripheral	————————>	Central
Magnitude of Resources	Small	————————>	Big
Scope of Activities	Narrow	————————>	Broad
Interaction Level	Infrequent	————————>	Intensive
Managerial Complexity	Simple	————————>	Complex
Strategic Value	Minor	————————>	Major

Source: Adapted from Austin (2000).

can be located at any point along this continuum. Depending on where they are on the continuum, collaborations vary in terms of the collaboration mind-set, the strategic alignment of the partners, the value that the collaboration has for each partner, and the management of the relationship.

- Simple collaborations involve only a little contact between partners. They are characterized by minimal interaction in defining activities, minimal fit beyond a shared interest in a particular issue, generic resource transfer, and contact between designated organizational personnel. An example would be client referral between social service agencies.

- Transactional collaborations, on the other hand, have a higher level of involvement between partners. These collaborations involve a partnering mind-set with increased understanding and trust, an overlap in mission and vision, a more equal exchange of resources—possibly involving core competencies—and extended relationships throughout the organization. An example would be a teen counseling organization and a recreation center collaborating on developing a program to build teen self-esteem.

- Integrative collaborations involve extensive, multidimensional involvement. These collaborations are characterized by a *we* instead of *us and them* mind-set, a broad scope of activities of strategic significance and high mission mesh and shared values, projects that are identified and developed at all levels of the organization and joint benefit creation, and deep personal relationships across the organizations with the culture of each organization influencing the other. An example would be several school districts jointly designing curriculum and providing teacher training.

For new entrepreneurial ventures, collaborations can provide many benefits, as we describe further in the next section. Because it takes time to develop transactional or integrative collaborations with other organizations, especially on new and untested products or services, it is likely that most initial collaborations will be simple. As partners gain more experience with each other, however, more significant collaborations can be established.

Collaboration and Innovation

Research on interorganizational relations has shown that four major components of collaboration are related to innovativeness. Collaboration can assist innovation by giving organizations access to information, technical assistance, information, and clients. Collaboration can transfer knowledge, enhance legitimacy, leverage the resources of individual organizations, and provide opportunities for shared learning and resource exchange.[8] Useful knowledge and information can be about unmet needs, new approaches and services, and new resources to fund innovation. More frequent contacts enhance the prospects for the diffusion of innovation among organizations.

Systematic research on these relationship benefits in nonprofit organizations is sparse. Although the research is somewhat mixed, several studies have found positive support.[9] One systematic study examined four components of collaboration and three types of innovation.[10] It examined the effect that linkages of resources, information, technical assistance, and sending and receiving clients had on administrative, product, and process innovations. The findings showed that the effects of interorganizational relations varied according to the type of innovation. The total number of innovations and product innovations were positively related to technical assistance and client links. Administrative innovation was positively related to technical assistance links.

We now consider how social ventures may benefit from involvements in networks of organizations.

ENGAGEMENT IN NETWORKS

We now move to the consideration of organizational collaborations among more than two organizations. Organizational networks are collaborations among groups of organizations and are characterized by unique characteristics, benefits, and challenges.

The Nature of Networks

Networks pervade our world today. One of the most dramatic recent developments is the spread of personal networks made possible by new media. Advances in science and technology have made the world smaller and more interconnected, and groups, organizations, communities, and nations are increasingly joined together in complex webs of relationships. In this section we examine the use of organizational networks for entrepreneurship and innovation. Nowhere is the increasing use of networks more prevalent than among organizations. An *interorganizational network* is a set of organizations that come together to reach goals that they could not reach separately. These networks have several key features:[11]

- *Conceptual systems*: Networks help members to understand and deal with complex and ambiguous problems and issues. Shared understandings make it possible to develop new ways of responding to problems.

- *Transcendent relations*: Networks develop shared vision, purpose, and goals that incorporate but go beyond the interests of individual members.

- *Loose coupling of members*: Members represent autonomous organizations and meet as needed to carry out the network goals. Membership is voluntary. Networks are hierarchically organized, but organizations do not have superior-subordinate relationships with each other.

- *Self-regulation*: Members control the network and its activities. They are responsible for developing the mission, vision, and goals and for planning, initiating, and managing network activities. Network governance can be horizontal or vertical.

For-profits and nonprofits increasingly use these networks to gain access to information and resources, to share risk, and to address complex market or social environments. Public agencies use them to avoid duplication of services and make better use of scarce resources. The newest and most innovative networks are being constructed to address complex problems that span sector boundaries, such as health care, community development, and education. These problems are really sets of interconnected problems. For example, health is related to community conditions and education. This makes these problems difficult to conceptualize and analyze and immune to simple solutions.[12] Dealing with them requires extensive collaboration among different types and levels of organizations from each sector. This is clearly shown in the example of the New Baldwin Corridor Coalition, which established a number of new networks among its members.

Another example is the policy field for early childhood education, which we presented in Chapter Four. In Figure 10.2 we again show the policy field first depicted in Figure 4.5.[13] Notably, this policy field is a network composed of relationships among the public and private organizations at local, state, regional, and national levels that are involved with early childhood education in Minnesota. Within the network, connections and flows between organizations can take

Figure 10.2

Early Childhood Education Policy Field in Minnesota, 2008

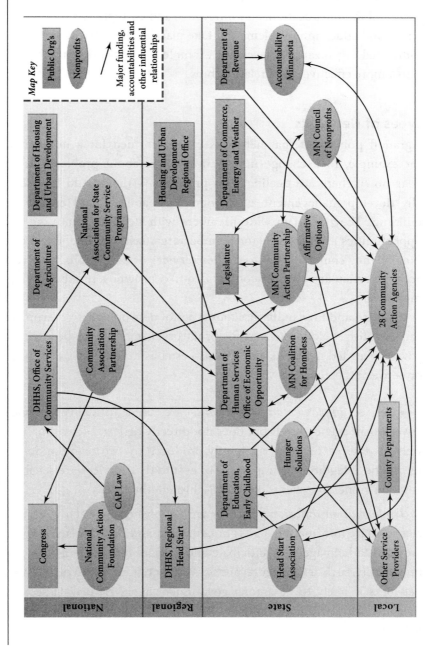

Map Key

Public Org's

Nonprofits

→ Major funding, accountabilities and other influential relationships

National

Congress

National Community Action Foundation

CAP Law

DHHS, Office of Community Services

Department of Agriculture

Department of Housing and Urban Development

National Association for State Community Service Programs

Community Association Partnership

Regional

DHHS, Regional Head Start

Housing and Urban Development Regional Office

State

Department of Education, Early Childhood

Department of Human Services Office of Economic Opportunity

Legislature

Department of Commerce, Energy and Weather

Department of Revenue

Hunger Solutions

MN Coalition for Homeless

MN Community Action Partnership

Affirmative Options

MN Council of Nonprofits

Accountability Minnesota

Head Start Association

Local

County Departments

28 Community Action Agencies

Other Service Providers

Source: Sandfort (2010, p. 640).[14]

place in terms of resources, administrative authority, information, or referrals. The network contains organizations that deal with various factors affecting early childhood education, and innovative and entrepreneurial solutions to early childhood education problems can take place at the network level as well as the individual organizational level. For example, the network could be reconfigured into a more effective set of relationships.

Types of Networks

Agranoff points out that networks can be formed for a number of reasons; for example, to exchange information, learn about problems in depth, and hear how others are dealing with problems.[15] They could be used to mutually develop management and program capabilities and engage in capacity building. They could provide members with new programming options and opportunities as blueprints for member organizations' interactive engagement. Finally, they could be used to deliver services or adopt collaborative courses of action. Particular networks could, of course, provide a number of these to their members.

Milward and Provan discuss four types of networks that government agencies can establish.[16] Nonprofit and for-profit organizations can be partners in these government-led networks and can also establish these types of networks within or between their sectors.

• *Service implementation networks* are used to deliver services that a government agency funds but does not directly deliver, such as many health and welfare services. Services are jointly produced by two or more other organizations, and integration is important to ensure that services are reliably produced and that vulnerable clients do not fall through the cracks.

• *Information diffusion networks* are established between government agencies to share information across organization and department boundaries. They are used to help agencies anticipate and prepare for problems that involve high uncertainty, such as disaster response. Although the bulk of collaboration in these networks is likely to be among government agencies, private sector organizations may also be valuable sources of information that government agencies find helpful.

• *Problem-solving networks* are designed to solve immediate and pressing problems, such as the impact of natural disasters. Public managers confront demands for quick action, and this shapes the nature of the network that is established. Collaborations may be temporary, and after the problem or issue is dealt with the network may disband or become dormant. As disaster or emergency response often involves nonprofit and for-profit organizations, they can be important members of these networks.

• *Community capacity-building networks* are established to help communities build the social capital they need to deal with both current and future needs, such as economic development or prevention of alcohol or drug abuse. Networks and partnerships build social capital in that they promote trust and norms of reciprocity between organizations. This makes coordinated or joint action between organizations easier. Given their important roles in communities, nonprofit organizations will be important partners in these networks.

In addition, a given network may provide a number of the benefits described in the following section, as in the case of the New Baldwin Corridor Coalition networks, which involved information diffusion, problem solving, and capacity building.

Network Governance

Provan and Kenis identify three types of network governance.[17] In *participant governed* networks, the members of the network govern themselves. Consequently, these networks are decentralized and flexible on the one hand, but inefficient on the other. In addition, a relatively high degree of agreement among members is needed. A group of hospitals meeting to discuss their responses to changes in health care legislation would be one example. *Lead organization–governed* networks are more centralized structures. In this case, one organization is in control of network governance. These networks can be more efficient and handle a greater degree of disagreement among network members. They are, however, less flexible. An example would be a city government-led network to design a new light-rail transportation system. The third type is a *network-administrative* type of governance. In this case, a separate organization serves as a network broker or coordinator. The collective impact model we describe next features this type of governance.

Key Success Factors

A recent study by John Bryson and colleagues described the following set of key factors for successful cross-sector networks:[18]

• Understanding prior initiatives and the overall environment in which the network will be working. Whenever possible, leverage existing networks (rather than creating a new one).

• Developing effective process, structures, and governance mechanisms so participants understand their scope and roles.

• Understand the role of key players, such as who has decision authority in network governance. This will likely shift over the course of a collaboration process, especially if the role of the network changes.

• Demonstrating leadership and key competencies. Typically the network sponsors have formal authority. On-the-ground network champions lack formal authority but have legitimacy, in the eyes of the other members of the network, to be their convener.

• Creating an outcome-oriented accountability system that collects data on the inputs, processes, and outcomes of the network and relies on transparency and relationships among the network members to self-enforce behaviors.

Community of Practice

The notion of communities of practice describes how innovation can be fostered in networks. Communities of practice are "groups of people who share a concern, a set of problems, or a passion about a topic, and who deepen their knowledge and expertise in this area by interacting on an ongoing basis."[19] They operate as learning environments in which participants connect and interact to solve problems, share ideas, set standards, build tools, and develop relationships with peers and stakeholders. If participants are organizational representatives, they are the interpersonal manifestation of the interorganizational networks we have just described. As such, they create the network features and determine network activities.

Snyder and Briggs outline the key elements of a community of practice:[20]

• *Community*: Members are at various levels, including conveners, core members, active members, and peripheral members.

• *Domain*: A focus on a specific area (such as "results for kids," as we describe shortly) and a collective passion for an issue and how it can contribute to society.

Often there is a political context that gives legitimacy to this domain and those affected by it.

- *Practice*: Techniques, methods, tools and professional attitudes, along with learning activities to build, share, and apply the practice.

- *Sponsorship and support*: This could be done top-down or via a professional association from the outside. This would include logistics (such as meeting space), communications, and coaching for network leaders.

Snyder and Briggs describe the *community* of practice for Boost4Kids.[21] Boost4Kids defined its *domain* as "results for kids." This includes a number of interrelated outcomes, such as school readiness, health insurance, nutrition, healthy behaviors, and preventing child abuse. The Boost4Kids *community* was a wide-ranging network of federal agencies in addition to various foundations and nonprofits. The network is shown in Figure 10.3. Nongovernment partners included the Annie E. Casey Foundation, the Hitachi Foundation, the Institute for Educational Leadership, the National Civic League, The Finance Project, and numerous local nonprofit organizations. Each member participated in the context of a "performance partnership" that consisted of a local community, a state, and a federal partner; each was assigned a federal agency champion to work with the partnership to help measure results and cut red tape.

Boost4Kids *practice* included a number of tools and techniques. Geographic information system tools and methods helped identify strategic sites for after-school programs and focused efforts to find kids who had no health insurance. Templates for electronic, "universal" applications were designed to allow families to apply for multiple related family services without getting bounced around from agency to agency to fill out dozens of forms. Best practices were developed for improving access to federal nutrition programs and for enhancing school readiness programs for kids, including better ways to use Department of Transportation funds to get young children to day-care facilities. Boost4Kids also developed additional methods for strengthening outreach to at-risk youth, to encourage them to join after-school programs.

Collective Impact

Collective impact (CI) is a methodology for organizing community collaboration to deal with complex problems. CI was first described by Kania, Kramer, and Hanleybrown in two articles in the *Stanford Social Innovation Review*.[22] CI

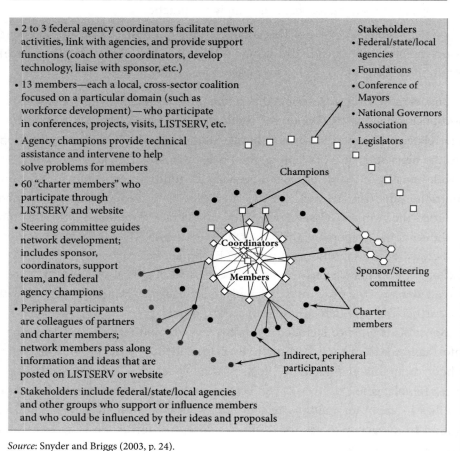

Figure 10.3
Boost4Kids Overall Community Network Structure

- 2 to 3 federal agency coordinators facilitate network activities, link with agencies, and provide support functions (coach other coordinators, develop technology, liaise with sponsor, etc.)

- 13 members—each a local, cross-sector coalition focused on a particular domain (such as workforce development)—who participate in conferences, projects, visits, LISTSERV, etc.

- Agency champions provide technical assistance and intervene to help solve problems for members

- 60 "charter members" who participate through LISTSERV and website

- Steering committee guides network development; includes sponsor, coordinators, support team, and federal agency champions

- Peripheral participants are colleagues of partners and charter members; network members pass along information and ideas that are posted on LISTSERV or website

- Stakeholders include federal/state/local agencies and other groups who support or influence members and who could be influenced by their ideas and proposals

Stakeholders
- Federal/state/local agencies
- Foundations
- Conference of Mayors
- National Governors Association
- Legislators

Champions

Coordinators

Members

Sponsor/Steering committee

Charter members

Indirect, peripheral participants

Source: Snyder and Briggs (2003, p. 24).

is based on the notion of creating a community response that is appropriate to the complex and dynamic problems communities face. Complex and dynamic problems, such as hunger or drug abuse, create a complex and dynamic problem environment in a community, which will need to be addressed by multiple sectors and stakeholders and will require multiple approaches. A basic principle of organizational science is that to deal with a complex environment, an organization must also become complex, essentially establishing separate units to deal with different aspects of the environmental complexity.[23] Given this, the community problem environment will need a complex and dynamic organizational initiative to respond to it. It is likely that simple organizations or initiatives (such as traditional collaborations) will not be adequately complex to deal with the problem complexity. CI initiatives, on the other hand, possess the required complexity and dynamism to deal with these most difficult community problems.

A key feature of CI initiatives is that they involve a combination of centralized and decentralized structures, which give CI initiatives the complexity they need. CI can then take advantage of the strengths of each type of structure.

• Centralized, more structured elements include a steering or overseeing committee and a backbone organization that provides coordination and resources. These elements set overall direction (policy, strategy) and coordinate activities of the CI initiative.

• Decentralized, more flexible elements include working groups directly related to all aspects of the problem. These are composed of appropriate service providers and programs. These elements collaborate and develop responsive and innovative solutions.

CI differs from other types of collaborations. Traditional collaborations entail several organizations with existing missions, strategies, and programs joining some of their activities to accomplish what they could not do alone. At the extreme, this may involve modifying, blending, or even merging programs or structures. It is important to note that the work of aligning the organizations (deciding goals, planning strategy and programs, and so on) is done up front. After this, the collaboration can proceed as planned. The organizations in CI initiatives, on the other hand, work out joint goals, activities, coordination, and alignment over time. For example, it could take up to several years to develop a strategic framework. CI is a process of social change that is launched without identifying any particular overall solution in advance.

WORKING ACROSS SECTORS

In this section we move to the consideration of larger boundaries; that is, the boundaries between the nonprofit, for-profit, and public sectors. Social entrepreneurial ventures can also be designed to work across these boundaries. This is becoming increasingly important as complex social problems span the sectors.

The Blurring of Sectoral Boundaries

Over the past few decades, the boundaries between the public, business, and nonprofit sectors have been blurring, as many pioneering organizations blend social and environmental aims with business approaches. There are many expressions of this trend. For-profits are moving further toward providing social value by using cause-based marketing, triple bottom lines, corporate social responsibility, social auditing, socially responsible investing, and sustainability reporting. At the same time, public and nonprofits are using more businesslike methods and market-based activity, including venture philanthropy, program-related investment, government reinvention, new public management, and social return on investment.

These developments have led some to speculate that although the mission and method of many organizations in the business, government, and nonprofit sectors are becoming steadily more similar, something more than simple blurring of the boundaries between sectors is occurring. They hold that organizations in the three sectors are converging toward fundamentally new, hybrid forms that integrate social purposes with business methods.[24]

Hybrid Organizations

According to the dictionary, "hybrid" is defined as things derived from heterogeneous sources, or composed of elements of different or incongruous kinds.[25] In terms of organizations, Billis adopts a "prime sector" approach and maintains that organizations have "roots" or primary adherence to the principles of one sector.[26] Hybrid organizations adhere to their prime sector while adopting some aspects of another sector. With this approach, each sector could form hybrids with the other two, yielding nine types of hybrids. For example, nonprofit hybrids could take the form nonprofit-public, nonprofit-business, and nonprofit-public-business. In each of these, their primary adherence is to principles of the nonprofit sector.

The past few decades have seen a proliferation of new hybrid organizational models formed to address a variety of societal challenges. These forms are hybrid in that their operations combine models from more than one sector. The number and variety of these models has led some to speculate that they constitute an emerging "fourth sector," as shown in Figure 10.4.[27] Fourth sector denotes that these organizations blend attributes and strategies from all sectors, making them hard to describe using the principles from only one sector. What

Figure 10.4
The Emergence of a New Fourth Sector

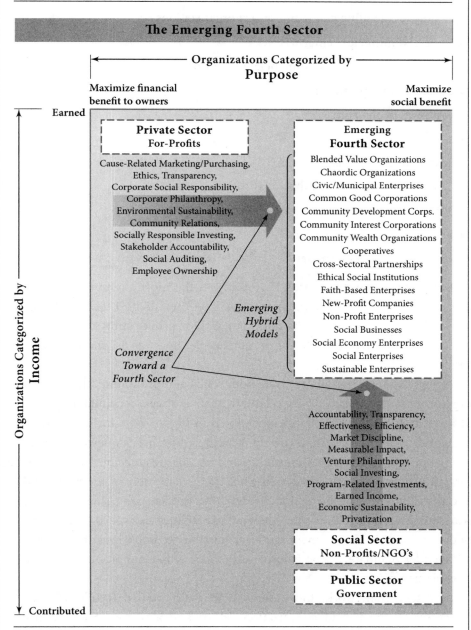

Source: Sabeti (2012, p. 8).

they do share is the coupling of the pursuit of social and environmental aims with the use of business methods. Numerous examples of hybrid organizational models have emerged in recent years, including:

- Chaordic (blending chaos and order) organizations
- Civic and municipal enterprises
- Community development financial institutions
- Cross-sectoral partnerships
- Faith-based enterprises
- Nonprofit enterprises
- Sustainable enterprises
- Community wealth organizations
- Social enterprises
- Blended value organizations
- Social economy enterprises

Nonprofit–for-profit hybrids have received the most attention in the literature. Kim Alter has also written extensively on these hybrid forms.[28] Table 10.2 shows the characteristics of the nonprofit and for-profit prime sectors and nonprofit–for-profit hybrids in terms of motives, methods, goals, and destination of funds.

All hybrid organizations generate both social and economic value and can be organized by how their activity relates to their motives, accountability, and use of income. Alter's Hybrid Spectrum, shown in Figure 10.5, includes four types of hybrid organizations.[29] On the right-hand side of her framework are corporations practicing social responsibility and socially responsible business. These for-profit hybrids create social value, but their main motives are profit-making and distribution of profit to shareholders. On the left-hand side of her framework are nonprofits with income-generating activities and social enterprises. For both of these hybrids, the main motive is mission accomplishment as dictated by stakeholder mandate. Social enterprises may be either nonprofits or for-profits, as explained next.

In Alter's framework, the difference in main motive (profit or mission) is central to the hybrid organization's ethos and activities. For this reason,

Table 10.2
Spectrum of Practitioners

	Purely Philanthropic	Hybrid	Purely Commercial
Motives	Appeal to goodwill	Mixed motives	Appeal to self-interest
Methods	Mission-driven	Balance of mission and market	Market-driven
Goals	Social value creation	Social and economic value creation	Economic value creation
Destination of Income/Profit	Directed toward mission activities of nonprofit organization (required by law or organizational policy)	Reinvested in mission activities or operational expenses, and/or retained for business growth and development (for-profits may redistribute a portion)	Distributed to shareholders and owners

Source: Alter (2013).

Figure 10.5
Hybrid Spectrum

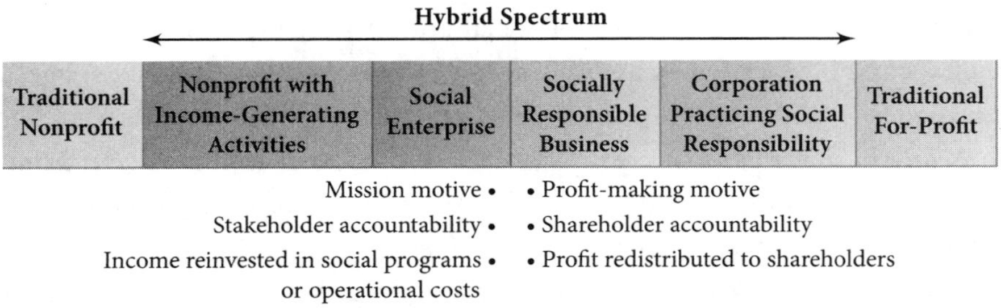

Hybrid Spectrum

Traditional Nonprofit	Nonprofit with Income-Generating Activities	Social Enterprise	Socially Responsible Business	Corporation Practicing Social Responsibility	Traditional For-Profit

Mission motive •   • Profit-making motive

Stakeholder accountability •   • Shareholder accountability

Income reinvested in social programs •   • Profit redistributed to shareholders
or operational costs

Source: Alter (2013).

organizations rarely evolve or transform in type along the full spectrum. Those that transform from social enterprise to socially responsible company or vice versa must first reorient their primary purpose, then realign their organization. Although nonprofits are founded to create social value, the need for financial sustainability may lead them to seek external or self-generated funds. The difference between nonprofits with income-generating activities and nonprofit social enterprises is a matter of the degree to which they rely on income generation. Income generation is more important for nonprofit social enterprises and may be integrated into the social services provided. On the other hand, whereas for-profits are established to create economic value through earned income, they may be compelled to make social contributions in response to market or other pressures. In for-profit social enterprises, however, the mission motive must be dominant. They must be created primarily for a social purpose. This differentiates them from the other for-profit hybrids, for which profit is still the primary purpose. This definition of social enterprise is consistent with that of the Social Enterprise Alliance, a major umbrella group. The Alliance maintains that: "The common good is its *primary* purpose, literally 'baked into' the organization's DNA, and trumping all others."[30] Other definitions, however, may relax this requirement and apply the term to other hybrid forms.[31] It is therefore important to be clear about an author's definition when encountering the term.

Social Enterprise

As early as 1996, the Roberts Foundation Homeless Economic Development Fund defined social enterprise as "a revenue generating venture founded to create economic opportunities for very low income individuals, while simultaneously operating with reference to the financial bottom-line."[32] Since then, numerous definitions have been offered, incorporating various elements of the function, funding, and ownership of social enterprises. We will adopt a definition of social enterprise that incorporates a number of the elements suggested and provides latitude for a broad range of practical applications: *A social enterprise is any business venture created for a social purpose—mitigating/reducing a social problem or a market failure—and to generate social value while operating with the characteristics of a private sector business.*[33]

Given that they seek social change, social enterprises benefit from entrepreneurship, innovation and market approaches. The business characteristics often cited include financial discipline, innovation, and determination.[34] Although some definitions restrict the term to nonprofit and for-profit organizations, on the basis of function it could also be applicable to public agencies. We discussed public-sector examples in Chapter Nine. Our discussion here focuses on nonprofit and for-profit social enterprises. Social enterprises may be structured as a department within an organization or as a separate legal entity, either a subsidiary nonprofit or for-profit. In either case, business success and social impact are interdependent.

Distinguished by their characteristic as creators of both social and economic value, social enterprises have the following characteristics:

- Use business tools and approaches to achieve social objectives
- Blend social and commercial capital and methods
- Create social and economic value
- Generate income from commercial activities to fund social programs
- Are market-driven and mission-led
- Measure financial performance and social impact
- Meet financial goals in a way that contributes to the public good
- Enjoy financial freedom from unrestricted income
- Incorporate enterprise strategically to accomplish the mission

Alter distinguishes several types of social enterprises, based on the level of integration between their social programs and business activities. The primary types are *embedded* social enterprises and *integrated* social enterprises.

In embedded social enterprises, business activities are embedded within the organization's operations and social programs and are central to its mission. Social programs are self-financed through enterprise activities; thus the embedded social enterprise also functions as a sustainable program strategy. The social mission is the central purpose of the business. The relationship between the business activities and the social programs are comprehensive; financial and social benefits are achieved simultaneously. Because of this mission focus, most embedded social enterprises are usually structured as nonprofits to protect against mission drift, but they may also be registered as for-profits, depending on the legal environment.

In integrated social enterprises, social programs overlap with business activities, often sharing costs and assets. Organizations create integrated social enterprises as a funding mechanism to support the nonprofit's operations and mission activities. The relationship between the business activities and the social programs is synergistic, adding value—financial and social—to one another. In many cases integrated social enterprises expand or enhance the organization's mission, enabling it to achieve greater social impact. Mission expansion may be achieved by commercializing the organization's social services and selling them to a new fee-paying market, or by providing new services to existing clients. Integrated social enterprises leverage tangible and intangible assets—such as expertise, program methodology, relationships, brand, and infrastructure—as the basis from which to create their businesses. The integrated social enterprise may be structured as a profit center or enterprise department within the nonprofit or as separate entity.

The framework is then utilized to describe a number of social enterprise operating models, summarized as follows:[35]

• *External Support Model* (embedded): Social programs are distinct from business activities. Nonprofits create external social enterprises to fund their social services and/or operating costs. The enterprise's activities are "external" from the organization's operations, but they support its social programs through supplementary financing. External social enterprises generally do not benefit from leveraging, cost sharing, or program synergies; therefore to serve their purpose, they must be profitable. A museum running a gift shop would be an example.

• *Entrepreneur Support Model* (embedded): The social enterprise sells business support and financial services to its target population or "clients," self-employed individuals or firms. Social enterprise clients then sell their products and services in the open market. Economic development organizations, including microfinance institutions, small and medium enterprises, and business development service programs use the entrepreneur support model.

• *Market Intermediary Model* (embedded): The social enterprise provides services to its target population or "clients"—small producers (individuals, firms, or cooperatives)—to help them access markets. Social enterprise services add value to client-made products; typically these services include product development, production and marketing assistance, and credit. The market intermediary either purchases the client-made products outright or takes them on consignment; it then sells the products in high-margin markets at a markup. Marketing supply cooperatives as well as fair trade, agriculture, and handicraft organizations frequently use the market intermediary model of social enterprise.

- *Employment Model* (embedded): The social enterprise provides employment opportunities and job training to its target populations or "clients": people with high barriers to employment, such as the disabled, the homeless, at-risk youth, and ex-offenders. The organization operates an enterprise employing its clients, and it sells its products or services in the open market. The employment model is widely used by disabilities and youth organizations, as well as social service organizations serving low-income women, recovering addicts, formerly homeless people, and welfare to work recipients.

- *Fee-for-Service Model* (embedded): The social enterprise commercializes its social services and then sells them directly to the target populations or "clients:" individuals, firms, communities, or to a third-party payer. Fee-for-service is one of the most commonly used social enterprise models among nonprofits. Membership organizations and trade associations, schools, museums, hospitals, and clinics are typical examples of fee-for-service social enterprises.

- *Low-Income Client as Market Model* (embedded): A variation of the fee-for-services model. The emphasis of this model is giving poor and low-income clients access to products and services for which price, distribution, product features, and other factors have barred access to this market. Examples of products and services may include health care (vaccinations, prescription drugs, eye surgery) and health and hygiene products (iodized salt, soap, eyeglasses, hearing aids, feminine hygiene products), and utility services (electricity, biomass, and water) for which they pay. These models are often advocated for use in developing countries.

- *Cooperative Model* (embedded): The social enterprise provides direct benefit to its target population or "clients"—cooperative members—through member services: market information, technical assistance and extension services, collective bargaining power, economies of bulk purchase, access to products and services, and access to external markets for member-produced products and services. The cooperative membership often comprises small-scale producers in the same product group or a community with common needs—such as access to capital or health care. Cooperative members are the primary stakeholders in the cooperative, reaping benefits of income, employment, or services, as well as investing in the cooperative with their own resources of time, money, products, and labor.

- *Market Linkage Model* (embedded or integrated): The social enterprise facilitates trade relationships between the target population or "clients"—small producers or local firms and cooperatives—and the external market. The social enterprise functions as a broker, connecting buyers to producers and vice versa, and charging fees for this service. Selling market information and research services is a second type of business common in the market linkage model. Unlike the market intermediary model, this type of social enterprise does not sell or market clients' products; rather, it connects clients to markets. Many trade associations, cooperatives, private sector partnerships, and business development programs use the market linkage model of social enterprise.

• *Service Subsidization Model* (integrated): The social enterprise sells products or services to an external market and uses the income it generates to fund its social programs. Business activities and social programs overlap, sharing costs, assets, operations, income, and often program attributes. Although the service subsidization model is employed primarily as a financing mechanism—the business mandate is separate from its social mission—the business activities may enlarge or enhance the organization's mission.

In addition to these hybrid social enterprise operating models, several new legal organizational hybrid forms for social enterprise have been developed in the United States. We describe them next.

NEW LEGAL FORMS

Social enterprises in the United States can now take advantage of two new legal for-profit forms of incorporation: they can incorporate as a low-profit limited liability company or a benefit corporation. These legal forms are available in a growing number of states. These are legally and explicitly hybrids, as in both forms social benefits must be a major purpose. This is a dramatic departure from the profit-maximizing mandate of traditional for-profits. Both forms are taxed at normal corporate tax rates.

Low-Profit Limited Liability Company (L3C)

A L3C must operate with a stated goal of achieving a social goal, with making a profit a secondary goal. Vermont was the first state to offer this corporate form. According to interSector Partners, L3C (an education and consulting firm), as of July 1, 2012, this corporate status was available in nine states and two Indian tribes. It is reported to be gaining ground in other states. In addition, there were 825 active L3Cs nationwide.[36]

L3Cs are encouraged to act in a manner consistent with nonprofit law. For example, the model state law providing for the establishment of the L3C states that the organization must meet these criteria:[37]

- Significantly furthers the accomplishment of one or more charitable or educational purposes within the meaning of section 170(c)(2)(B) of the Internal Revenue Code of 1986, as amended

- Would not have been formed but for the organization's relationship to the accomplishment of charitable or educational purposes

Unlike a nonprofit, a L3C can distribute the profit to owners or investors. Returns, however, could be lower than other for-profit investments, given the nature of its social mission. The L3C was designed to attract private investments and philanthropic capital in ventures designed to provide social benefit. For example, it is easier for foundations to make program-related investments (PRIs) in L3Cs. Although foundations are designed to be primarily grant-making nonprofits, they can make investments (PRIs) under some circumstances. A PRI is an investment with a socially beneficial purpose that is consistent with and furthers a foundation's mission. PRIs must be approved by the Internal Revenue Service (IRS). However, when using an L3C, with its explicit social mission, foundations do not need a special ruling by the IRS that the investment qualifies as a PRI.

Benefit Corporation

The benefit corporation is a new class of corporation required to create a material positive impact on society and the environment and to meet higher standards of accountability and transparency.[38] At the time of this writing, this new legal form was available in fourteen states, and legislation to establish them has been introduced in thirteen others.[39] The enacting state's benefit corporation statutes are so placed in existing state corporation codes that the enacting state's existing corporation code applies to benefit corporations in every respect except those explicit provisions unique in the benefit corporation form. The major characteristics of the benefit corporation form are as follows:[40]

- A requirement that a benefit corporation must have a corporate purpose to create a material positive impact on society and the environment

- An expansion of the duties of directors to require consideration of nonfinancial stakeholders as well as the financial interests of shareholders

- An obligation to report on its overall social and environmental performance using a comprehensive, credible, independent, and transparent third-party standard.

The benefit corporation grew out of the work of B Lab, a nonprofit organization that certifies the social responsibility of corporations in the same way that TransFair certifies Fair Trade coffee.[41] Corporations are certified as "B Corps" (note that this is not the same as a benefit corporation) if they voluntarily agree to meet social and environmental performance standards, ensure accountability, and provide transparency. At the time of this writing, there were over 807 certified B Corps in 27 countries across 60 different industries.[42]

B Lab has gone beyond this certification system based on voluntary compliance. B Lab and others have extended the B Corps principles into a set of legal requirements that are now being included in state incorporation laws. The results are benefit corporations, which have a legal obligation to create social benefits as just outlined. Patagonia, the well-known outdoor clothing manufacturer, became one of the first organizations to register in California as a benefit corporation. This underscores Patagonia's commitment to environmental causes, which is expressed on its website: "For us at Patagonia, a love of wild and beautiful places demands participation in the fight to save them, and to help reverse the steep decline in the overall environmental health of our planet. We donate our time, services and at least 1% of our sales to hundreds of grassroots environmental groups all over the world who work to help reverse the tide."[43]

CONCLUDING THOUGHTS

In this chapter we considered how social entrepreneurs can work across boundaries to enhance their ventures. Working across organizational boundaries and partnering with another organization can allow a social venture to provide more or different social value than it could have provided by itself. Partnerships can be tailored in a great variety of ways and can be more or less central to an organization's operations. Networks simultaneously extend the benefits of partnering to more organizations and facilitate more widespread and coordinated action to provide social value. Social entrepreneurs can also work across sector boundaries. This is becoming more important as more complex problems span sectors. Just as organizations working together can increase their overall social impact, sectors working together will be more effective social problem solvers.

In the next chapter we examine the impact on social entrepreneurship of additional new developments. The rapid development and increasing use of new media is transforming many aspects of our lives. Similarly, new media are also impacting social entrepreneurship. New media facilitate communication among those involved in social ventures, help them coordinate their work, and enhance fundraising and advocacy for social causes.

EXERCISES

Exercise 10.1

Why is interorganizational collaboration important for social entrepreneurship? What particular aspects of the social entrepreneurship process would benefit the most from interorganizational collaboration? Illustrate your points by describing how a social venture that is carried out by a single organization might be improved through collaboration.

Exercise 10.2

How can participation in a network benefit social entrepreneurship? How might participation in a network be more beneficial for social entrepreneurship than participating in an interorganizational collaboration? Use your example from Exercise 10.1 to illustrate your points.

Exercise 10.3

What benefits would a for-profit–nonprofit hybrid structure provide for social entrepreneurship? What challenges or difficulties might this structure need to address? Illustrate your points with an example.

New Media and Social Entrepreneurship

Invisible Children is a San Diego-based nonprofit advocacy organization dedicated to bringing awareness to the activities of indicted Ugandan war criminal Joseph Kony. The organization was founded by three young filmmakers—Jason Russell, Bobby Bailey, and Laren Poole—after they traveled to Africa in the spring of 2003 and were shocked by what they saw in Northern Uganda: children displaced and fearful of being forced into service for a rogue militant group. Upon returning in the summer, they produced a documentary, *Invisible Children: Rough Cut*, which was well received. Based on the outpouring of support and their own desire to make a difference, they formed Invisible Children, Inc., an advocacy organization that according to the mission statement "uses film, creativity, and social action to end the use of child soldiers in Joseph Kony's rebel war and restore Northern Uganda to peace and prosperity."

On March 5, 2012, Invisible Children started an Internet video campaign called *Kony 2012*. The goal of the short film was to make Kony so notorious internationally that he would be arrested by year's end. Within three days, the *Kony 2012* video quickly became one of the greatest viral successes in the short history of social media, drawing millions of viewers on YouTube. Within three weeks, it spurred action on Capitol Hill: over one third of U.S. senators introduced a bipartisan resolution condemning Kony and his troops for "unconscionable crimes against humanity."

The *Kony 2012* film also called on young people to "cover the night" on April 20, a worldwide canvassing campaign in which engaged supporters were to place posters in public areas and at their homes to raise more awareness to stop Kony's atrocities. However, as one commentator observed, "That date has now come and gone, and the actual turnout—almost everywhere—was lackluster and desultory. Some 3.5 million people had pledged or signed up with Invisible Children to participate in 'cover the night' activities, but the planned blanketing of communities with Kony posters, murals, and stickers doesn't seem to have happened on the massive scale first expected, as the enthusiasm waned after the release of the video on March 8, 2012."[1]

A telling example of the attention span of the public on this topic was described in an NPR story: on the day that was supposed to be designated as "cover the night," young people at William & Mary had moved on to the next internet viral phenomenon: a world record–breaking public spooning event. An organizer of the public spooning event explained their strategy for organizing the event: "We didn't start advertising this until this week, because we didn't want to kill the buzz. So many things are so viral and go by so quickly, it's harder than ever to keep people's attention." As of April 19, 2012, 625 people had "liked" the spooning event listing on Facebook, whereas the Kony 2012 William & Mary page had just sixteen likes.[2]

Public support for the cause on social media came and went like a fast-moving thunderstorm.

On April 5, 2012, Invisible Children released a follow-up video, titled *Kony 2012: Part II—Beyond Famous*. It garnered less than 1 percent of the viewership of the original. The failure to repeat the success of the original video clearly indicated that the campaign had lost its momentum.

INTRODUCTION

In the course of just two decades, the Internet and social media have quickly become an inseparable part of our lives. As of 2012, more than 2.4 billion people—over a third of the world's human population—had used the services of the Internet. As of 2013, Facebook, a leading social networking site founded by several Harvard University students in February 2004, boasted over one billion active users, and Twitter, an online social networking and microblogging service that enables its users to send and read brief text-based messages, had over five hundred million registered users and generated over 340 million tweets on a daily basis.[3]

These new media channels have greatly enhanced the ability of both citizens and organizations to engage in meaningful interactions in cyberspace. On the citizen side, the incredible democratization of information and the access to advanced web-based technologies have fundamentally changed not only the way we shop, work, socialize, interact, and play, but also the way we learn and get our information. On the organizational side, the Internet and social media enable organizations not only to self-disclose organizational information but also to target, mobilize, and interact with their constituents in ways not possible in other situations or through other media.[4]

This chapter examines how this rapid diffusion of new media generates new possibilities for social entrepreneurship—and poses new challenges. The Internet and social media have provided new convening platforms for public and nonprofit organizations to communicate with multiple stakeholders, coordinate work within and across organizational boundaries, and fundraise and advocate for social causes. We examine the various ways in which social entrepreneurs are experimenting with using social media for social good. We then introduce the notion of "attention philanthropy" and its implications for social entrepreneurship.

NEW MEDIA, NEW POSSIBILITIES

The direct, efficient, and low-cost features of the Internet renders it an important alternative broadcast and communication medium for organizations in the public and nonprofit sectors, especially those organizations that are small and resource-poor.[5] As individuals rely more and more on the Internet as their primary information source, they can decide which nonprofit to give to, volunteer with, and interact with, based on the online presentation of the nonprofit.[6] Evidence has shown that the amount of disclosure provided by an organization on its website, especially disclosure of performance and annual reports, increases the level of charitable contributions to the organization.[7] The Internet also offers dialogic interaction (or two-way communication), a highly engaging function that leads to meaningful and rigorous exchanges and transactions between the nonprofit and its stakeholders.[8]

Furthermore, based on the sophisticated interactivity made available by Web 2.0, social media such as blogs, MySpace, Cyworld, Twitter, and Facebook offer a low-cost and user-friendly alternative for the public to participate in discussion with larger audiences and draw attention to issues that might otherwise have been ignored by traditional mass media. Social networking sites like Facebook and Twitter are free and have built-in interactivity, so organizations of any size can create a site and start building a network of friends and followers with whom they are in almost real-time contact. With social media, organizations can develop dialogic interactions with interested publics, including donors, supporters, clients, and the media.[9]

Social media can be broadly defined as internet- and mobile-based technologies that allow for the creation and exchange of user-generated material. Beyond this general definition, there are various types of social media. Researchers Kaplan and Haenlein have created a classification scheme based on the two key dimensions that form the term "social media."[10] The media dimension concerns the richness of the media (the amount of information the media allow to be transmitted in a given time interval in order to resolve ambiguity and uncertainty) and the degree of social presence (that is, the acoustic, visual, and physical contact that can be achieved) that the media allow to emerge between two communication partners. The social dimension looks at the degree of self-disclosure (that is, the conscious or unconscious revelation of personal information such as thoughts, feelings, likes, and dislikes that is consistent with the image one would like to present) that the media require and the type of self-presentation they allow.

The juxtaposition of both dimensions results in a typology of social media visualized in Figure 11.1. Along the dimension of social presence and media richness, applications such as collaborative projects (such as Wikipedia) and blogs are at the low end of the continuum, as they are often text-based and therefore only allow for a relatively simple exchange. Content communities (such as YouTube) and social networking sites (such as Facebook) lie

Figure 11.1
Classification of Social Media

	Social presence/Media richness		
Self-presentation/Self-disclosure	**Low**	**Medium**	**High**
High	Blogs	Social networking sites (e.g., Facebook)	Virtual social worlds (e.g., Second Life)
Low	Collaborative projects (e.g., Wikipedia)	Content communities (e.g., YouTube)	Virtual game worlds (e.g., World of Warcraft)

Source: Kaplan & Haenlein (2010).

somewhere in the middle of the continuum, as they not only provide text-based communication but also enable the sharing of pictures, videos, and other forms of media. On the high end of the continuum are virtual game and social worlds (such as World of Warcraft and Second Life), which attempt to replicate all dimensions of face-to-face interactions in a virtual environment. In the area of self-presentation and self-disclosure, blogs usually score higher than collaborative projects, as the latter tend to be focused on specific content domains. Similarly, social networking sites such as Facebook allow for more self-disclosure than content communities like YouTube. Finally, virtual social worlds require a higher level of self-disclosure than virtual game worlds, as the latter are ruled by strict guidelines that force users to behave in a certain way.[11]

With the introduction of Web 2.0, the entire premise of the Internet changed. It became much more participatory and collaborative. Users are not just consumers of information on the Internet anymore; websites are designed to be user-centered and interactive. People have also become contributors through virtual communities, blogs, video sharing, and social media platforms, which further facilitate the creation and sharing of user-generated content and communication among individuals, businesses, nonprofits, and even governments.

MYTHS AND REALITIES ABOUT SOCIAL MEDIA

In a recent study, researchers Ogden and Starita provide an overview of myths and realities about the use of social media among nonprofit organizations:[12]

- *"It's free."* In reality, while it is "free" to join social media platforms, it takes a great deal of time and resources to actually use the tools.

- *"Everyone is doing it."* In reality, the more that people use social media the more difficult and expensive it becomes to rise above the noise.

- *"It's another channel to reach people."* In reality, yes, it offers a new channel, but none of the older channels are yet going away. So now the organization must keep using all the old channels plus the new channels.

- *"It's the way to reach the next generation."* In reality, the benefits of reaching the next generation now through social media are still unclear.

- *"You can build relationships with donors and volunteers."* In reality, there is no evidence yet that social networking creates lasting relationships.

- *"You must act, or you'll be left behind."* In reality, in most technology revolutions there is little downside to waiting for best practices to emerge.

Although nonprofits are starting to adopt the new channel of social media to change how they communicate, coordinate, advocate, and fundraise, some organizations have yet to adopt social media applications. Resource constraints and organizational culture may explain the existence of laggards. Despite the cost efficiency of social media, the maintenance of an updated presence is time consuming and may create extra administrative loads, which indicates that the organization needs to allocate more resources to it. Moreover, not every nonprofit has an inclination to conduct two-way communication with their stakeholders or the public. They may instead put a priority on fundraising, advocacy, or memberships to meet their strategic goals.[13]

Social media can be an efficient medium for the organization to reach and engage multiple stakeholders. In fact, what best distinguishes the second generation of web technologies is precisely its ability to facilitate intense interactions between actors. Interactive blogs, discussion lists, bulletin boards, real-time consultations, online training, virtual conferences, personalizable intranets and extranets, and social networking software can play a valuable role in strengthening bonds, building trust, and communicating strategically with key stakeholders. More recently, the increasing popularity of collaborative wikis, online surveying and polling tools, and tagging and social bookmarking projects has facilitated intense, decentralized, and highly participatory problem-solving, decision-making, brainstorming, and knowledge-creation efforts.

Prior research identifies three key communicative functions in social media messages (such as tweets and Facebook status updates) sent by nonprofit organizations:[14]

- *Information.* The "information" function covers messages that spread information about the organization's activities, highlights from events, or other news, facts, reports, or anything of potential interest to an organization's stakeholders.

- *Community.* The "community" function covers messages that serve to interact, share, and converse with stakeholders in a way that fosters relationships, creates networks, and ultimately builds an online community.

- *Action.* The "action" function covers messages that aim to get stakeholders to "do something" for the organization—anything from donating money or buying T-shirts to attending events and launching advocacy campaigns.

Consistent with these three key functions, we next discuss how new media can help social entrepreneurs further their cause.

NEW MEDIA AND INFORMATION SHARING

One main area in which social entrepreneurs have a large potential to use these kinds of services is information sharing. As mission-driven organizations rely on the public trust, it is vitally important for social entrepreneurs to communicate their activities to stakeholders. Social media allow organizations to accomplish this via Facebook, which provides unlimited daily updates, and Twitter, which can provide minute-by-minute updates—say, during a crisis—using a hashtag (for example, #redcross will bring up every tweet that anyone has sent out containing that term). The user-focused and user-generated information makes the cause much more personal, and it is a great tool for getting information disseminated.

Social media like Facebook, Twitter, and others are an important way for nonprofit organizations to "push" information to the masses. For example,

Athens Nurses Clinic has a Facebook page that fans can Like and follow. The director purposely uploads a new picture and makes a post about the work of the clinic every other day in order to keep the Nurses Clinic in the cycle of their fans' newsfeeds. Having this continuous information flow also provides a "pull" for fans to check the page often and see what updates the clinic has made. Volunteers may see their pictures posted; donors can see the outcomes of their donations for clinic patients.

Social media also make marketing a significantly more time-consuming task and lead to a new role for a public relations director. Instead of simply issuing a press release to a local newspaper about a big event, an organization now must also update the website, post on Facebook, tweet about it, send an email to all the organization's stakeholders, and write a blog about the news—and must do all of these tasks for small events too. It can be more than a full-time job managing all the media outlets now available.

Text4baby offers an interesting example. Text4baby is a mobile information service designed to promote maternal and child health. The idea seems simple: "all you need to do is send a text message to the number 511411 with the word BABY or BEBE (for Spanish messages). You will be prompted for your due date or your child's birth date, and your zip code, and immediately, you will begin receiving three messages a week offering actionable, evidence-based information relevant to your stage in pregnancy or your child's development."[15] This text4baby service is provided for free to its clients, and is made possible through the support of the Wireless Foundation as well as cell phone companies. This is the beauty of marrying new media to social entrepreneurship: taking something simple and harnessing it in a way that is helpful to other people or creating something people want.

NEW MEDIA AND FUNDRAISING

The Pew Research Center's Internet & American Life Project has documented, through years of polling, that the number of people who donate online has grown consistently over the last two decades. Findings show that one in five U.S. adults (20%) today have made a charitable donation online, and that one in ten (9%) have made a charitable donation using the text messaging feature on their mobile phone. Not surprisingly, the number of political campaigns and advocacy groups that have purposefully developed an online fundraising mechanism has also increased.

Web 2.0 and social media are also great ways to expand in order to gain interested parties for donations. Throughout all of the social media applications, great governance and accountability gains can be made. Therefore social media and Web 2.0 should be a part of all nonprofit strategic planning in order to keep up with the times.

Recently, American Express and Twitter linked up to offer American Express cardholders a new way to shop: they sync their card with their Twitter accounts, and they can purchase items using specially created #hashtags. An organization called Chirpify offers nonprofits a way to fundraise; all that people have to do is tweet back with certain words and the amount they want to donate using PayPal. Chirpify has created an easy way to integrate our constant use of social media as a platform for a new social enterprise and a new stream for fundraising for nonprofits.[16]

Through social media, MoveOn.org has successfully mobilized fundraising and grassroots action in the United States for both political candidates and political issues. MoveOn's online communications blend website and social media formats and seamlessly combine the mobilization of local groups (called "councils") with coordinated fundraising appeals. Most important, MoveOn has demonstrated a sustained ability to financially support the election of candidates friendly to its policy positions. On the conservative side, the Tea Party movement also reflects an ability to use social media to harness decentralized social networks in order to mobilize support (volunteer and financial) for endorsed candidates. Additionally, issue advocacy organizations, such as environmental groups, and organizations that engage in both charitable work and advocacy activities, such as organizations that serve the disabled or other target populations, also use social media for fundraising in conjunction with community-building messages and content.

NEW MEDIA AND STAKEHOLDER ENGAGEMENT

New media offer social entrepreneurs fresh ways to get their message across. If they were to harness the potential of the engagement tools social media offer, the possibilities would be limitless. For example, some American Red Cross (ARC) chapters craftily use social media to keep their community-based AmeriCorps interns responsive to the needs of the local community. The interns manage a microblog that offers ongoing, journal-style daily accounts of the work of the

ARC in Southeast Louisiana. When a fire breaks out or a minor disaster requires the response of the ARC, this team of online journalists acts as one of the first responders.[17] Nonprofit managers could reap bountiful lessons from this style of online engagement. The organization is inadvertently highlighting how well they serve their mission in the community with every updated blog entry.

As new media have changed the landscape of communication for almost all organizations, including nonprofits, it has brought both opportunities to seize and threats to manage. First, new media have greatly increased an organization's opportunity for external exposure, publicity, and communication. It is focused on being a forum for two-way communication, which gives nonprofits an opportunity to go beyond promoting themselves to engage in a conversation with stakeholders. One nonprofit that does a good job of engaging stakeholders through new media is Compassion International, a Christian child sponsorship organization through which donors can sponsor children living in poverty to support their long-term development. Compassion engages people through its Facebook page, Twitter account, blog, and interactive website. In addition to asking for donations and sponsorships, it makes things personal by providing encouraging updates on the progress of sponsored children; highlights about exceptional staff, volunteers, and donors; links to interesting articles related to poverty; and more. The Compassion website allows potential sponsors to browse pictures and descriptions of children awaiting sponsorship, and it provides a platform for donors to write letters to their sponsored child online, a method more familiar and convenient than pen and paper for many in this age of email and electronic devices.

New media create an expanded public relations role, but they also have other major managerial and governance consequences. Web 2.0 tools like Google Docs can encourage collaboration among organizations or even facilitate work between different departments of the same organization, whether they are in the same geographic location or not. Web-based solutions for financial and program management abound, like QuickBooks or a diabetes state management software that a nonprofit health network purchases for its member clinics to provide its diabetes programming in each of the clinics. Programs like Skype are useful in connecting people who cannot be in the same physical location, which could facilitate more attendance and engagement at board or membership meetings of a nonprofit.

A "PYRAMID" MODEL OF SOCIAL MEDIA–BASED STRATEGY

Guo and Saxton present a pyramid model of social media-based advocacy that entails a three-stage process.[18] Through inductive analyses, they identify a series of new types of social media-based advocacy work, which they grouped into three broader categories that form the basis for an original pyramid model of social media-based advocacy. This hierarchical model entails a three-stage process: (1) reaching out to people, (2) keeping the flame alive, and (3) stepping up to action. The organization first reaches out to current and potential supporters and raises awareness of the organization's cause. Once a constituency is built, the next step is to sustain the constituency and keep alive the flame of passion among supporters. When the timing is right, the final step is to mobilize the supporters to act. The hierarchy implicit in the model reflects how each successive layer of the model is built on the one below. Given the greater number of messages at the earlier stages, the three elements of social media–based advocacy can be depicted as a pyramid (Figure 11.2).

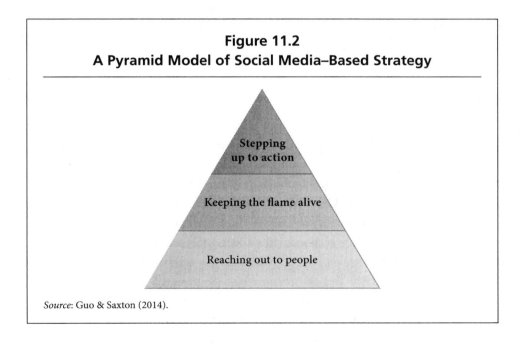

Figure 11.2
A Pyramid Model of Social Media–Based Strategy

Stepping up to action

Keeping the flame alive

Reaching out to people

Source: Guo & Saxton (2014).

Though the three components represent "stages," all three can happen simultaneously—the stage is conceived with respect to the organization's relationship with a specific group of stakeholders at any given time. In the fluid social media environment, an organization must always be seeking to reach out to new audiences (stage one), deepen that audience's knowledge and sustain its interest (stage two), and then motivate it to act (stage three). In other words, the organization is always cultivating and organizing new supporters. In effect, it is a model of mobilization-driven relationship-building—a model for how organizations can generate and mobilize network support through communicative relationship-building strategies.

This pyramid model of mobilization-driven relationship-building offers a framework for understanding the process through which social entrepreneurs use targeted stakeholder communication on social media to further their cause. The model is descriptive rather than normative, in that it aims to describe how the function of social media *actually* varies with the stage of the engagement process, not how it *should* vary. At stage one, the organization's priority is to reach out and bring awareness of the cause to the public. At stage two, the priority becomes sustaining communities of interest and networks of supporters. At stage three, the priority becomes mobilization, be that a request for donations or a call to action.

NEW MEDIA, NEW CHALLENGES

New media have also posed new challenges. We live in an increasingly information-saturated world, characterized by the twenty-four-hour news cycle, countless social media outlets, and the wealth of information at our fingertips. In the nonprofit sector, organizations' increasing transparency and disclosure adds to the glut of information. Compounding matters is the increasing prevalence of "information intermediaries" such as GuideStar and rating agencies such as Charity Navigator, all of which provide additional venues for organizational information. For social entrepreneurs who are working on an innovative solution to a social problem, the campaign must be pursued on multiple fronts. Beyond the traditional off-line fundraising and the website, a nonprofit might be involved in raising money on Facebook Causes or on numerous "crowdfunding" sites such as GoFundMe, Kickstarter, or Crowdrise.

With the wealth of information on any given organization that is now available, the "problem" for the philanthropist is no longer *information asymmetry*, in the sense of the donor or philanthropist not having enough information on the organization's mission, projects, or performance. Rather, the challenge becomes *information overload*. Put differently, the information environment of nonprofit organizations has changed. It is markedly "richer," yet more difficult to navigate. With so much to look at but limited information-processing capacity, there is an attention deficit problem: for the philanthropist, it can be difficult to know where to pay attention; and for the organization, it can be difficult to capture and hold the philanthropist's attention.

Welcome to the age of *attention philanthropy*. To understand the characteristics and boundaries of this new concept, it is helpful to define the term "attention philanthropy" as understood by various researchers. Guo and Saxton define attention philanthropy as "philanthropy in which all players (e.g. donors, funders, supporters, nonprofits, etc.) are potentially overwhelmed by information overload and confronted with the challenges of attention deficit."[19] Shenk defines attention philanthropy as the "gift of notice" whereby organizations facilitate getting good ideas and noble enterprises noticed in the first place.[20] Steffen defines it as the process of "shining a light on work that's worth supporting, yet falls outside the notice of the usual sources of acclaim."[21] In summary, these definitions share an acknowledgment of the problem of information overload for consumers of nonprofit organizations; however, they differ as to the source of these problems.

Given the altered information landscape, attention philanthropy has as its starting point the problem of attention deficit. Donors and supporters today pay attention to a much wider variety of organizations than they used to. Yet this wider scope of attention comes with a price: their attention to any particular organization is necessarily diluted. This attention dilution is manifested in several main aspects of philanthropy. In terms of charitable giving, a dramatic increase in the number of nonprofits in recent years has triggered a heated debate among donors and funders: some lament that the nonprofit sector is becoming a cottage industry and that there are too many nonprofits to choose from, whereas others see this growth as "a sign of vitality and creativity."[22] Both sides are aware of the reality that nonprofits are competing with each other more strongly than ever for attention from donors and funders. In terms of volunteering, a notable trend is the growing popularity of "episodic" or short-term volunteering:[23] this trend, along with the decline in the number of volunteers in recent years, raises concerns about the ability of nonprofit leaders to get volunteers to pay attention to their organizations.

The problem of attention dilution in philanthropy has two possible broad implications. First, there is less predictability in who gets attention. This month it could be child soldiers in Uganda; next month it could be strip mining in West Virginia. More likely, it will be a large-scale famine or natural disaster like the Haitian earthquake of 2010. While these catastrophes are definitely worthy of garnering our attention and support, they have a tendency to divert our support from smaller, but still very important local causes. Attention philanthropy seems to exacerbate these issues. Second, and perhaps more important, donors and supporters may be more likely to notice attention-grabbing stories and "focusing events" such as natural disasters and crises. This tendency is consistent with the observation that nonprofits often rely on anecdotal, personalized stories and narratives, rather than systematic evaluations, to convey organizational performance to the public.[24] Such a tendency is particularly strong in the context of online giving.

In effect, attention philanthropy presents opportunities as well as challenges for nonprofit leaders. Leaders must be more vigilant than before in innovating new ways to reach their target audiences if they hope to gain support. An excellent example can be seen in TOMS Shoes, a shoe company with a charitable mission ("for every pair sold, a new pair will be donated to a child in need of shoes"). Although the company famously spends very little on formal channels of advertising, they have developed a unique grassroots marketing approach that involves a series of attention-grabbing events, such as the "One Day without Shoes" campaign. These clever strategies have exposed many people to the TOMS message in a unique way that is bound to stay with them, and which is crucial to TOMS' business and philanthropic success. Since TOMS launched in 2006, over a million pairs of shoes have been given to children in more than twenty countries.[25]

The excess of information available on the Internet can serve crucial marketing purposes. Take, for example, the creative marketing used by supporters of the Susan G. Komen for the Cure Foundation on Facebook every October during Breast Cancer Awareness Month. Komen is already known for creative marketing tactics, and, in spite of some bad press in 2012,[26] the organization does a great job of gaining attention through social media like Facebook. In years past, a viral Facebook phenomenon of unknown origin encouraged women to (mysteriously) state where they like to leave their purse when they walk in the door. The status posts, reading "I like it on the floor" or "I like it on the kitchen counter" get people talking. As more women become aware of the status messages, they post their own, causing curiosity and spreading the discussion. In the first year of this exercise in viral marketing, the tactic apparently funneled 140,000 new fans to the official Susan G. Komen Facebook page.[27] Though Komen did not take credit for the phenomenon, the organization embraced it. "We think it's terrific," a spokeswoman for Komen said at the time. "It's a terrific example of how little things get started on the Internet and go a long way to raise cancer awareness."[28]

The challenge of attention philanthropy for social entrepreneurs, which is tied to attention deficit, becomes twofold: rising above all of the other potential sources of information through creativity and ingenuity, and turning that attention into action. The key for a nonprofit like Komen is to take the fleeting attention of Facebook status posts and inspire some sort of activity. Though the Internet allows people to become informed quickly and easily, it also enables "armchair activism" or "slacktivism." In this regard *Kony 2012* again serves as a good example. Though the video got millions of views on Facebook, critics alleged that the campaign would do little to cause real change.[29]

Bonk writes about the crucial role that strategic communications can play in developing nonprofits—with a particular emphasis on targeted audiences reached through targeted messages.[30] Because of the Internet, media are becoming stratified, and the ways that people find information—news or otherwise—are diversifying and becoming more specialized. Gainer makes the point that, while marketing tends to be a one-way relationship in the for-profit world (businesses communicate to consumers), marketing is a two-party exchange in the nonprofit world.[31] But this means that the process of receiving information can become a lot more fun for the recipient—and it opens up new avenues for engagement. Facebook and Twitter give people the opportunity to interact with this information—and to become mobile, freelance marketers of the causes they care about. It adds to the information at our disposal, yes, but it also provides a way for the rest of us to sort through information by seeing what our Facebook friends and Twitter followers are discussing, promoting, or criticizing.

One way to combat the attention deficit problem is to get better at reaching the audience that has the problem. Good, targeted communication is important. Allowing for two-way exchange should open up new avenues for involvement by those people who stumble across the shallow, surface-level information that is easily available. Beneath the surface of the creative, fun, eye-catching message, there must be incrementally more deeply involved opportunities for engagement and for learning and retrieving information. Once someone reposts a Facebook status, there should be follow-up that encourages the signing of petitions or a visit to the nonprofit's website. From there, nonprofits can encourage particular ways of donating time or money and encouraging others to do so. The opportunities to transition from shallow to deeper levels of engagement must be seamless, and they must be simple—one click.

Yet it can be difficult for organizations to know how much of their very limited resources to dedicate to attention philanthropy. Should you hire a web specialist? A public relations guru? A consulting firm with revolutionary ideas, along the lines of Worldchanging?[32] This will surely cost a hefty sum, and results are never guaranteed. Even if an organization is successful in getting attention from a lot of people, its own success can be its biggest failing, as individuals can be overloaded with your message—which could cause apathy or even a backlash toward the organization and the mission. It seems that over the past few years this has slowly been happening to the cause of breast cancer awareness. More specifically, the color pink, representing the cause is seen everywhere in our daily lives, from soup cans to NFL football jerseys. Although the marketing may raise attention, some feel that this is not enough, as the campaign has not contributed to serious progress in prevention and treatment of the disease. Many believe that the real problems of breast cancer and the mission of associated charities have gotten lost in all the pink advertising, as the public succumbs to "pink fatigue."[33]

This scenario could have dire consequences for social entrepreneurs themselves, as they become so wrapped up in attention philanthropy and the associated byproducts, like marketing, that they lose their sense of why they are there in the first place. This sounds like it is already happening in the case of some breast cancer charities; they are putting all their efforts into grabbing attention, yet their mission of eradicating breast cancer is taking a back seat.

Guo and Saxton attribute the problem of getting organizations to notice information overload and individual challenges of coping with all of the information—that is, attention deficit. Steffen, on the other hand, attributes the real problem to the gatekeepers of attention in the media, political, and philanthropic spheres. He cites as evidence the fact that those experts who are charged with evaluating nonprofits—the gatekeepers—are unable to sufficiently evaluate the innovations and new ideas of outsiders to the benefit of their colleagues and protégées. This sets the boundary for the extent of attention deficit when it comes to philanthropy. Donors and funders may not suffer from attention deficit when it comes to established organizations because not only do they have the name recognition of established nonprofits, but they also have "gatekeepers" like GuideStar or Charity Navigator to filter information. However, attention deficit does come into play for organizations that are new and have not sufficiently established themselves. New expert evaluators might be necessary to facilitate communication with new innovative nonprofits and overcome the consumers' attention deficit. Therefore, organizations like Worldchanging, RealClimate, GOOD, SciDev, Global Voices, and NextBillion may be necessary to capture the energetic, youthful, and engaged audiences looking to find innovative nonprofits.[34]

Not all new innovative ventures are equally viable or worthy of investment, and there is still a need to filter. Steffen shares this view, noting that a system that aggregates votes may devolve into a zero-sum popularity contest wherein popularity is not a measure of effectiveness or viability. Steffen's suggestion to control this process calls for "curated participation," in which experts may make suggestions for attention philanthropy based on their reputation. Their reputations depend on the users who support them, their contributions to the site, or being referred by a reputable member of the site. This process sets up a mini-democratic process in which the best and brightest trend-spotters could be utilized while still including input from the masses. The implication for social entrepreneurs is that their popularity and viability may be more easily recognized if they have merit, even if more traditional gatekeeper organizations overlook them.

This strategy of coping with attention deficit by using attention philanthropy websites has strengths and weaknesses. It has strength because it is more flexible and can publicize nonprofits that are on the cutting edge of innovation. It also allows other interested parties to help craft these innovative strategies and builds a base of supporters once the project gets established. It provides a way for consumers to deal with attention deficit by having an expert as an intermediary. However, this approach is problematic, because the criteria for selection of these cutting-edge organizations are neither systematic nor clearly defined. Relying on the reputation of an expert is not that far removed from relying on a popular vote.

Social entrepreneurs can conquer attention deficit by being viable and innovative, and by crafting legitimate solutions to problems of public concern. If they have a forum to make themselves presentable to a larger audience—that is, if they have a legitimate gatekeeper—attention deficit can be conquered. Whether by using evaluators like GuideStar or Charity Navigator, or attention philanthropy websites like Worldchanging, or a future iteration of any of these, social entrepreneurs and nonprofit leaders must find the best ways to make themselves marketable to a large audience while at the same time maintaining their reputations as legitimate. This balancing act—maintaining popularity, credibility, and legitimacy—needs constant attention as strategies are developed for communicating and working with key stakeholders in the community.

CONCLUDING THOUGHTS

Social entrepreneurs and nonprofit leaders need to be cognizant of the important role that social networking sites provide for their causes. More and more people all over the world depend on the Internet for information, and an organization with a poor online showing will not stand much of a chance of surviving long enough to carry out its mission. When it comes to attention philanthropy, nonprofit leaders must be careful not to put all their eggs in one basket. It is still important to keep a focus on attracting donors, volunteers, staff, and board members in the old-fashioned way. This includes phone calls, word of mouth, and especially face-to-face meetings. Ultimately, a tweet or a Facebook "Like" is not going to pay for the services that a charity provides or satisfy the volunteers enough to keep them coming back.

In decades past, it was harder to achieve a critical mass of support for a cause as Invisible Children did with the *Kony 2012* push. However, if an organization was successful, the success lasted long enough to achieve serious results. The aid to Ethiopian famine victims in the mid-1980s is a case in point. Before the Internet, organizers used radio, MTV, and massive concerts like Live Aid to raise awareness and money to help starving people in Africa. This philanthropic venture was so successful that it is still being talked about—even being replicated—over twenty-five years later. Yet, our TVs and radios did not have the capability to bombard us with thousands of causes that our computers and smartphones have today. It is nearly impossible to concentrate on just one thing when there is that much information at our fingertips. Hence, if social entrepreneurs and nonprofits want to achieve big results in awareness and donations, they cannot depend on social media alone.

EXERCISES

Exercise 11.1

What are the three stages of the pyramid model of social media–based strategy? Use an example to illustrate the three stages. Then identify a social venture that has been relying on traditional tools and platforms for advocacy and relationship building, and propose a social media–based strategy to improve its advocacy coverage and organizational effectiveness.

Exercise 11.2

What is "attention philanthropy"? What are its implications and the consequences for social entrepreneurs? Illustrate your points with an example.

Exercise 11.3

How can organizations adapt to the new information environment without losing their sense of mission? Identify a social venture that you consider has adapted well to the new information era but still kept its original mission. Describe in specific detail one or two initiatives of the venture.

CONCLUSION: THE ROAD TRAVELED AND THE JOURNEY AHEAD

This book set out to provide a critical overview and assessment of the rapidly growing field of social entrepreneurship, and to offer social entrepreneurs and innovators the necessary knowledge, tools, and skillsets to tackle some of the most difficult problems in our society.

We have taken a theory-based approach that draws extensively on the existing entrepreneurship and innovation literatures. In particular, we have followed the spirit of evidence-based management to educate current and future social entrepreneurs in evidence-based practices. We believe that such an approach is most effective not only in helping students understand the potentials and limits of social entrepreneurship but also in preparing students to find innovative solutions to social problems.

This focus on the use of research and scientific evidence to guide practice echoes organization scholars Herbert A. Simon's and Andrew H. Van de Ven's view that scholars and educators in professional schools such as management, public administration, and social work should "conduct research that contributes knowledge to a scientific discipline, on the one hand, and . . . apply that knowledge to the practice of management as a profession, on the other."[1] Viewed through this lens, "nothing is so practical as a good theory."[2]

THE TAKEAWAYS

In this section, we highlight some of key points and important takeaways from this book.

Social Mission Is the Compass of Social Entrepreneurship

Public and nonprofit organizations need to experiment with new ideas and promote innovative initiatives in order to accomplish their social mission. However, it is important to remember that being innovative and proactive is just a means to an end—the social mission. Notwithstanding the value of developing new sources of revenue and finding creative ways of supporting the work of the organization, such social entrepreneurial initiatives should be designed and implemented without losing sight of mission.

The centrality of mission is clearly demonstrated in the construct of social entrepreneurial orientation (SEO), introduced in Chapter Two. Serving as an indicator of an organization's propensity to engage in social entrepreneurship, SEO consists of three relatively independent dimensions: the degree of entrepreneurship, the frequency of entrepreneurship, and the alignment with social mission. A major implication of this construct is that SEO varies across organizations and by dimension: an organization can display a high degree and frequency of entrepreneurship but still rank low in terms of mission alignment. For example, for those organizations that engage in earned-income ventures, a healthy dose of self-sufficiency increases security about their future capabilities and therefore should be encouraged. Yet a preoccupation with business ventures may lead to mission drift, wherein the businesses are tempted to change their mission according to their commercial bottom line rather than keep it focused on the cause.

Another implication of the SEO construct is that a mission-driven organization cannot always be social entrepreneurial: SEO can change over time and according to the life stage of the organization. During its early years, for example, a start-up job training agency might actively experiment with a variety of innovative programs and services in an effort to identify the most effective model for placing noncustodial parents in jobs, thus demonstrating a higher degree of SEO along all three dimensions. Upon receiving feedback on these exploratory initiatives, the organization might decide to focus on one or two programs or services that prove to be most cost-effective for accomplishing their goals and objectives. As a result, the organization's SEO will decline in subsequent years, which is only natural as the organization progresses toward a mature stage and builds its core competency. Throughout the process, however, it is always important for the organization to be mindful of mission alignment.

Social Entrepreneurship Is Opportunity Driven

Opportunity development clearly stands out as a vital step in social entrepreneurship. Every social entrepreneurial organization or initiative begins with the identification of an opportunity. In Chapters Three and Four, we have discussed the process by which social entrepreneurs identify a social entrepreneurial opportunity and implement the opportunity by establishing a new organization (that is, an independent start-up). We have discussed possible theories about how individuals go about the process, as well as the implications for practitioners, educators, and researchers in the field. Entrepreneurship, especially social entrepreneurship, remains a field of which we still have an incomplete picture. However, the current research provides a firm foundation and a clear direction for future research.

We have identified several important steps toward the successful launch of a social entrepreneurial organization: recognizing an innovative opportunity, evaluating benefits and costs of exploiting the opportunity, and developing a plausible business model that includes an effective operating model and a viable resource strategy. While these steps are helpful for planning purposes, the actual process of turning an opportunity into a viable program or organization does not necessarily follow these steps in a sequential order. In reality, the pursuit of an entrepreneurial initiative is often more organic and opportunistic, and entrepreneurs are usually in the right place at the right time and prepared to exploit the situation. The process is not so much subject to tight planning and control as it is to adept adaptation to circumstances and good timing.

Social Entrepreneurship Is Not the Patent of Start-Up Organizations

Most of the current scholarly and practitioner-related literature has focused primarily on start-up organizations. However, large and established organizations can be social entrepreneurial, too. In an effort to learn more about "how to make an elephant dance," we have spent two chapters looking into the process of social intrapreneurship; that is, the processes and mechanisms by which social entrepreneurial opportunities emerge and develop into new programs, services, and ventures in an existing organization.

A unique challenge in managing the social intrapreneurial process is to strike an appropriate balance between exploratory and exploitative opportunities. The former are unrelated or only marginally related to an organization's core competency; the latter are related. Large and established organizations tend to favor exploitative opportunities because these opportunities are inside their comfort zone: the chance of success is higher when a homeless shelter develops an innovative initiative in collaboration with a local restaurant to add nutritious meal items to the offerings of its soup kitchen, because the nutritious meal service is closely related to its core competency (sheltering and soup kitchen); the chance of success is much lower if the homeless shelter decides to pursue an opportunity that would help homeless individuals and families to start small businesses. Yet although it seems safer in the short run to stay inside the comfort zone, that becomes problematic in the long run as the organization falls prey to a competency trap.[3] We highlight the crucial role of middle managers in the social intrapreneurial process: not only are they responsible for identifying an exploratory opportunity and obtaining relevant information, but they also must be able to sell the opportunity to top management for further exploitation.

Social Entrepreneurship Is Not Confined to a Particular Sector

Although most of the discussions in this book focus on organizations in the nonprofit sector, the key concepts, theories, and principles can potentially be applied to understanding social entrepreneurial behavior in other sectors. In Chapter Nine, we directed the reader's attention to social entrepreneurship in the public sector. We identified the unique challenges and opportunities, as well as recent practices and future trends to promote public sector entrepreneurship. In Chapter Ten, we extended the discussion to social entrepreneurship that spans organizational and sector boundaries, and we examined how individuals and organizations work across sector boundaries to develop innovative solutions. Such boundary-spanning initiatives are increasingly important, as more complex problems require the collective efforts and commitments of nonprofits, government agencies, businesses, and communities. By working together, organizations and sectors become more effective social problem solvers and maximize their social impact.

FURTHER QUESTIONS

Our book also touches on some additional questions, but very briefly. Here, we list these questions for further consideration.

• *What are the pitfalls of the hybridization of social entrepreneurship (blending of for-profit and non-profit)?* Does this desire to thoroughly integrate concepts from the for-profit sector and yet maintain a nonprofit-like mission pose a threat to the validity of a social enterprise? And where do we draw the line between money-making entity and social change agent? The concept of a double bottom line was discussed earlier in the book, and it is useful to think further about the factors influencing these lines. In an ideal world, we could always make a profit while also receiving social returns on the investment. However, what happens when the two bottom lines clash with each other? As social entrepreneurs, what do we fall back on when forced to make a tough choice between financial and social benefits?

• *How can we learn from entrepreneurial failures?* When speaking of social entrepreneurs, we tend to refer to those individuals who are *successful* in their attempts at new, innovative responses to social problems. People can participate in that process without succeeding in their efforts, but does that make them less of a social entrepreneur? Thomas Edison famously failed thousands of times before he successfully invented the first commercially practical incandescent light. By learning from our past mistakes, we better understand our opportunities and can more fully develop innovative solutions. If we want to better understand the social entrepreneurial process, it may well be more fruitful to study the person who fails than the instant success.

• *How do we hold social entrepreneurs accountable?* As discussed earlier in the book, multiple stakeholders are involved in the development of a social entrepreneurial organization. Social entrepreneurs need to ask donors and supporters to contribute to their organization in the form of time, finances, or partnerships. These contributions are critical to the functioning of the social entrepreneurial organization, but they do not come without a price: when someone makes a contribution, in return they expect social entrepreneurs to be accountable for their time and resources by practicing good stewardship. In the wake of nonprofit and business scandals, such as Angel Food Ministries and Enron, social entrepreneurs cannot ignore the accountability expectations of stakeholders. But are there adequate mechanisms to ensure accountability?

• *Can social entrepreneurs make a social impact in a virtual world?* The Internet and social media have provided a wonderful platform for aspiring social entrepreneurs to experiment their innovative approaches to achieving a social mission. Yet to what extent can virtual social entrepreneurs create a real impact? For instance, many people have raised doubts about the effectiveness of advocacy campaigns carried out in online forums or organized through social media, calling them "clicktivism." In response to such skepticism, Avaaz—the world's largest online activist network—offers an interesting opinion. Alice Jay, a campaigns director for Avaaz, was quoted as follows: "I think the clicktivism debate is just silly. I don't think anyone doubts that iTunes has changed music, or eBay has changed commerce. No one calls that clicktivism. . . . No one calls Gandhi a 'walkavist,' or Rosa Parks a 'sitavist.' The Internet is really just the place where this change is happening."[4]

- *What is the "dark side" of attention philanthropy?* The concept of attention philanthropy (introduced in Chapter Eleven) is rooted in the idea that attention and recognition come from creating buzz or a sense of urgency. Donors and supporters may focus only on the attention-grabbing stories or natural disasters and crises that are well publicized. The problem with buzz is that it is fundamentally short-lived: the initial allure diminishes before long, and then the organization must start the cycle of attracting donors all over again. Buzz is also problematic because it works better for large, popular nonprofit organizations than for smaller organizations; the latter also support worthy missions but find it hard to compete. Nonprofits don't necessarily have the budget to support flashy advertising campaigns like their for-profit counterparts, and even if they do, donors aren't typically fond of having their donations go to such expenditures. With an abundance of watchdog agencies and a culture of increased transparency, it is also imperative for social entrepreneurs to remain transparent about how they spend donations and prepared to defend any decisions consistently across all levels.

CONCLUDING REMARKS

In closing, we declare ourselves cautious advocates of the social entrepreneurship movement. The idea of this book was inspired by the tension between the believers and the skeptics, as acutely observed by Michael Edwards in his book *Just Another Emperor? The Myths and Realities of Philanthropcapitalism*: "For some, social enterprise constitutes a new or fourth sector that is distinct from the public, private and conventional non-profit worlds, while for others it seems more a case of old wine in new bottles, re-packaging the traditional service providing functions of civil society under a new and fancier title, perhaps to garner more resources."[5]

In working through this book and examining the accumulated body of knowledge that is forming a solid foundation for this emerging field, it has become clear that social entrepreneurship is no silver bullet that can magically solve society's intractable problems, and yet it is certainly not a fraud or a "devil in disguise." Social entrepreneurship cannot replace the hard work of numerous traditional civil society organizations and government agencies—but it suggests exciting directions for the future.

INTRODUCTION

1. Goldsmith, S., & Eggers, W. (2004). *Governing by network: The new shape of the public sector*. Washington, DC: Brookings Institution Press (p. 7).

2. For more on these types of problems, see Groupsmith. (2013). Technical problems vs. adaptive challenges. Retrieved from http://www.groupsmith .com/uploads/file/technical%20problems%20vs%20%20adaptive%20 challenges.pdf

3. Friedman, T. (2005). *The world is flat: A brief history of the twenty-first century*. New York: Farrar, Straus and Giroux (pp. 449–459).

4. Phills, J., Deiglmeier, K., & Miller, D. (2008). Rediscovering social innovation. *Stanford Social Innovation Review*, 6, Fall 2008. Retrieved from http:// www.ssireview.org/articles/entry/rediscovering_social_innovation

5. Murphy, R. M., & Sachs, D. (2013, May 2). The rise of social entrepreneurship suggests a possible future for global capitalism. *Forbes*. Retrieved from http://www.forbes.com/sites/skollworldforum/2013/05/02/the-rise-of -social-entrepreneurship-suggests-a-possible-future-for-global-capitalism

6. The following points about social entrepreneurship are from Light, P. (2006). Searching for social entrepreneurs: Who they might be, where they might be found, what they do. In R. Mosher-Williams (Ed.), *Research on social entrepreneurship: Understanding and contributing to an emerging field* (pp. 13–38). ARNOVA Occasional Paper Series, Volume 1, Number 3. Indianapolis, IN: ARNOVA.

7. Brock, D., & Ashoka U. (2008). *Social entrepreneurship teaching resources handbook*. Arlington, VA: Ashoka Global Academy for Social Entrepreneurship (pp. 46–50).

8. David, V. (2005). *The market for virtue: The potential and limits of corporate social responsibility*, Washington, DC: Brookings Institution Press (p. 28).

9. Brock, D., & Ashoka U. (2008) (p. 9).

10. Ibid.

11. Ibid.

12. Ashoka U & Brock, D. (2011). *Social entrepreneurship education resource handbook*. Arlington, VA: Ashoka U, the University Division of Ashoka: Innovators for the Public (p. 4).

13. Ibid. (p. 5).

14. Tracey, P., & Phillips, N. (2007). The distinctive challenge of educating social entrepreneurs: A postscript and rejoinder to the special issue on entrepreneurship education. *Academy of Management Learning and Education*, 6: 264–271.

15. Harvard Business Review On Point. (2006). Evidence-based management (p. 1). Accessed from: http://hbr.org/product/evidence-based-management -hbr-onpoint-enhanced-edition/an/298X-PDF-ENG

16. Ibid.

17. Rousseau, D. (2006). Is there such a thing as "evidence-based management"? *Academy of Management Review*, 31(2): 256–69 (p. 256).

18. Schön, D. (1987). *Educating the reflective practitioner*. San Francisco: Jossey-Bass (pp. 25–26).

19. Ibid. (p. 33).

20. Ibid. (p. 34).

21. Ibid. (p. 35).

22. Ibid. (p. 13).

CHAPTER ONE

1. Boschee, J. (2001). Eight basic principles for nonprofit entrepreneurs. *Nonprofit World*, 19(4): 15–18; Zietlow, J. T. (2001). Social entrepreneurship: Managerial, finance, and marketing aspects. *Journal of Nonprofit and Public Sector Marketing*, 9(1/2): 19–43.

2. Dees, J. G., & Anderson, B. B. (2006). Framing a theory of social entrepreneurship: Building on two schools of practice and thought. In R. Mosher-Williams (Ed.), *Research on social entrepreneurship: Understanding and contributing to an emerging field. ARNOVA Occasional Paper Series*, 1(3): 39–66. Indianapolis, IN: ARNOVA.

3. Austin, J., Stevenson, H., & Wei-Skillern, J. (2006). Social and commercial entrepreneurship: same, different, or both? *Entrepreneurship Theory and Practice*, 30(1): 1–22.

4. Brinckerhoff, P. (2000). *Social entrepreneurship: The art of mission-based venture development*. New York: Wiley.

5. Center for the Advancement of Social Entrepreneurship (CASE) (2008). Developing the field of social entrepreneurship: A report from the Center for Advancement of Social Entrepreneurship (CASE). Duke University, Fuqua School of Business. Retrieved from http://www.caseatduke.org/documents/CASE_Field-Building_Report_June08.pdf

6. Dees, J. G. (1998). The meaning of social entrepreneurship. Duke University, Fuqua School of Business. Retrieved from http://www.caseatduke.org/documents/dees_sedef.pdf

7. Frumkin, P. (2002). *On being nonprofit: A conceptual and policy primer*. Cambridge, MA: Harvard University Press.

8. Light, P. (2006a). Reshaping social entrepreneurship. *Stanford Social Innovation Review*, 4(3): 47–51.

9. Martin, R., & Osberg, S. (2007). Social entrepreneurship: The case for definition. *Stanford Social Innovation Review*, Spring: 29–39.

10. Mort, G. S., Weerawardena, J., & Carnegie, K. (2003). Social entrepreneurship: Towards conceptualization. *International Journal of Nonprofit and Voluntary Sector Marketing*, 8(1): 76–88.

11. Peredor, A. M., & McLean, M. (2006). Social entrepreneurship: A critical review of the concept. *Journal of World Business*, 41(1):56–65.

12. Pomerantz, M. (2003). The business of social entrepreneurship in a "down economy." *In Business*, 25(2): 25–28.

13. Thompson, J., Alvy, G., & Lees, A. (2000). Social entrepreneurship: A new look at the people and the potential. *Management Decision*, 38(5): 328–338.

14. Young, D. R. (1986). Entrepreneurship and the behavior of nonprofit organizations: Elements of a theory. In S. Rose-Ackerman (Ed.), *The economics of nonprofit institutions: Studies in structure and policy* (pp. 161–184). Oxford/New York: Oxford University Press.

15. Austin, J., Stevenson, H., & Wei-Skillern, J. (2006); Dees, J. G. (1998); Dees, J. G., Emerson, J., & Economy, P. (2001). *Enterprising non-profits: A toolkit for social entrepreneurs.* New York: Wiley; Light, P. C. (2006b). Searching for social entrepreneurs: Who they might be, where they might be found, what they do. In R. Mosher-Williams (Ed.), *Research on social entrepreneurship: Understanding and contributing to an emerging field. ARNOVA Occasional Paper Series*, 1(3): 13–38. Indianapolis, IN: ARNOVA; Peredor, A. M., and McLean, M. (2006).

16. Hoogendoorn, B., Pennings, H., & Thurik, A. (2010). What do we know about social entrepreneurship: An analysis of empirical research. *International Review of Entrepreneurship*, 8(2): 71–112.

17. Boschee, J. (2001) (p. 15); Zietlow, J. T. (2001).

18. Tschirhart, M., & and Bielefeld, W. (2012). *Managing nonprofit organizations.* San Francisco: Jossey-Bass (p. 36).

19. Austin, J., Stevenson, H., & Wei-Skillern, J. (2006).

20. Martin, R. L., & Osberg, S. (2007) (p. 30).

21. Peredor, A. M., & McLean, M. (2006).

22. Martin, R., & Osberg, S. (2007). Peredor, A. M., & McLean, M. (2006).

23. Dees, J. G. (1998).

24. Mort, G. S., Weerawardena, J., & Carnegie, K. (2003).

25. Peredor, A. M., & McLean, M. (2006).

26. Young, D. R. (1986).

27. See also Light, P. C. (2006b).

28. Drayton, W. (2002). The citizen sector: Becoming as entrepreneurial and competitive as business. *California Management Review*, 44(3): 120–132.

29. Boschee, J., & National Center for Non-profit Boards (US) (1998). *Merging mission and money: A board member's guide to social entrepreneurship.* National Center for Non-profit Boards.

30. Mair, J., & Noboa, E., (2003). Social entrepreneurship: How intentions to create a social enterprise get formed. Barcelona: IESE Business School Working Paper No. 521.

31. Gartner, W. B. (1988). "Who is an entrepreneur?" is the wrong question. *American Journal of Small Business*, 12(4): 11–32.

32. Bornstein, D. (2012, November 13). The rise of social entrepreneur. *New York Times*. Retrieved from http://opinionator.blogs.nytimes.com/2012/11/13/the-rise-of-social-entrepreneur/

33. Steinberg, R. (2006). Economic theories of nonprofit organizations. In W. Powell & R. Steinberg, (Eds.), *The nonprofit sector: A research handbook* (pp. 117–139). Princeton: Yale University Press.

34. Bielefeld, W. (2009). Issues in social enterprise and social entrepreneurship. *Journal of Public Affairs Education*, 15(1): 69–86.

35. Shrestha, L. B., & Heisler, E. J. (2011). The changing demographic profile of the United States [electronic version]. Washington, DC: Congressional Research Service.

36. Parliamentary Assembly Report (2012, January 9). Demographic trends in Europe: turning challenges into opportunities. Doc. 12817. Retrieved from http://www.assembly.coe.int/ASP/Doc/XrefViewPDF.asp?FileID=12916&Language=EN

37. Lee, Y.-J. (2009). The determinants of sector choice: What attracts people to the nonprofit sector and are there gender differences? Paper presented at the Public Management Research Conference, Columbus, OH; Pynes, J. E.

(2000). Are women underrepresented as leaders of nonprofit organizations? *Review of Public Personnel Administration*, 20(2): 35–49.

38. Harding, R. (2004). Social enterprise: The new economic engine? *Business Strategy Review*, 15(4): 39–43.

39. Naidu, S. (2013). More women at B schools. *Women 2.0*. Retrieved from http://women2.com/the-rise-of-social-entrepreneurship-women-and-b-schools-play-a-role/

40. Hoskisson, R. E., Hitt, M. A., & Ireland, D. (2004). *Competing for advantage*. Mason, OH: South-Western/Thomson Learning.

41. Powell, W., & Owen-Smith, J. (1998). Universities and the market for intellectual property in the life sciences. *Journal of Policy Analysis and Management*, 17(2): 253–277.

42. Zidisha set to "expand" in peer-to-peer microfinance. (2010, February 7). *Microfinance Focus*.

43. Murphy, R. M., & Sachs, D. (2013, May 2). The rise of social entrepreneurship suggests a possible future for global capitalism. *Forbes*. Retrieved from http://www.forbes.com/sites/skollworldforum/2013/05/02/the-rise-of-social-entrepreneurship-suggests-a-possible-future-for-global-capitalism.

44. Lyons, T., & Liang, K. (2011, September). What works! Conference paper, "Prospects for Collaborative Research in Social Entrepreneurship" workshop, Northeast Regional Center for Rural Development, Philadelphia, PA 2011.

45. Nagler, J. (2007). The importance of social entrepreneurship for development. Retrieved from http://www.business4good.org/2007/04/importance-of-social-entrepreneurship.html

46. Noya, A. (2010). Social Entrepreneurship and Social Innovation, in SMEs, Entrepreneurship and Innovation (pp. 185–215). OECD Publishing.

47. Harding, R. (2004).

48. Nagler, J. (2007).

49. Ibid.

50. Mulgan, G. (2008). *The art of public strategy: Mobilizing power and knowledge for the common good*. Oxford, UK: Oxford University Press.

51. City of Phoenix Public Works Department. (2011). Annual report, FY 2010–2011.

52. Mulgan, G. (2007). Ready or not? Taking innovation in the public sector seriously. *NESTA Provocation*, *3*.

53. Ibid.

54. Social Innovator. (2013). Public sector unions. Retrieved from http://socialinnovator.info/ways-supporting-social-innovation/public-sector/innovation-workforce/public-sector-unions

55. TOMS Shoes. (2013). One for one. Retrieved from http://www.toms.com/evolving-our-giving

56. Hochberg, L. (2009, March 26). Seattle coffee company uses profits to aid bean growers. *Newshour*. Retrieved from http://www.pbs.org/newshour/bb/social_issues/jan-june09/coffee_03–26.html

57. RingCentral. (2012). Five successful examples of social entrepreneurship. Retrieved from http://blog.ringcentral.com.

58. *Real Change* 2012 annual report. (2013, March 13). *Real Change*.

59. Seelos, C., & Mair, J. (2005). Social entrepreneurship: Creating new business models to serve the poor. *Business Horizons*, *48*(3): 241–246.

60. Shears, A. R. (2006, September 25). Curing the third world. *Philanthropy Magazine*. Retrieved from http://www.philanthropyroundtable.org/topic/excellence_in_philanthropy/curing_the_third_world

61. Cause Marketing Forum (2013). Background and Basics. Retrieved from http://www.causemarketingforum.com/site/c.bkLUKcOTLkK4E/b.6443937/k.41E3/Background_and_Basics.htm

62. Varadarajan, P. Rajan, & Menon, Anil. (1988). Cause-related marketing: A co-alignment of marketing strategy and corporate philanthropy. *The Journal of Marketing*, *52*(3): 58–74.

63. Grameen Bank. (2013). A short history of Grameen Bank. Retrieved from www.grameen-info.org.

64. University of Virginia. (2013). Steven I. Cooper bio. Retrieved from http://www2.commerce.virginia.edu/cmit/activities/CooperBio.htm

65. Sources: Fathy, H. (2010). *Architecture for the poor: an experiment in rural Egypt*. University of Chicago press. Miles, M. (2006). Utopias of Mud? Hassan Fathy and Alternative Modernisms. *Space and Culture*, *9*(2), 115–139.

CHAPTER TWO

1. Case details are taken from interviews with Aliyya Shelley Mattos, executive director of the PaperSeed Foundation, and the Foundation website, http://www.paperseed.org

2. Lumpkin, G. T., & Dess, G. G. (1996). Clarifying the entrepreneurial orientation construct and linking it to performance. *Academy of Management Review*, 21(1): 135–172.

3. Morris, M. H., & Sexton, D. L. (1996). The concept of entrepreneurial intensity: Implications for company performance. *Journal of Business Research*, 36: 5–13.

4. See Guo, C., Shockley, G., & Tang, R. (2009). At the intersection of two worlds: Religion, social enterprise, and Partners in Christ International. *GIVING—International Journal on Philanthropy and Social Innovation*, 2: 71–82; Weerawardena, J., & Mort, G. S. (2006). Investigating social entrepreneurship: A multidimensional model. *Journal of World Business*, 41: 21–35; Young, D. R. (2000). Nonprofit entrepreneurship. In S. J. Ott (Ed.), *Understanding Nonprofit Organizations: Governance, Leadership, and Management* (pp. 218–222). Boulder, CO: Westview Press.

5. Miller, D. (1983). The correlates of entrepreneurship in three types of firms. *Management Science*, 29(7): 770–791.

6. Covin, J. G., & Slevin, D. P. (1991). A conceptual model of entrepreneurship as firm behavior. *Entrepreneurship Theory and Practice*, 16: 7–25; Lumpkin, G. T., & Dess, G. G. (1996); Miller D., & Friesen, P. H. (1982). Innovation in conservative and entrepreneurial firms: two models of strategic momentum. *Strategic Management Journal*, 3: 1–25.

7. Covin, J. G., & Lumpkin, G. T. (2011). Entrepreneurial orientation theory and research: Reflections on a needed construct. *Entrepreneurship Theory and Practice*, 35(5): 855–872.

8. Covin, J. G., & Slevin, D. P. (1989). Strategic management of small firms in hostile and benign environments. *Strategic Management Journal*, 10: 75–87; Miller, D. (1983). The correlates of entrepreneurship in three types of firms. *Management Science*, 29: 770–791.

9. Lumpkin, G. T., & Dess, G. G. (1996).

10. Mort, G. S., Weerawardena, J., & Carnegie, K. (2003). Social entrepreneurship: Towards conceptualization. *International Journal of Nonprofit Sector Marketing*, 8(1): 76–88.

11. Weerawardena, J., & Mort, G. S. (2006).

12. Cools, E., & Vermeulen, S. (2008). What's in a name? An inquiry on the cognitive and entrepreneurial profile of the social entrepreneur. Vlerick Leuven Gent Management School Working Paper Series 2008–02, Vlerick Leuven Gent Management School.

13. Emerson, J. (2001). Understanding risk: The social entrepreneur, and risk management. In J. G. Dees, J. Emerson, & P. Economy (Eds.), *Enterprising Nonprofits: A Toolkit for Social Entrepreneurs* (pp. 125–160). Wiley.

14. Interview with Aliyya Shelley Mattos, executive director of the PaperSeed Foundation.

15. Trinity Effect. (n.d.). Retrieved from http://www.trinityeffect.org

16. The 2010 annual report, Goodwill Industries of Lane and South Counties.

17. The 2011 annual report, Goodwill Industries of Northwest North Carolina.

18. Miller, D., & Friesen, P. H. (1982). Innovation in conservative and entrepreneurial firms: two models of strategic momentum. *Strategic Management Journal*, 3(1): 1–25.

19. Morris, M. H., & Joyce, M. (1998). On the measurement of entrepreneurial behavior in not-for-profit organizations: Implications for social marketing. *Social Marketing Quarterly*, 4(4): 1–23.

20. Helm, S. T., & Andersson, F. O. (2010). Beyond taxonomy: An empirical validation of social entrepreneurship in the nonprofit sector. *Nonprofit Management and Leadership*, 20(3): 259–276.

21. Morris, M. H., Coombes, S., Schindehutte, M., & Allen, J. (2007). Antecedents and outcomes of entrepreneurial and market orientations in a nonprofit context: Theoretical and empirical insights. *Journal of Leadership & Organizational Studies*, 13(4): 12–39.

22. See, for example, Covin, J. G., & Slevin, D. P. (1989). Strategic management of small firms in hostile and benign environments. *Strategic Management Journal*, 10: 75–87; Lyon, D. W., Lumpkin, G. T., & Dess, G. G. (2000).

Enhancing entrepreneurial orientation research: Operationalizing and measuring a key strategic decision making process. *Journal of Management,* 26(5): 1055–1085; Miller, D. (1983). The correlates of entrepreneurship in three types of firms. *Management Science,* 29: 770–791; Wiklund, J. (1999). The sustainability of the entrepreneurial orientation-performance relationship. *Entrepreneurship Theory and Practice,* 24(1): 37–48.

23. Rauch, A., Wiklund, J., Lumpkin, G. T., & Frese, M. (2009). Entrepreneurial orientation and business performance: An assessment of past research and suggestions for the future. *Entrepreneurship Theory and Practice,* 33(3): 761–787.

24. Andersson, F. O., & Helm, S. T. (2013). Do socially entrepreneurial nonprofits perform better? An empirical exploration. Working paper, University of Missouri-Kansas City. Retrieved from http://bloch.umkc.edu/faculty-staff/documents/andersson-helm-conference.pdf

25. Pearce, I. I., John, A., Fritz, D. A., & Davis, P. S. (2010). Entrepreneurial orientation and the performance of religious congregations as predicted by rational choice theory. *Entrepreneurship Theory and Practice,* 34(1): 219–248.

26. Caruana, A., Ewing, M. T., & Ramaseshan. (2002). Effects of some environmental challenges and centralization on the entrepreneurial orientation and performance of public sector entities. *Service Industries Journal,* 22(2): 43–58.

27. Coombes, S. M., Morris, M. H., Allen, J. A., & Webb, J. W. (2011). Behavioral orientations of nonprofit boards as a factor in entrepreneurial performance: Does governance matter? *Journal of Management Studies,* 48(4): 829–856.

28. Helm, S. T., & Andersson, F. O. (2010). Beyond taxonomy: An empirical validation of social entrepreneurship in the nonprofit sector. *Nonprofit Management and Leadership,* 20(3): 259–276.

29. Morris, H. M., Coombes, S., Schindehutte, M., & Allen, J. (2007).

30. Morris, M. H., & Joyce, M. (1998). Morris, M. H., Webb, J. W., & Franklin, R. J. (2011). Understanding the manifestation of entrepreneurial orientation in the nonprofit context. *Entrepreneurship Theory and Practice,* 35(5): 947–971.

31. Morris, M. H., & Sexton, D. L. (1996).

32. Morris, H. M., & Lewis, P. S. (1995). The determinants of entrepreneurial activity: implications for marketing. *European Journal of Marketing*, 29(7): 31–48; Morris, M. H., & Sexton, D. L. (1996).

33. Thomke, S. (2002). Innovations at 3M Corporation (A). Harvard Business School Case 9–699–012.

34. Kuratko, D. F., Hornsby, J. S., & Goldsby, M. G. (2007). The relationship of stakeholder salience, organizational posture, and entrepreneurial intensity to corporate entrepreneurship. *Journal of Leadership & Organizational Studies*, 13(4): 56–72.

35. Morris, M. H., & Sexton, D. L. (1996).

36. Morris, M. H., Webb, J. W., & Franklin, R. J. (2011).

37. Frumkin, P. (2002). *On Being Nonprofit*. Cambridge, MA: Harvard University Press.

38. Adapted and extended from Helm & Andersson (2010).

CHAPTER THREE

1. Case details are taken from Holcim Foundation for Sustainable Construction. The power of small changes: Stories of microcredit introduced in Bangladesh by Muhammad Yunus. Proceedings of the first Holcim Forum for Sustainable Construction. Retrieved from www .holcimfoundation.org/portals/1/docs/firstforum_yunus.pdf

2. Shane, S., & Venkataraman, S. (2000). The promise of entrepreneurship as a field of research. *Academy of Management Review*, 225(1): 17–226.

3. Short, J. C., Ketchen, D. J., Jr., Shook, C. L., & Ireland, R. D. (2010). The concept of "opportunity" in entrepreneurship research: Past accomplishments and future challenges. *Journal of Management*, 36(1): 40–65.

4. Haugh, H. (2005). A research agenda for social entrepreneurship. *Social Enterprise Journal*, 1(1): 1–12; Lehner, O. M., & Kaniskas, J. (2012). Opportunity recognition in social entrepreneurship: A thematic meta-analysis. *Journal of Entrepreneurship*, 21(1): 25–58.

5. Bygrave, W. D., & Hofer, C. W. (1991). Theorizing about entrepreneurship. *Entrepreneurship Theory and Practice*, 16(1): 13–22; Eckhardt, J. T., & Shane, S. A. (2003). Opportunities and entrepreneurship. *Journal of Management*, 29(3): 333–349.

6. Russell, R. D. (1999). Developing a process model of corporate entrepreneurial systems: A cognitive mapping approach. *Entrepreneurship Theory and Practice*, 23 (3): 65–84.

7. Baucus, D. A., & Human, S. E. (1994). Second-career entrepreneurs: A multiple case study analysis of entrepreneurial processes and antecedent variables. *Entrepreneurship Theory and Practice*, 19(2): 41–71; Bygrave, W. D., & Hofer, C. W. (1991). Theorizing about entrepreneurship. *Entrepreneurship Theory and Practice*, 16(1): 13–22; Van De Ven, A. H. (1992). Suggestions for studying strategy process: A research note. *Strategic Management Journal*, 13: 169–188.

8. Shane, S., & Venkataraman, S. (2000), p. 220.

9. Short, J. C., Ketchen Jr, D. J., Shook, C. L., & Ireland, R. D. (2010), p. 55.

10. Hansen, D. J., Shrader, R., & Monllor, J. (2011). Defragmenting definitions of entrepreneurial opportunity. *Journal of Small Business Management*, 49(2): 283–304.

11. Berglund, H. (2007). Opportunities as existing and created: a study of entrepreneurs in the Swedish mobile internet industry. *Journal of Enterprising Culture*, 15(3): 243–273; Cajaiba-Santana, G., & Lyon, E. M. (2010). Socially constructed opportunities in social entrepreneurship: A structuration model. *Handbook of Research on Social Entrepreneurship*, 88–106.

12. Alvarez, S. A., & Barney, J. B. (2007). Discovery and creation: Alternative theories of entrepreneurial action. *Strategic Entrepreneurship Journal*, 1(1–2): 11–26.

13. Gartner, W. B., Carter, N. M., & Hills, G. E. (2003). The language of opportunity. In C. Steyaert & D. Hjorth (Eds), *New movements in entrepreneurship* (pp. 103–124). Cornwall: MPG Books Ltd.

14. Drucker, P. F. (2006). *Innovation and entrepreneurship*. Harper Business.

15. Brooks, A. C. (2009). *Social entrepreneurship: A modern approach to social value creation*. Pearson Education.

16. Austin, J., Stevenson, H., & Wei-Skillern, J. (2006). Social and commercial entrepreneurship: same, different, or both? *Entrepreneurship Theory and Practice*, 30(1): 1–22.

17. Guclu, A., Dees, J. G., & Anderson, B. B. (2002). The process of social entrepreneurship: Creating opportunities worthy of serious pursuit. Center for the Advancement of Social Entrepreneurship (CASE), Duke University, Fuqua School of Business.

18. Clarkin, J. E., Deardurff, D. D., & Gallagher, A. (2012). Opportunities for social entrepreneurship: An analysis of the social sector in six Midwest US areas. In J. Kickul & S. Bacq (Eds.), *Patterns in Social Entrepreneurship Research* (pp. 15–41). Cheltenham, UK: Edward Elgar.

19. Monllor, J. (2010). Social entrepreneurship: A study on the source and discovery of social opportunities. In K. Hockerts, J. Mair, & J. Robonsin, (Eds.), *Values and Opportunities in Social Entrepreneurship* (pp. 99–120). Hampshire, UK: Palgrave Macmillan.

20. Guclu, A., Dees, J. G., & Anderson, B. B. (2002), p. 1.

21. Light, P. C. (2006). Reshaping social entrepreneurship. *Stanford Social Innovation Review*, 4(3), 47–51.

22. Monllor, J. (2010).

23. Dees, J. G., Emerson, J., & Economy, P. (Ed). (2001). *Enterprising nonprofits: A toolkit for social entrepreneurs*. New York: Wiley.

24. Austin and colleagues (2006); Dorado and colleagues (2006); Hockerts (2006); Mair & Marti (2006); Robinson (2006).

25. Jack, S. L., & Anderson, A. R. (2002). The effects of embeddedness on the entrepreneurial process. *Journal of Business Venturing*, 17(5): 467–487.

26. Frumkin, P. (2005). *On Being Nonprofit: A Conceptual and Policy Primer*. Harvard University Press.

27. Ardichvili, A., Cardozo, R., & Ray, S. (2003). A theory of entrepreneurial opportunity identification and development. *Journal of Business Venturing*, 18(1): 105–123.

28. Guclu, A., Dees, J. G., & Anderson, B. B. (2002).

29. Guo, C., Brown, W. A., Ashcraft, R. F., Yoshioka, C. F., & Dong, H.K.D. (2011). Strategic human resources management in nonprofit organizations. *Review of Public Personnel Administration*, 31(3): 248–269.

30. Seelos, C., Mair, J., Battilana, J., & Dacin, M. T. (2011). The embeddedness of social entrepreneurship: Understanding variation across local communities. Working paper, IESE Business School, University of Navarra, Spain.

31. York, J., Sarasvathy, S., & Larson, A. (2010). The thread of inchoate demand in social entrepreneurship. In Hockerts, K. (Ed.), *Values and opportunities in social entrepreneurship* (pp. 141–162). New York: Palgrave.

32. Kirzner, I. (1973). *Competition and Entrepreneurship*. Chicago: University of Chicago Press; Ardichvili, A., Cardozo, R., & Ray, S. (2003). A theory of entrepreneurial opportunity identification and development. *Journal of Business Venturing*, 18: 105–123; Gaglio, C. M., & Katz, J. A. (2001). The psychological basis of opportunity identification: Entrepreneurial alertness. *Small Business Economics*, 16: 95–111.

33. Dees, J. G., Emerson, J., & Economy, P. (Eds.). (2001).

34. Baron, R. A., & Ensley, M. D. (2006). Opportunity recognition as the detection of meaningful patterns: Evidence from comparisons of novice and experienced entrepreneurs. *Management Science*, 52(9), 1331–1344.

35. Shane, S., & Venkataraman, S. (2000).

36. Roberts, P. (2013). New research suggests start-up experience doesn't help social entrepreneurs. *Harvard Business Review*. Retrieved from http://blogs.hbr.org/cs/2013/02/for_social_venture_founders_ex.html.

37. Ibid.

38. Arenius, P., & Clercq, D. D. (2005). A network-based approach on opportunity recognition. *Small Business Economics*, 24(3): 249–265.

39. Burt, R. (1992). *Structural Holes: The Social Structure of Competition*. Cambridge: Harvard University Press.

40. Hills, G., Lumpkin, G. T., Singh, R. P. (1997). Opportunity recognition: perceptions and behaviors of entrepreneurs. *Frontiers of Entrepreneurship Research* (pp. 203–218). Babson College, Wellesley, MA.

41. Granovetter, M. (1973). The strength of weak ties. *American Journal of Sociology*, 6, 1360-1380.

42. Perry-Smith, J. E., & Shalley, C. E. (2003). The social side of creativity: A static and dynamic social network perspective. *Academy of Management Review*, 28(1): 89–106.

43. Ruef, M. (2002). Strong ties, weak ties and islands: Structural and cultural predictors of organizational innovation. *Industrial and Corporate Change*, 11(3): 427–449.

44. Kitzi, J. (2001). Recognizing and assessing new opportunities. In J. G. Dees, J. Emerson, & P. Economy (Eds.), *Enterprising nonprofits: A toolkit for social entrepreneurs* (pp. 43–62). New York: Wiley.

45. Zahra, S. A., Rawhouser, H. N., Bhawe, N., Neubaum, D. O., & Hayton, J. C. (2008). Globalization of social entrepreneurship opportunities. *Strategic Entrepreneurship Journal*, 2(2): 117–131.

CHAPTER FOUR

1. Case details are taken from Emerson, J., & Twersky, F. (1996). *New social entrepreneurs: the success, challenges and lessons of non-profit enterprise creation*. San Francisco: The Roberts Foundation (pp. 75–80).

2. Guclu, A., Dees, J. G., & Anderson, B. B. (2002). *The process of social entrepreneurship: creating opportunities worthy of serious pursuit*. Center for the Advancement of Social Entrepreneurship: Duke—The Fuqua School of Business.

3. SEKN (Social Enterprise Knowledge Network), Austin, J., Gutierrez, R.,Ogliastri, E., & Reficco, E. (2006). *Effective management of social enterprises: Lessons from businesses and civil society organizations in Iberoamerica*. Cambridge, MA: Harvard University David Rockefeller Center for Latin American Studies (p. 252).

4. Ibid (p. 264).

5. Wei-Skillern, J., Austin, J. E., Leonard, H., & Stevenson, H. (2007). *Entrepreneurship in the social sector*. Los Angeles: Sage (p. 23).

6. SEKN (p. 265).

7. Alter, K. S. (2000). *Managing the double bottom line: A business planning reference guide for social enterprises*. Save the Children Federation.

8. BlendedValue. (2013). Retrieved from www.blendedvalue.org

9. Anderson, A. A. (2005). *A community builder's approach to theory of change: A practical guide to theory development*. New York: The Aspen Institute Roundtable on Community Change.

10. Knowlton, L. W., & Phillips, C. C. (2013). *The logic model guidebook: Better strategies for great results.* Los Angeles: Sage.

11. Ibid. (p. 21).

12. W. K. Kellogg Foundation. (2000). Developing a theory-of-change logic model for your program. In *Using logic models to bring together planning, evaluation and action: Logic model development guide* (Chapter Three). Battle Creek, MI: W. K. Kellogg Foundation.

13. Knowlton, L. W., & Phillips, C. C. (2013) (p. 35).

14. Porter, M. E. (1985). *Competitive advantage.* New York: Free Press.

15. Porter, M. E., & Kramer, M. R. (2006, December). Strategy and society: The link between competitive advantage and corporate social responsibility. *Harvard Business Review* (pp. 77–92).

16. Sommerrock, K. (2010). *Social entrepreneurship business models: Incentive strategies to catalyze public goods provision.* New York: Palgrave Macmillan (p. 45).

17. A number of guides are available for conducing feasibility studies. See SCORE. (2011). *Business planning tools for non-profit organizations* (2nd ed.). SCORE Foundation and Office Depot Foundation. Retrieved from http://www.score.org/resources/business-planning-tools-nonprofit-organizations (p. 18); Larson, R. (2002). *Venture forth: the essential guide to starting a moneymaking busiess in your nonprofit organization.* St. Paul, MN: Amherst H. Wilder Foundation.

18. Compiled from SCORE and Larson. Also, thanks to Milissa Stone for suggestions regarding feasibility assessment.

19. Tschirhart, M., & Bielefeld, W. (2012). *Managing nonprofit organizations.* San Francisco: Jossey-Bass (p. 43).

20. Even the government provides business plans, through the Small Business Administration; see http://www.sba.gov/

21. Kickul, J., & Lyons, T. S. (2012). *Understanding social entrepreneurship: The relentless pursuit of mission in an ever changing world.* New York: Routledge (p. 75); Rooney, J. (2001). Planning for social enterprise. In J. G. Dees, J. Emerson, & P. Economy (Eds.), *Enterprising nonprofits: A toolkit for social entrepreneurs.* New York: Wiley.

22. Wolk, A., & Kreitz, K. (2008). *Business planning for enduring social impact: A social-entrepreneurial approach to solving social problems.* Cambridge, MA: Root Cause (p. 60).

23. Morris, M. H., Kuratko, D. F., & Covin, J. G. (2011). *Corporate entrepreneurship & innovation* (3rd ed.). Mason, OH: South-Western Cengage Learning (p. 66).

24. Ibid. (p. 67).

25. Emerson, J. (2001). Understanding risk, the social entrepreneur, and risk management. In J. G. Dees, J. Emerson, & P. Economy (Eds.), *Enterprising nonprofits: A toolkit for social entrepreneurs.* New York: Wiley; Brooks, A. C. (2009). *Social entrepreneurship: A modern approach to social value creation.* Upper Saddle River, NJ: Pearson Prentice Hall (pp. 60–61).

26. Dickson, P. R., & Giglierano, J. J. (1986). Missing the boat and sinking the boat: A conceptual model of entrepreneurial risk. *Journal of Marketing*, 50: 43–51.

27. For example, see Sargeant, A. (2009). *Marketing management for nonprofit organizations* (3rd ed.). New York: Oxford University Press; Andreasen, A. R., & Kotler, P. (2008). *Strategic marketing for nonprofit organizations* (7th ed.). Upper Saddle River, NJ: Pearson Prentice Hall.

28. Majeska, K. (2001). Understanding and attracting your "customers." In J. G. Dees, J. Emerson, & P. Economy (Eds.), *Enterprising nonprofits: A toolkit for social entrepreneurs.* New York: Wiley.

29. Andreasen, A. R., & Kotler, P. (2008) (pp. 153–157).

30. Ibid. (pp. 224–226).

31. Stone, M., & Sandfort, J. (2009). Building a policy fields framework to inform research on nonprofit organizations. *Nonprofit and Voluntary Sector Quarterly*, 38(6): 1054–1075.

32. Sandfort, J., & Stone, M. (2008). Analyzing policy fields: Helping students understand complex state and local contexts. *Journal of Public Affairs Education*, 14(2): 129–148 (p. 129).

33. Sandfort, J. (2010). Nonprofits in policy fields. *Journal of Public Policy Analysis and Management*, 29(3): 637–644.

34. Stone, M., & Sandfort, J. (2009) (pp. 1063–1070).

35. Shaw, E., & Carter, S. (2007). Social entrepreneurship: Theoretical antecedents and empirical analysis of entrepreneurial processes and outcomes. *Journal of Small Business and Enterprise Development*, 14(3): 418–434.

36. Weerawardena, J., & Mort, G. S. (2006). Investigating social entrepreneurship: A multidimensional model. *Journal of World Business*, 41: 21–35.

37. Dees, J. G. (2001). Mobilizing resources. In J. G. Dees, J. E. Emerson, & P. Economy (Eds.), *Enterprising nonprofits: A toolkit for social entrepreneurs.* New York: Wiley (pp. 63–102).

38. Brooks, A. C. (2009). *Social entrepreneurship: A modern approach to social value creation.* Upper Saddle River, NJ: Pearson Prentice Hall (p. 88).

CHAPTER FIVE

1. Details of this case come from Chertavian, G. (2012). *A year up: How a pioneering program teaches young adults real skills for real jobs—with real success.* New York: Viking; Year Up. (2007). Year Up growth plan and capital requirements. Retrieved from http://nonprofitfinancefund.org/files/docs/Year_Up.pdf

2. Year Up. (2007) (pp. 13–19).

3. Roder, A., & Elliott, M. (2011). *A promising start: Year Up's initial impacts on low-income young adult's careers.* New York: Economic Mobility Corporation. Retrieved from http://www.yearup.org/pdf/emc_study.pdf

4. Scott, W. R., & Davis, G. F. (2007). *Organizations and organizing: Rational, natural, and open system perspectives.* Upper Saddle River, NJ: Pearson Prentice Hall (p. 326).

5. Hancock, J. (2003). Scaling-up the impact of good practice in rural development: A working paper to support implementation of the World Bank's Rural Development Strategy. Report number 26031. Washington, DC: The International Bank for Reconstruction and Development. (Public Disclosure Authorized) (p. 14).

6. Herman, R. D., & Renz, D. O. (1999). Theses on nonprofit organizational effectiveness. *Nonprofit and Voluntary Sector Quarterly*, 28(2): 107–126.

7. Murray, V., & Tassie, B. (1994). Evaluating the effectiveness of nonprofit organizations. In R. D. Herman & Associates, *The Jossey-Bass handbook*

of nonprofit leadership and management (pp. 303–324). San Francisco: Jossey-Bass.

8. Ibid; also Tschirhart, M., & Bielefeld, W. (2012). *Managing nonprofit organizations.* San Francisco: Jossey-Bass/Wiley (pp. 13–17).

9. Sharir, M., & Lerner, M. (2006). Gauging the success of social ventures initiated by individual social entrepreneurs. *Journal of World Business*, 41: 6–20.

10. Wei-Skillern, J., Austin, J. E., Leonard, H., & Stevenson, H. (2007) (see chap. 4, n. 5).

11. This concept was developed by Mark Moore: Moore, M. (1997). *Creating public value: strategic management in government.* Cambridge, MA: Harvard University Press.

12. Tschirhart, M., & Bielefeld, W. (2012) (p. 20).

13. Quinn, R. E., & Rohrbaugh, J. (1981). A competing values approach to organizational effectiveness. *Public Productivity Review*, 5(2): 122–140.

14. Cameron, K. (2009). An introduction to the competing values framework. Haworth organizational culture white paper. Retrieved from http://www.haworth.com/en-us/Knowledge/Workplace-Library/Documents/An-Introduction-to-the-Competing-Values-Framework.pdf

15. Quinn, R. E., & Rohrbaugh, J. (1981).

16. See, for example, Bryson, J. M., & Crosby, B. C. (1992). *Leadership for the common good: Tackling public problems in a shared-power world.* San Francisco: Jossey-Bass/Wiley.

17. Herman, R. D., & Renz, D. O. (1999).

18. Kushner, R. J., & Poole, P. P. (1996). Exploring structure-effectiveness relationships in nonprofit arts organizations. *Nonprofit Management and Leadership*, 7(2): 119–136.

19. Kaplan, R. S., & Norton, D. P. (1996). *The balanced scorecard.* Boston, MA: Harvard Business School Press (pp. 25–29).

20. Ibid. (pp. 30–31).

21. Niven, P. R. (2003). *Balanced scorecard step-by-step for government and nonprofit agencies.* Hoboken, NJ: Wiley.

22. Niven, P. R. (2003) (p. 30).

23. Ibid. (pp. 34–35).

24. Gitlow, H. S. (2005). Organizational dashboards: Steering an organization towards its mission. *Quality Engineering*, 17: 345–357.

25. Paton, R. (2003). *Managing and measuring social enterprises.* Thousand Oaks, CA: Sage (pp. 139–146).

26. Ibid. (p. 142).

27. Year Up (2007) (p. 9).

28. Examples of outcome and impact evaluation of environmental education programs come from MEERA. (2013). My environmental education evaluation resource assistant. University of Michigan, School of Natural Resources and environment. Retrieved from http://meera.snre.umich.edu/plan-an-evaluation/related-topics/outcomes-and-impacts

29. Ibid.

30. Ibid.

31. Harrell, A., Burt, M., Hatry, H., Rossman, S., Roth, J., and Sabol, W. (1996). *Evaluation strategies for human service programs: A guide for policymakers and providers.* Washington, DC: The Urban Institute.

32. Roder, A., & Elliot, M. (2011). *A promising start: Year Up's initial impacts.* New York: Economic Mobility Corporation. Retrieved from http://www.yearup.org/pdf/emc_study.pdf

33. National Action Plan for Energy Efficiency. (2007). *Model energy efficiency program impact evaluation guide.* Prepared by S. R. Schiller, Schiller Consulting. www.epa.gov/eeactionplan. Retrieved from http://www.epa.gov/cleanenergy/documents/suca/evaluation_guide.pdf (p. ES-3).

34. Ibid. (p. 4-2).

35. Tuan, M. (2008). *Measuring and/or estimating social value creation: Insights into eight integrated cost approaches.* Seattle, WA: Bill & Melinda Gates Foundation (p. 10).

36. Karoly, L. A. (2008). *Valuing benefits in benefit-cost studies of social programs.* Santa Monica, CA: RAND (p. 6).

37. Brooks, A. C. (2009). *Social entrepreneurship: A modern approach to social value creation.* Upper Saddle River, NJ: Pearson Prentice Hall (pp. 71–72).

38. Taylor, M. A., Dees, J. G., & Emerson. J. (2002). The question of scale: finding an appropriate strategy for building on your success. In J. G. Dees, J. Emerson, & P. Economy (Eds.), *Strategic tools for social entrepreneurs: Enhancing the performance of your enterprising nonprofit* (pp. 235–266). New York: Wiley.

39. Bloom, P. N. (2012). *Scaling your social venture: Becoming an impact entrepreneur.* New York: Palgrave Macmillan.

40. Kalafatas, J. (2013). *Approaches to scaling social impact.* Durham, NC: Duke University, Center for the Advancement of Social Entrepreneurship. Retrieved from http://www.caseatduke.org/knowledge/scalingsocialimpact/frameworks.html

41. Dees, J. G., & Anderson, B. B. (2004, Spring). Scaling social impact: Strategies for spreading social innovations. *Stanford Social Innovation Review.* Dees, J. G., & Anderson, B. B. (2013). *Scaling for social impact: Exploring strategies for spreading social innovations.* Durham, NC: Center for the Advancement of Social Entrepreneurship, Duke University. Retrieved from http://www.setoolbelt.org/resources/379

42. Taylor, M. A., Dees, J. G., & Emerson. J. (2002) (pp. 240–242).

43. KaBoom. (2013). Our mission. Retrieved from http://kaboom.org/about_kaboom/our_mission_vision

44. KIPP. (2013). About KIPP. Retrieved from http://www.kipp.org/about-kipp

45. Habitat for Humanity. (2013). Retrieved from http://www.habitat.org/

CHAPTER SIX

1. Case details drawn from Herrnaz, J. Jr., Council, L. R., & McKay, B. (2011). Tri-value organization as a form of social enterprise: The case of Seattle's FareStart. *Nonprofit and Voluntary Sector Quarterly*, 40(5): 829–849; FareStart. (2013). Good food. Better lives. Retrieved from http://farestart.org/

2. FareStart. (2013). FareStart's mission, vision, and values. Retrieved from http://farestart.org/about/mission/index.html

3. FareStart. (2013). Good food. Better lives.

4. U.S. Government Revenue. (2013). Government revenue details. Retrieved from http://www.usgovernmentrevenue.com/year_revenue_2012USbn_14 bs1n#usgs302

5. Fair Tax Blog. (2013). What is a government enterprise? Retrieved from http://www.fairtaxblog.com/20081019/what-is-a-government-enterprise/

6. U.S. Government Revenue. (2013). Government revenue details. Retrieved from http://www.usgovernmentrevenue.com/year_revenue_2012USbn_14 bs1n#usgs302

7. Borins, S. (1998). *Innovating with integrity: How local heroes are transforming American government.* Washington, DC: Georgetown University Press (pp. 92–96).

8. Ash Center for Democratic Governance and Innovation. (2013). Innovations in government. Harvard University. Retrieved from http://www.ash.harvard.edu/ash/Home/Programs/Innovations-in-Government

9. Social Enterprise Knowledge Network (SEKN), Austin, J., Gutierrez, R.,Ogliastri, E., & Reficco, E. (2006). *Effective management of social enterprises: Lessons from businesses and civil society organizations in Iberoamerica.* Cambridge, MA: Harvard University David Rockefeller Center for Latin American Studies (p. 51).

10. Ibid. (p. 192).

11. Blackwood, A. S., Roeger, K. L., & Pettijohn, S. L. (2010). *The nonprofit sector in brief: Public charities, giving, and volunteering, 2012.* Washington, DC: Urban Institute (p. 3).

12. Salamon, L. M. (2012). *America's nonprofit sector: A primer* (3rd ed.). New York: Foundation Center (p. 103).

13. Ibid. (p 105).

14. Froelich, K. A. (1999). Diversification of revenue strategies: Evolving resource dependence in nonprofit organizations. *Nonprofit and Voluntary Sector Quarterly*, 28(3): 146–268.

15. Department of Trade and Industry (DTI). (2002). *Social enterprise: A strategy for success.* London: HM Treasury.

16. Wallace, B. (2005). Exploring the meaning(s) of sustainability for community-based social entrepreneurs. *Social Enterprise Journal*, 1(1): 78–89.

17. Young, D. (2010). Nonprofit finance: Developing nonprofit resources. In David O. Renz and Associates, *The Jossey-Bass Handbook of Nonprofit Leadership and Management* (3rd ed., pp. 482–504). San Francisco: Jossey-Bass (p. 498).

18. Wei-Skillern, J., Austin, J. E., Leonard, H., & Stevenson, H. (2007). *Entrepreneurship in the social sector.* Thousand Oaks, CA: Sage (pp. 138–140).

19. Social Enterprise Knowledge Network (SEKN), Austin, J., Gutierrez, R., Ogliastri, E., & Reficco, E. (2006) (pp. 170–171).

20. Young (2010) (p. 500).

21. Salamon, L. M. (2012) (p. 41).

22. *Giving USA 2012: The annual report on philanthropy for the year 2011.* Indianapolis, IN: The Center on Philanthropy (p. 8).

23. Ibid. (p. 10).

24. Blackwood, A. S., Roeger, K. L., & Pettijohn, S. L. (2012) (p. 6).

25. Citing personal communication from Hank Rosso: Fogal, R. E. (2010). Designing and managing the fundraising program. In D. O. Renz, & Associates, *The Jossey-Bass handbook of nonprofit leadership and management* (3rd ed., pp. 505–523). San Francisco: Jossey-Bass (pp. 506–507).

26. Froelich, K. A. (1999).

27. Grace, K. S. (2002). Treating your donors as investors. In J. G. Dees, J. Emerson, & P. Economy (Eds.), *Strategic tools for social entrepreneurs: Enhancing the performance of your enterprising nonprofit* (pp. 117–139). New York: Wiley (p. 119).

28. The White House, Office of Social Innovation and Civic Participation. (2013). Social innovation fund. Retrieved from http://www.whitehouse.gov/administration/eop/sicp/initiatives/social-innovation-fund

29. Salamon, L. M. (2012) (p. 69).

30. Young, D. R. (2010) (p. 494).

31. Ibid. (p. 494).

32. Smith, S. R. (2010). Managing the challenges of government contracts. In David O. Renz and Associates, *The Jossey-Bass Handbook of Nonprofit Leadership and Management* (3rd ed., pp. 553–579). San Francisco: Jossey-Bass (pp. 564–570).

33. Bielefeld, W. (2007). Social entrepreneurship and social enterprise. In C. Wankel (Ed.), *21st Century management: A reference handbook* (pp. 22–31). Thousand Oaks, CA: Sage (p. 28).

34. Wei-Skillern, J., Austin, J. E., Leonard, H., & Stevenson, H. (2007) (pp. 140–141).

35. Hurwit & Associates. (n.d.). Taxation of unrelated business income. Retrieved from http://www.hurwitassociates.com/l_unrelated_income.php

36. Brooks, A. C. (2009). *Social entrepreneurship: A modern approach to social value creation.* Upper Saddle River, NJ: Pearson Prentice Hall (p. 90); James, E., & Young, D. R. (2006). Fee income and commercial ventures. In D. R. Young (Ed.), *Financing nonprofits: Putting theory into practice* (pp. 93–120). Lanham, MD: AltaMira Press.

37. Anderson, B. B., Dees, J. G., & Emerson, J. (2002). Developing viable earned income strategies. In J. G. Dees, J. Emerson, & P. Economy (Eds.), *Strategic tools for social entrepreneurs: Enhancing the performance of your enterprising nonprofit* (pp. 191–233). New York: Wiley.

38. Worth, M. J. (2012). *Nonprofit management: principles and practice* (2nd ed.). Los Angeles: Sage (p. 306).

39. Ibid. (p. 302).

40. Ibid. (p. 303).

41. Susan G. Komen Minnesota. (2013). Komen race for the cure. Retrieved from http://www.komenminnesota.org/Komen_Race_for_the_Cure_.htm

42. Center on Philanthropy. (2013). *Leveraging the power of foundations: An analysis of program-related investments.* Indianapolis, IN: Center on Philanthropy.

43. Ibid.

44. RSI Social Finance. (2013). PRI funds. Retrieved from http://rsfsocialfinance.org/services/investing/pri/

45. Kaplan, R. S., & Grossman, A. S. (2010, October). The emerging capital market for nonprofits. *Harvard Business Review*, pp. 110–118.

46. Ibid. (p. 114).

47. For a full discussion, see Bugg-Levine, A., & Emerson, J. (2011). *Impact investing: Transforming how we make money while making a difference*. San Francisco: Jossey-Bass (p. 9).

48. Freireich, J., & Fulton, K. (2009). *Investing for social and environmental impact: A design for catalyzing an emerging industry*. San Francisco: Monitor Institute. Retrieved from http://monitorinstitute.com/downloads/what-we-think/impact-investing/Impact_Investing.pdf

49. Ibid.

50. RSF Social Finance. (2013). Social investment fund. Retrieved from http://rsfsocialfinance.org/services/investing/social/

51. Harji, K., & Jackson, E. (2012). *Accelerating impact: Achievements, challenges and what's next in building the impact investing industry*. New York: The Rockefeller Foundation.

52. Social Finance. (2012). *A new tool for scaling impact: How social impact bonds can mobilize private capital to advance social good*. Boston, MA: Social Finance.

CHAPTER SEVEN

1. Case details are taken from Guo, C., Shockley, G., & Tang, R. (2009). At the intersection of two worlds: Religion, social enterprise, and Partners in Christ International. *GIVING—International Journal on Philanthropy and Social Innovation*, 2: 71–82.

2. McGaw, N. (2013, February 8). Have a real impact; keep your day job. *Harvard Business Review*. Retrieved from http://blogs.hbr.org/cs/2013/02/have_a_real_impact_keep_your_d.html

3. Farid, M. (2005). Organizational attributes of nonprofit intrapreneurship: An empirical study. *Academy of Entrepreneurship Journal*, 11(2): 1–18.

4. Frumkin, P. (2002): *On being nonprofit: A conceptual and policy primer*. Cambridge, MA: Harvard University Press.

5. Pinchot, G., & Pinchot, E. (1978, Fall) *Intra-corporate entrepreneurship*. Tarrytown School for Entrepreneurs. Retrieved from http://www.intrapreneur.com/MainPages/History/IntraCorp.html

6. Stevenson, H. H., & Jarillo, J. C. (1990). A paradigm of entrepreneurship: Entrepreneurial management. *Strategic Management Journal*, 11(5): 17–27.

7. Antoncic, B., & Hisrich, R. D. (2003). Clarifying the intrapreneurship concept. *Journal of Small Business and Enterprise Development*, 10(1), 7–24.

8. Zahra, S. A. (1991). Predictors and financial outcomes of corporate entrepreneurship: An exploratory study. *Journal of Business Venturing*, 6: 259–285.

9. Burgelman, R. A. (1983). Corporate entrepreneurship and strategic management: Insights from a process study. *Management Science*, 29(12), 1349–1364.

10. Antoncic, B., & Hisrich, R. D. (2003). Clarifying the intrapreneurship concept. *Journal of Small Business and Enterprise Development*, 10(1): 7–24.

11. Zahra, S. A. (1991).

12. Brooks, A. C. (2008). *Social entrepreneurship*. Upper Saddle River, NJ: Pearson Prentice Hall.

13. Grayson, D., McLaren, M., & Spitzeck, H. (2011). *Social intrapreneurs: An extra force for sustainability*. Doughty Center for Corporate Responsibility Occasional Paper.

14. Kistruck, G. M., & Beamish, P. W. (2010). The interplay of form, structure, and embeddedness in social intrapreneurship. *Entrepreneurship Theory and Practice*, 34(4): 735–761.

15. Mair, J., & Marti, I. (2006). Social entrepreneurship research: A source of explanation, prediction, and delight. *Journal of World Business*, 41(1): 36–44.

16. Schmitz, B., & Scheuerle, T. (2012). Founding or transforming? Social Intrapreneurship in three German Christian-based NPOs. *ACRN Journal of Entrepreneurship Perspectives*, 1(1): 13–36.

17. Yusuf, J. (2005). Putting entrepreneurship in its rightful place: A typology for defining entrepreneurship across private, public and nonprofit sectors. *Academy of Entrepreneurship Journal*, 11(2): 113–127.

18. Antoncic, B., & Hisrich, R. D. (2001).

19. Garton, C. (2010, November 24). Panera opens doors to second "Cares Café" charity store. *USA Today*. Retrieved from http://yourlife.usatoday.com/mind-soul/doing-good/kindness/post/2010/11/panera-opens-doors-to-their-second-cares-cafe-charity-store/132353/1

20. Takagi, G. (2012). Parent-subsidiary structures—Part I: Control and separateness. *Nonprofit Law Blog*. Retrieved from http://www.nonprofitlawblog.com/home/2012/06/parent-subsidiary-structures-part-i.html

21. Khan, M. A. (2008). Red Cross attracts $190K in pledges via Text 2HELP program. *Mobile Marketer*. Retrieved from http://www.mobilemarketer.com/cms/news/messaging/2226.html

22. Suspended Coffees. (n.d.). https://www.facebook.com/suspendedcoffeess

23. Breathe California of Los Angeles County. (n.d.). BREATHE LA history. Retrieved from http://www.breathela.org/about/breathe-la-history

24. Thornberry, N. E. (2003). Corporate entrepreneurship: Teaching managers to be entrepreneurs. *Journal of Management Development*, 22(4): 329–344.

25. Lumpkin, G. T., & Dess, G. G. (1996). Clarifying the entrepreneurial orientation construct and linking it to performance. *Academy of Management Review*, 21(1): 135–172.

26. Antoncic, B., & Hisrich, R. D. (2001).

27. Walker, R. (2007). An empirical evaluation of innovation types and organizational and environmental characteristics: Towards a configuration framework. *Journal of Public Administration Research and Theory*, 8 (59): 591–615.

28. Kearney, C., Hisrich, R., & Roche, F. (2008). A conceptual model of public sector corporate entrepreneurship. *International Entrepreneurship and Management Journal*, 4(3): 295–313.

29. Ibid.

30. Sadler, R. J. (2000). Corporate entrepreneurship in the public sector: The dance of the chameleon. *Australian Journal of Public Administration* (Australia), 59(2): 25–43.

31. Kearney, C., Hisrich, R., & Roche, F. (2008).

32. Jennings, D. F., & Lumpkin, J. R. (1989). Functionally modeling corporate entrepreneurship: An empirical integrative analysis. *Journal of*

Management, 15(3): 485–503; Hornsby, J. S., Kuratko, D. F., & Zahra, S. A. (2002). Middle managers' perception of the internal environment for corporate entrepreneurship: Assessing a measurement scale. *Journal of Business Venturing*, 17: 253–273.

33. Hornsby, J. S., Kuratko, D. F., & Zahra, S. A. (2002).

34. Denison, D. R. (1996). What is the difference between organizational culture and organizational climate? A native's point of view on a decade of paradigm wars. *Academy of Management Review*, 21(3), 619–654; Jaskyte, K., & Dressler, W. W. (2005). Organizational culture and innovation in nonprofit human service organizations. *Administration in Social Work*, 29(2), 23–41.

35. Sadler, R. J. (2000). Corporate entrepreneurship in the public sector: The dance of the chameleon. *Australian Journal of Public Administration*, 59(2): 25–43.

36. Damanpour, F., & Schneider, M. (2006). Phases of the adoption of innovation in organizations: Effect of environment, organization, and top managers. *British Journal of Management*, 17: 215–236.

37. Cyert, R. M., & March, J. G.. (1963/1992). *A behavioral theory of the firm* (2nd ed). Englewood Cliffs, NJ: Prentice Hall.

38. Bourgeois, L. J. (1981). On the measurement of organizational slack. *Academy of Management Review*, 6: 29–39.

39. McDonald, R. E. (2007). An investigation of innovation in nonprofit organizations: The role of organizational mission. *Nonprofit and Voluntary Sector Quarterly*, 36(2): 256–281.

40. Zahra, S. A. (1993). Environment, corporate entrepreneurship, and financial performance: A taxonomic approach. *Journal of Business Venturing*, 8: 319–340.

41. Dess, G. D., & Beard, D. W. (1984). Dimensions of organizational task environments. *Administrative Science Quarterly*, 30: 52–73.

42. Hambrick, D. C., & Finkelstein, S. (1987). Managerial discretion: A bridge between polar views of organizational outcomes. In L. L. Cummings & B. M. Staw (Eds.), *Research in organizational behavior* (pp. 369–406). Greenwich, CT: JAI Press.

43. Miller, D., & Friesen, P. H. (1982). Innovation in conservative and entrepreneurial firms: Two models of strategic momentum. *Strategic Management Journal*, 3: 1–25; Osborne, D., & Gaebler, T. A (1992). *Reinventing government: How the entrepreneurial spirit is transforming the public sector.* Reading, MA: Addison-Wesley; Nutt, P. C., & Backoff, R. W. (1993). Transforming public organizations with strategic management and strategic leadership. *Journal of Management*, 19: 299–349.

44. Morris, M. H., & Jones, F. F. (1999). Entrepreneurship in established organizations: The case of the public sector. *Entrepreneurship Theory and Practice*, 24(1): 71–91.

45. Levine, C. H., Backoff, R. W., Cahoon, A. R., & Siffin, W. J. (1975). Organizational design: A post Minnowbrook perspective for the "new" public administration. *Public Administration Review*, 35: 425–435.

46. Covin, J. G., & Slevin, D. P. (1991). A conceptual model of entrepreneurship as firm behavior. *Entrepreneurship Theory and Practice*, 16: 7–25.

47. Peters, T. J., & Waterman, R. H. (1982). *In search of excellence: Lessons from America's best-run companies.* New York: Harper and Row; Kanter, R. M. (1984). *The change masters.* New York: Simon & Schuster; Pinchot, G. (1985). *Intrapreneuring.* New York: Harper & Row.

48. Kearney, C., Hisrich, R., & Roche, F. (2008). A conceptual model of public sector corporate entrepreneurship. *International Entrepreneurship and Management Journal*, 4(3): 295–313.

49. Peters, T. J., & Waterman, R. H. (1982).

50. Ahuja, G., & Morris Lampert, C. (2001). Entrepreneurship in the large corporation: A longitudinal study of how established firms create breakthrough inventions. *Strategic Management Journal*, 22(6–7): 521–543.

51. Mulgan, G., & Albury, D. (2003). *Innovation in the public sector.* Strategy Unit, Cabinet Office, October 2003.

52. Borins, S. (2001). The challenge of innovating in government. *The PricewaterhouseCoopers Endowment for the Business of Government*, February 2001.

53. Kistruck, G. M., & Beamish, P. W. (2010). The interplay of form, structure, and embeddedness in social intrapreneurship. *Entrepreneurship Theory and Practice*, 34(4): 735–761.

54. Ibid.

55. Ibid.

56. Ibid.

57. Borins, S. (2001).

58. Ren, C. R., & Guo, C. (2011). Middle managers' strategic role in the corporate entrepreneurial process: Attention-based effects. *Journal of Management*, 37(6): 1586–1610.

CHAPTER EIGHT

1. Case details are taken from Jones, T. (2008). BANK ON IT: Sometimes you have to break the rules to succeed. Vodafone had to create them from scratch. *PM Network*, 22(6): 58–63; Omwansa, T. K., & Sullivan, N. P. (2012). *Money, real quick: The story of M-Pesa*. New York: Guardian Books.

2. Weiss, L. (2012, December 7). An interview with Aaron Hurst, social innovator. Taproot Foundation. Retrieved from http://www.taprootfoundation. org/about-probono/blog/interview-aaron-hurst-social-innovator

3. See Bygrave, W. D., & Hofer, C. W. (1991). Theorizing about entrepreneurship. *Entrepreneurship Theory and Practice*, 16(2): 13–22; Eckhardt, J. T., & Shane, S. A. (2003). Opportunities and entrepreneurship. *Journal of Management*, 29(3): 333–349.

4. Van De Ven, A. H. (1992). Suggestions for studying strategy process: A research note. *Strategic Management Journal*, 13: 169–188.

5. Burgelman, R. A. (1983). A model of the interaction of strategic behavior, corporate context, and the concept of strategy. *Academy of Management Review*, 8: 61–70.

6. Jansen, J.J.P., Van den Bosch, F.A.J., & Volberda, H. W. (2006). Exploratory innovation, exploitative innovation, and performance: Effects of organizational antecedents and environmental moderators. *Management Science*, 52: 1661–1674.

7. Ren, C. R., & Guo, C. (2011). Middle managers' strategic role in the corporate entrepreneurial process: Attention-based effects. *Journal of Management*, 37(6), 1586–1610.

8. Burgelman, R. A. (1983). Corporate entrepreneurship and strategic management: Insights from a process study. *Management Science*, 29(12): 1349–1364.

9. Ibid.

10. Ren, C. R., & Guo, C. (2011).

11. Ocasio, W. (1997). Towards an attention-based view of the firm. *Strategic Management Journal*, 18(S1): 187–206.

12. Kingdon, J. W. (2002). *Agendas, alternatives, and public policies* (Longman Classics edition). London: Longman Publishing Group.

13. Peters, T. J., & Waterman, R. H. (2004). *In search of excellence: Lessons from America's best-run companies.* New York: HarperBusiness; Zahra, S. A. (1991). Predictors and financial outcomes of corporate entrepreneurship: An exploratory study. *Journal of Business Venturing*, 6: 259–285.

14. Floyd, S. W., & Woolridge, B. (1999). Knowledge creation and social networks in corporate entrepreneurship: The renewal of organizational capability. *Entrepreneurship Theory and Practice*, 23(3): 123–143.

15. Guo, C. (2003). Environmental constraints, governance patterns, and organizational responsiveness: A study of representation in nonprofit organizations. Unpublished dissertation, University of Southern California, Los Angeles, CA.

16. Burgelman, R. (1984). Managing the internal corporate venturing process. *Sloan Management Review*, 25(2): 33–48.

17. Ocasio, W. (1997).

18. Maidique, M. A. (1980). Entrepreneurs, champions, and technological innovation. *MIT Sloan Management Review*, 21(2): 59–76.

19. Borins, S. (2002). Leadership and innovation in the public sector. *Leadership & Organization Development Journal*, 23(8): 467–476.

20. Nohria, N., & Gulati, R. (1996). Is slack good or bad for innovation? *Academy of Management Journal*, 39: 1245–1264.

21. Ren, C. R., & Guo, C. (2011).

22. Howlett, M. (1998). Predictable and unpredictable policy windows: Institutional and exogenous correlates of Canadian federal agenda-setting. *Canadian Journal of Political Science*, 31: 495–524.

23. Levitt, B., & March, J. G. (1988). Organizational learning. *Annual Review of Sociology*, 14, 319–340.

24. Levinthal, D. A., & March, J. G. (1993). The myopia of learning. *Strategic Management Journal*, 14: 95–112.

25. March, J. G. (1994). *A primer on decision making: How decisions happen.* New York: Free Press.

26. Louis, M. R., & Sutton, R. I. (1991). Switching cognitive gears: From habits of mind to active thinking. *Human Relations*, 44: 55–76.

27. Dutton, J. E., & Jackson, S. E. (1987). Categorizing strategic issues: Links to organizational action. *Academy of Management Review*, 12: 76–90.

28. Cohen, R. (2011, July 25). Staying alive: Nonprofit innovation in a traditional setting. *Nonprofit Quarterly.* Retrieved from http://www.nonprofitquarterly.org

29. Nonprofit Quarterly. (2013, June 6). NPQ's report to you, its community. Retrieved from http://nonprofitquarterly.org/governancevoice/22412-npq-s-report-to-you-its-community.html

30. George, E., Chattopadhyay, P., Sitkin, S. B., & Barden, J. (2006). Cognitive underpinnings of institutional persistence and change: A framing perspective. *Academy of Management Review*, 31: 347–385.

31. Quinn, J., Mintzberg, J., & James, R. (1988). *The strategy process: Concepts, context, and cases.* Upper Saddle River, NJ: Prentice Hall.

32. Borins, S. (2002). Leadership and innovation in the public sector. *Leadership & Organization Development Journal*, 23(8): 467–476.

33. Maidique, M. A. (1980). Entrepreneurs, champions, and technological innovation. *MIT Sloan Management Review*, 21(2): 59–76.

34. Burgelman, R. A. (1983). A process model of internal corporate venturing in the diversified major firm. *Administrative Science Quarterly*, 28: 223–244.

35. Interview with Aliyya Shelley Mattos, executive director of the PaperSeed Foundation.

36. Mintzberg, H. (1989). *Mintzberg on management.* New York: Free Press.

37. Floyd, S. W., & Wooldridge, B. (1992). Middle management involvement in strategy and its association with strategic type: A research note. *Strategic Management Journal*, 13(S1): 153–167.

38. Floyd, S. W., & Wooldridge, B. (1999). Knowledge creation and social networks in corporate entrepreneurship: The renewal of organizational capability. *Entrepreneurship Theory & Practice*, 23: 123–143.

39. Ren, C. R., & Guo, C. (2011).

40. See Kouzes, J. M., & Posner, B. Z. (1987). *The leadership challenge*. San Francisco: Jossey-Bass; Jaskyte, K. (2004). Transformational leadership, organizational culture, and innovativeness in nonprofit organizations. *Nonprofit Management and Leadership*, 15(2): 153–167.

41. Simons, R. (1987). Accounting control systems and business strategy: An empirical analysis. *Accounting, Organizations and Society*, 12: 357–374.

42. Sadler, R. J. (2000). Corporate entrepreneurship in the public sector: The dance of the chameleon. *Australian Journal of Public Administration*, 59(2): 25–43.

CHAPTER NINE

1. Case details taken from Moore, M. H. (2013). Diana Gale and the Seattle solid waste utility. In *Recognizing public value* (pp. 244–291). Cambridge, MA: Harvard University Press.

2. Dictionary.com. (2013). Government. Retrieved from http://dictionary. reference.com/browse/government

3. Palmer, J. L,, & Sawhill, I. V. (1982). The Reagan experiment: an examination of economic and social policies under the Reagan administration. Washington, DC: The Urban Institute.

4. Lewis, E. (1980). *Public entrepreneurship: toward a theory of bureaucratic power*. Bloomington, IN: Indiana University Press; Doig, J. W., & Hargrove, E. C. (1987). *Leadership and innovation: Entrepreneurs in government*. Baltimore, MD: Johns Hopkins University Press.

5. Morris, M. H., Kuratco, D. F., & Covin, J. G. (2011). *Corporate entrepreneurship and innovation: Entrepreneurial development within organizations* (3rd ed.). Mason, OH: South-Western Cengage Learning (p. 132).

6. Morris, M. H., Kuratco, D. F., & Covin, J. G. (2011) (pp. 130–131).

7. Cooper, T. L., & Wright N. D. (1992). *Exemplary public administrators: Character and leadership in government*. Baltimore, MD: John Hopkins University Press.

8. Drucker, P. F. (1995, February). Really reinventing government. *Atlantic Monthly*, pp. 49–61; Schneider, M., Teske, P., & Mintrom, M. (1995). Public entrepreneurs: Agents for change in American government. Princeton, NJ: Princeton University Press.

9. Nutt, P. C., & Backoff, R. W. (1993). Transforming public organizations and strategic management and strategic leadership. *Journal of Management*, 19(2): 299–349.

10. Osborne, D., & Gaebler T. A. (1992). *Reinventing government: How the entrepreneurial spirit is transforming the public sector*. Reading MA: Addison-Wesley.

11. Savas, E. (2000). *Privatization and public-private partnerships*. New York: Chatham House Publishers; Wolk, A. (2008). *Advancing social entrepreneurship: Recommendations for policy makers and government agencies*. Washington, DC: The Aspen Institute and Root Cause.

12. Ramamuurti, R. (1986). Public entrepreneurs: Who they are and how they operate. *California Management Review*, 28(3): 142–158; Morris, M. H., Kuratco, D. F., & Covin, J. G. (2011) (p. 135).

13. Ramamuurti, R. (1986).

14. Morris, M. H., & Jones, F. (1999). Entrepreneurship in established organizations: the case of the public sector. *Entrepreneurship Theory and Practice*, 24(1): 71–91.

15. Ibid. (p. 84).

16. Palmer, J. L., & Sawhill, I. V. (1982).

17. Osborne, D., & Gaebler, T. A. (1992).

18. Denhardt, J. V., & Denhardt, R. B. (2011). *The new public service: Serving, not steering*. Armonk, NY: M. E. Sharpe (pp. 17–18).

19. Bumgarner, J., & Newswander, C. (2009). The irony of NPM: The inevitable extension of the role of the American state. *American Review of Public Administration*, 39(2): 189–207.

20. Box, R. C., Marshall, G. S., Reed, B. J., & Reed, C. M. (2001). New public management and substantive democracy. *Public Administrative Review*, 61(5): 608–619.

21. Stone, D. (2008). Global public policy, transnational policy communities and their networks. *Journal of Policy Sciences*, 36(1): 19–38.

22. Denhardt, R. B., & Denhardt, J. V. (2000). The new public service: Serving rather than steering. *Public Administration Review*, 60(6): 549–59 (p. 557).

23. Ibid. (pp. 553–556).

24. Ibid. (p. 557).

25. Ibid.

26. Eggers, W. D., & Singh, S. K. (2009). *The public innovator's playbook: Nurturing bold ideas in government*. Cambridge, MA: Deloitte and Ash Institute of Harvard Kennedy School.

27. Ibid. (p. 29).

28. Wolk, A. (2008).

29. Brass, C. T. (2012). Changes to the Government Performance and Results Act (GPRA): Overview of the new framework of products and processes. Washington, DC: Congressional Research Service.

30. Ibid.

31. Federal FY2014 Budget. (2013). Analytical perspectives, performance and management, 7. Delivering a High Performance Government (p. 87).

32. Moynihan, D. (2013). *The new federal performance system: Implementing the GPRA Modernization Act*. Washington, DC: IBM Center for the Business of Government.

33. Federal FY2014 Budget. (2013).

34. Brenner, S., & Smith, B. (2009, October). Louisiana first state in the nation to launch an institute to incubate innovative social programs. *Philadelphia Social Innovations Journal*. Retrieved from http://www.philasocialinnovations.org/site/index.php?option=com_content&view=article&id=39:louisiana-is-first-state-in-the-nation-to-launch-an-institute-to-incubate-innovative-social-programs&catid=20:what-works-and-what-doesnt&Itemid=31

35. Perry, S. (2011, March 24). Minnesota explores "pay for performance" bonds. *Chronicle of Philanthropy*. Retrieved from http://philanthropy.com/blogs/state-watch/minnesota-explores-pay-for-performance-bonds/397

CHAPTER TEN

1. Details taken from Chisholm, R. F. (1998). *Developing network organizations: Learning from practice and theory*. Reading, MA: Addison-Wesley (pp. 60–107).

2. Bloom, P. N., & Dees, J. G. (2008). Cultivate your ecosystem. *Stanford Social Innovation Review*, Winter: 45–53.

3. Oliver, C. (1990). Determinates of interorganizational relationships: Integration and future directions. *Academy of Management Review*, 15: 241–265 (p. 241).

4. Thompson, A. M. (2002). Collaboration: Meaning and measurement. In T. Taillieu (Ed.), *Collaborative strategies and multi-organizational partnerships* (pp. 267–276). Leuven–Kessel-Lo, Belgium: Garant (p. 271).

5. Bailey, D., & Kooney, K. (2000). *Strategic alliances among health and human service organizations*. Thousand Oaks, CA: Sage; Tschirhart, M., & Bielefeld, W. (2012). *Managing nonprofit organizations*. San Francisco: Wiley (pp. 358–362).

6. Austin, J. (2000). *The collaboration challenge: How nonprofits and businesses succeed through strategic alliances*. San Francisco: Jossey-Bass; Tschirhart, M., & Bielefeld, W. (2012). *Managing nonprofit organizations*. San Francisco: Wiley (pp. 363–365).

7. For a similar typology of collaboration among nonprofit organizations, see Guo, C., & Acar, M. (2005). Understanding collaboration among nonprofit organizations: Combining resource dependency, institutional, and network perspectives. *Nonprofit and Voluntary Sector Quarterly*, 34(3): 340–361.

8. Nohria, N., & Eccles, R. G. (1992). *Networks and organizations*. Boston: Harvard University Press; Sagawa, S., & Segal, E. (2000). Common interest, common good: Creating value through business and social sector interorganizational relationships. *California Management Review*, 42(2): 105–122; Osborne, S. P., & Flynn, N. (1997, October-December). Managing the innovative capacity of voluntary and non-profit organizations in the provision of public services. *Public Money and Management*, 31–39; Young, D. (2003). New trends in the U.S. nonprofit sector: Toward market integration? In *The nonprofit sector in a changing economy*. Paris: Organization for Economic Co-operation and Development (OECD).

9. Osborne, S. P., & Flynn, N. (1997); Goes, J. B., & Park, S. H. (1997). Interorganizational relationships and innovation: The case of hospital services. *Academy of Management Review*, 40(3): 673–696; Ostrower, F. (2003). Cultural collaborations: Building partnerships for arts participation. Retrieved from http//www.urban.org/url.cfm?ID=310616

10. Jaskyte, K., & Lee, M. (2006). Interorganizational relationship: A source of innovation in nonprofit organizations? *Administration in Social Work*, 30(3): 43–54.

11. Chisholm, R. E. (1998). *Developing network organizations: Learning from practice and theory*. Reading, MA: Addison-Wesley (p. 6).

12. Ackoff, R. R. (1974). *Redesigning the future*. New York: Wiley Interscience.

13. Stone, M., & Sandfort, J. (2009). Building a policy fields framework to inform research on nonprofit organizations. *Nonprofit and Voluntary Sector Quarterly*, 38(6): 1054–1075.

14. Sandfort, J. (2010). Nonprofits in policy fields. *Journal of Public Policy Analysis and Management*, 29(3): 637–644.

15. Agranoff, R. (2007). *Managing within networks: Adding value to public organizations*. Washington, DC: Georgetown University Press.

16. Milward, B., & Provan, K. (2006). *A manager's guide to choosing and using collaborative networks*. Arlington, VA: IBM Center for the Business of Government.

17. Provan, K., & Kenis, P. (2007). Modes of network governance: Structure, management, and effectiveness. *Journal of Public Administration Research and Theory*, 18: 229–252.

18. Bryson, J. M., Crosby, B. C., Stone, M. M., & Saunoi-Sandgren, E. (2009). *Designing and managing cross-sector collaboration: A case study in reducing traffic congestion*. Arlington, VA: IBM Center for the Business of Government (p. 79).

19. Wenger, E. C., & Snyder, W. M. (2000, January-February). Communities of practice: The organizational frontier. *Harvard Business Review*, pp. 139–145.

20. Snyder, W. M., & Briggs, X. (2003). *Communities of practice: A new tool for government managers*. Arlington, VA: IBM Center for the Business of Government (p. 8).

21. Ibid. (pp. 35–25).

22. Kania, J., & Kramer, M. (2011, January). Collective impact. *Stanford Social Innovation Review*, Winter; Hanleybrown, F., Kania, J., & Kramer, M. (2012). Channeling change: Making collective impact work. *Stanford Social Innovation Review*.

23. Daft, R. L. (1998). *Organization theory and design* (6th ed.). Cincinnati, OH: South-Western College Publishing (pp. 90–91).

24. Fourth Sector. (2013). About the fourth sector. Retrieved from http://www .fourthsector.net/learn/fourth-sector

25. Dictionary.com. (2013). Hybrid. Retrieved from http://dictionary .reference.com/browse/hybrid

26. Billis, D. (2010). *Hybrid organizations and the third sector: Challenges for practice, theory and policy*. New York: Palgrave Macmillan (pp. 56–58).

27. Sabeti, H. (2012). *The emerging fourth sector*. Washington, DC: The Aspen Institute (p. 8).

28. Alter, K. (2013). Hybrid spectrums. Retrieved from http://www.4lenses. org/setypology/hybrid_spectrum

29. Ibid.

30. Social Enterprise Alliance. (2013). The case for social enterprise alliance. Retrieved from https://www.se-alliance.org/what-is-social-enterprise

31. Young, D. R. (2001). Social enterprise in the United States: Alternate identities and forms. Paper presented at the EMES Conference: The Social Enterprise: A Comparative Perspective, Trento, Italy, December 13–15, 2001.

32. Emerson, E., & Twersky, F. (1996). New social entrepreneurs: The success, challenge and lessons of nonprofit enterprise creation. San Francisco: The Roberts Foundation Homeless Economic Development Fund (p. ix).

33. Incorporates most of the elements suggested by Virtue Ventures and Kim Alter. Retrieved from http://www.virtueventures.com/

34. Alter, K. (2013). Definition of social enterprise. Retrieved from http:// www.4lenses.org/setypology/definition

35. Alter, K. (2013). Fundamental models. Retrieved from http://www.4lenses .org/setypology/models

36. interSector Partners, L³C. (2013). Here's the latest L³C tally. Retrieved from http://www.intersectorl3c.com/l3c_tally.html

37. Americans for Community Development. (2013). The concept of the L³C. Retrieved from http://www.americansforcommunitydevelopment.org/

38. Benefit Corp. (2013). Benefit Corp information center. Retrieved from http://benefitcorp.net/

39. Ibid.

40. Clark, W. H. Jr., & Vranka, L. (2013). The need and rationale for the benefit corporation. White paper retrieved from: http://benefitcorp.net/storage/documents/Benecit_Corporation_White_Paper_1_18_2013.pdf

41. Certified B Corporation. (2013). Retrieved from http://www.bcorporation.net/

42. Ibid.

43. Patagonia. (2013). Our reason for being. Retrieved from http://www.patagonia.com/us/patagonia.go?assetid=2047&ln=140

CHAPTER ELEVEN

1. Cohen, R. (2012). Why did Kony 2012 fizzle out? *Nonprofit Quarterly*, April 26. Retrieved from http://www.nonprofitquarterly.org/policysocial-context/20216-why-did-kony-2012-fizzle-out.html

2. Greenblatt, A. (2012). The social media shuffle: From Kony to spooning. Retrieved from http://www.npr.org/2012/04/19/150964208/young-people-turn-from-kony-to-spooning-record

3. Sources: World Stats. (2012, June 30). Internet World Stats. Miniwatts Marketing Group. Retrieved from http://www.internetworldstats.com/stats.htm; Facebook tops billion-user mark. (2012, October 4). *Wall Street Journal*. Retrieved from http://online.wsj.com/news/articles/SB1000087239639044363540457803616402738112; Twitter passed 500m users in June 2012, 140M of them in US; Jakarta "biggest tweeting" city. (2012, July 30). *TechCrunch*. Retrieved from http://techcrunch.com/2012/07/30/analyst-twitter-passed-500m-users-in-june-2012-140m-of-them-in-us-jakarta-biggest-tweeting-city

4. Saxton, G. D., Guo, S. C., & Brown, W. A. (2007). New dimensions of nonprofit responsiveness: The application and promise of Internet-based technologies. Public performance & management review, 31(2), 144–173.

5. Waters, R. D. (2007). Nonprofit organizations' use of the Internet: A content analysis of communication trends on the internet sites of the Philanthropy 400. *Nonprofit Management & Leadership*, 18(1): 59–76.

6. Gordon, T. P., Knock, C. L., & Neely, D. G. (2009). The role of rating agencies in the market for charitable contributions: An empirical test. *Journal of Accounting and Public Policy*, 28: 469–484.

7. Saxton, G. D., Neely, D., & Guo, C. (in press). Web disclosure and the market for charitable contributions. *Journal of Accounting and Public Policy*.

8. Saxton, G. D., Guo, C., & Brown, W. (2007).

9. Hackler, D., & Saxton, G. D. (2007). The strategic use of information technology by nonprofit organizations: Increasing capacity and untapped potential. *Public Administration Review*, 67(3): 474–487.

10. Kaplan, A. M., & Haenlein, M. (2010). Users of the world, unite! The challenges and opportunities of social media. *Business Horizons*, 53(1): 59–68.

11. Ibid.

12. Ogden, T., & Starita, L. (2009). Social networking and mid-size non-profits: What's the use? *Philanthropy Action*, 1–21.

13. Greenberg, J., & MacAulay, M. (2009). NPO 2.0? Exploring the web presence of environmental nonprofit organizations in Canada. *Global Media Journal* (Canadian edition), 2(1): 63–88.

14. Lovejoy, K., & Saxton, G. D. (2012). Information, community, and action: How nonprofit organizations use social media? *Journal of Computer-Mediated Communication*, 17(3): 337–353. Saxton, G. D., Guo, C., Chiu, I-H., & Feng, B. (2011). Social media and the social good: How nonprofits use Facebook to communicate with the public. *China Third Sector Research [Chinese]*, 1: 40–54.

15. Bornstein, D. (2011, February 7). Mothers-to-be are getting the message. *New York Times*. Retrieved from http://opinionator.blogs.nytimes.com/2011/02/07/pregnant-mothers-are-getting-the-message, or www.text4baby.com

16. To learn more about Chirpify, visit https://chirpify.com

17. For an account of National Preparedness and Response Corps AmeriCorps members who are serving their assignment with the American Red Cross in Southeast Louisiana, visit http://redcrossselanprc.wordpress.com

18. Guo, C., & Saxton, G. (2014). Tweeting Social Change: How Social Media Are Changing Nonprofit Advocacy. *Nonprofit and Voluntary Sector Quarterly*, in press.

19. Guo, C., & Saxton, G. D. (2012). May I have your attention, please? Rethinking nonprofit strategies for the age of attention philanthropy. Presented at the Association for Research on Nonprofit Organizations and Voluntary Action's 41st Annual Conference, Indianapolis, IN.

20. Shenk, D. (1997). *Data smog: Surviving the information glut.* San Francisco: Harper Edge.

21. Steffen, A. (2011). Attention philanthropy: Giving reputation a boost. In H. Masum & M. Tovey (Eds.), *The reputation society: How online opinions are reshaping the offline world* (pp. 89–96). Cambridge, MA: The MIT Press.

22. Hall, J. (2005, June 20). Too many ways to divide donations? *Christian Science Monitor*.

23. Handy, F., Brodeur, N., & Cnaan, R. (2006). Summer on the island: Episodic volunteering. *Voluntary Action*, 7(3): 31–46; Macduff, N. (1990). Episodic volunteering. In T. Connors (Ed.), *The volunteer management handbook* (pp. 187–205). New York: Wiley.

24. See Cornelissen, J. P. (2012). Sensemaking under pressure: The influence of professional roles and social accountability on the creation of sense. *Organization Science*, 23(1): 118–137; Fisher, W. R. (1985). The narrative paradigm: An elaboration. *Communications Monographs*, 52(4): 347–367.

25. TOMS Shoes (2013). One for one. Retrieved from http://www.toms.com/evolving-our-giving

26. Bassett, L. (2012, February 1). Susan G. Komen loses support after Planned Parenthood decision. *Huffington Post*. Retrieved from http://www.huffingtonpost.com/2012/02/01/susan-g-komen_n_1247262.html

27. Mackey, J. M. (2010, October 23). Facebook status "inches," "I like it . . ." in support of Susan G. Komen Foundation. *USA Live Headlines*. Retrieved from http://www.usaliveheadlines.com/1558/facebook-status-inches-i -like-it-in-support-of-susan-gkomen-foundation.htm.

28. James, S. (2010, January 8). Bra color status on Facebook goes viral. *ABC News*. http://abcnews.go.com/Health/bra-color-status-facebook-raises-curiosity -money-viral/story?id=9513986#.UZjuSsrkonM

29. Savvides, L. (2012, April 24). Kony 2012's online activism doesn't guar- antee offline success. *CNET Australia*. Retrieved from http://www.cnet .com.au/kony-2012s-onlineactivism-doesnt-guarantee-offline-success -339336460.htm

30. Bonk, K. (2010). Strategic communications. In *The Jossey-Bass Handbook of Nonprofit Leadership and Management* (3rd ed., pp. 329–346). San Francisco: Wiley.

31. Gainer, B. (2010). Marketing for nonprofit organizations. In *The Jossey-Bass Handbook of Nonprofit Leadership and Management* (3rd ed., pp. 301– 328). San Francisco: Wiley.

32. Attention Philanthropy 2010. (2009). Retrieved from http://www.world changing.com/archives/011191.html

33. National Public Radio. (2011, October 16). "Amid Breast Cancer Month, is there pink fatigue?"

34. Steffen, A. (2011).

CONCLUSION

1. Simon, H. A. (1967). The business school: A problem in organiza- tional design. *Journal of Management Studies*, 4(1): 1–16; Van de Ven, A. H. (1989). Nothing is quite so practical as a good theory. *Academy of Management Review*, 14(4): 486–489.

2. Lewin, K. (1945). The research center for group dynamics at Massachusetts Institute of Technology. *Sociometry*, 8(2): 126–136.

3. Levitt, B., & March, J. G. (1988). Organizational learning. *Annual Review of Sociology*, 14: 319–340.

4. Ball, J. (2013, January 14). Avaaz: Can online campaigning reinvent politics? *Guardian*. Retrieved from http://www.theguardian.com/world/2013/jan/15/avaaz-online-campaigning-reinvent-politics

5. Edwards, M. (2008). *Just another emperor? The myths and realities of philanthrocapitalism*. New York: Demos: A Network for Ideas & Action (p. 18).

ACKNOWLEDGMENTS

We would like to thank the Jossey-Bass/Wiley team for their support. In particular, words cannot express our gratitude to our most skillful book editor: Alison Hankey, Senior Editor at Jossey-Bass/Wiley. We are grateful not only for her great patience and warm encouragement, but also for her constructive advice that kept us focused and balanced. Deep thanks and appreciation must also go to Nina Kreiden, Senior Content Manager at Jossey-Bass/Wiley, who masterfully shepherded our book through the production process up until it became a finished, printed product. We also appreciate the wonderful work of Liz Albritton, our proofreader; Rob Brandt, Editorial Projects Manager; Dani Scoville, Editorial Program Coordinator; and Sheri Gilbert, permission review.

We owe an immense debt of gratitude to Dr. John Bryson, McKnight Presidential Professor of Planning and Public Affairs of the Hubert H. Humphrey School of Public Affairs at the University of Minnesota, and to Dr. Dennis Young, Bernard B. and Eugenia A. Ramsey Chair of Private Enterprise of the Andrew Young School of Policy Studies at Georgia State University. As the consulting editor for Jossey-Bass's public administration series, John showed his faith in us by recommending us to write this book, and always provided timely support and invaluable advice when we needed them most. Dennis offered gentle guidance and insightful comments when this book was still in the proposal stage, and continued to direct us to useful sources of information as we moved forward with our project.

The book has benefited tremendously from the thoughtful and critical comments of the anonymous reviewers. Their excellent suggestions on content and presentation have deepened our thinking and helped to improve our work. We also are also grateful to our colleagues Peter Frumkin (University of Pennsylvania), Ruth McCambridge (*Nonprofit Quarterly*), Gordon Shockley (Arizona State University), and Dennis Young (Georgia State University), who spent quality time reading through our manuscript and provided generous endorsements to our book.

Many other academic and practitioner colleagues have shared their insights and offered help during the process: Fredrik Andersson (University of Wisconsin–Milwaukee), Will Brown (Texas A&M), Alnoor Ebrahim (Harvard University), Peter Frank (Wingate University), Scott Helm (University of Missouri-Kansas City), Udaiyan Jatar (Blue Earth Network), Aliyya Mattos (PaperSeed Foundation), Morgan Marietta (University of Massachusetts Lowell), Charlotte Ren (University of Pennsylvania), Dave Renz (University of Missouri-Kansas City), John Ronquillo (DePaul University), Greg Saxton (University at Buffalo), Les Lenkowsky (Indiana University), among others. Their encouragement and kind offers to help have been important to our book and deserve special recognition.

The book would not have been possible without the participation and contributions of the many bright graduate students who have taken our social entrepreneurship courses at the University of Georgia and Indiana University-Purdue University Indianapolis. The numerous classroom discussions, blog posts, and email exchanges with them have inspired us to explore some really fabulous ideas that have eventually been reflected in this book. We also acknowledge the contributions of Kukkyoung Moon and Min Qi, who provided research assistance and helped prepare some of the tables and figures that enrich our book.

Finally and more personally, we are indebted to our loving families, who tolerated our absences and shouldered the household responsibilities when we were busy writing.

Throughout the process of writing this book, the people we have acknowledged above have given us their unstinting support and by so doing they have contributed in a very real way to the benefit our book will provide to students and future social entrepreneurs.

INDEX

Page references followed by *fig* indicate an illustrated figure; followed by *t* indicate a table; followed by *e* indicate an exhibit.

195–196; information diffusion networks between different agencies of, 214; setting policy for social entrepreneurship, 195; support for social entrepreneurship by, 194–195. *See also* Public sector entrepreneurship

Government enterprises, 119–121

Government funding: of nonprofit social entrepreneurship, 126*t*, 132–133; "pay for performance" bonds for public sector entrepreneurship, 199–200

Government Performance and Results Act (GPRA), 196

GPRA Modernization Act of 2010 (GPRAMA), 196–197

Grameen Bank: innovative social entrepreneur opportunity created by, 53, 59; micro loans made by, 22, 47; origins of the micro lending by, 47–49

Grayson, D., 147*t*

Great Recession (2008): financial challenges threatening new program launches during, 173–174; housing bubble collapse triggering the, 13; social entrepreneur potential during, 16; windows of opportunity for innovation during the, 173

Guclu, A., 52*t*, 53, 56, 69

GuideStar, 244, 249, 250

Guo, C., 166–167, 248

H

Habitat for Humanity International, 114

Haenlein, M., 236, 237

Hale, V., 20

Hancock, J., 91

Hanleybrown, F., 217

Harrell, A., 104

Harvard Business Review, 173

Harvard Law School, 58

Harvard University, 235

"Have a Real Impact; Keep Your Day Job" (McGraw), 144–145

Helm, S. T., 32

Heskowitz, A., 20

Hills, G. E., 51, 62

Hisrich, R., 150

Hitachi Foundation, 217

Homeless Economic Development Fund (HEDF) [Roberts Foundation], 68

Horowitz, S., 61

Housing and Urban Development (HUD), 132

Hughes, N., 161, 162, 174

Hurricane Gustav relief, 148

Hurricane Ike relief, 148

Hurricane Katrina American Red Cross call center, 22

Hurst, A., 162

Hybrid organizations: Alter's Hybrid Spectrum on, 222, 223*fig*; characteristics of different types of, 222, 223*t*; description of, 61–62, 220; emergence as new fourth sector, 220, 221*fig*, 222; examples of, 222

I

IBM, 36

IBM Center for the Business of Government, 190

Idea generation: illustrated diagram of, 56*fig*; pattern recognition contribution to, 58–60; prior experience contribution to, 60–62; public sector social entrepreneurship, 193*fig*–194; social assets contribution to, 57–58; social needs contribution to, 57; social networks contribution to, 60, 62

Nonprofit social entrepreneurship: comparing EO and EI in public, business, and, 37–38; description and examples of, 20–21; funding, 122–139; interface between public and, 21; levels of proactiveness and innovativeness in, 29; producing hybrid organizations, 61–62; relationship between EO and organizational performance in, 33–34

Nonprofit social entrepreneurship funding: earned income, 133–137; government funding, 126t, 132–133; income portfolios and commercial activity, 126t, 127–128; loans and equity finance, 137–139; philanthropy and, 126t, 128–130; revenue sources, 122–127; venture philanthropy, 130–131

Norton, D. P., 98

O

Obama administration, 172, 198, 200
Obama, B., 173, 196
Office of Management and Budget, 196
Office of Social Entrepreneurship, 198–199
Ogden, T., 238
Oliver, J., 19
"One Day without Shoes" campaign, 246
170(c)(2)(B) (Internal Revenue Code), 229
OneWorld Health, 20–21
Open systems model, 96–97
Operating model: creating social value in the value chain using, 75–76; description of the, 69fig, 73; program logic model used to develop, 73fig–75
Operational efficiency, 207–208
Opportunistic behavior, 9
Opportunities: comparing commercial and, 54–55; context of, 55; definitions of, 50–54; exploratory and exploitative, 164; how Muhammad Yunus created

his own, 47–49; "mountain climbing" vs. "mountain building" metaphors of, 51; moving to action from, 67–88; opportunity recognition theory on, 55–56; process of discovering and assessing, 55–66; process-oriented model to explain, 49; seven types of, 53–54; social entrepreneurship driven by, 255; stakeholders of, 55; two-phase model on selecting intrapreneurial, 166–170. *See also* Social entrepreneurship

Opportunity assessment: description of, 62; Kitzi's model on three criteria for, 62, 63t–65t; Shaker Zhahra's criteria for, 65–66

Opportunity assessment criteria: accessibility as, 65–66; market potential, 63t–64t; pervasiveness as, 65; radicalness as, 66; relevance as, 65; social value potential, 63t; sustainability potential, 64t–65t; urgency as, 65

Opportunity development process: developing the operating model, 69fig, 73fig–76; phase one: idea generation, 56fig, 57–62; phase two: opportunity assessment, 56fig, 62–66; resource strategy with supporting analysis, 69fig, 80–87fig; social impact theory, resource strategy, and operating model of, 69fig; social impact theory used to elaborate opportunity, 69fig–72; venture feasibility and planning, 69fig, 76–80

Organization or operational risk, 81
Organizational alignment, 8
Organizational boundaries: collaboration between organizations stretching, 207–211; collaboration and blurring of sectoral, 220; engagement in networks stretching, 211–219; logic model

and evaluation of, 93*fig*–94; social entrepreneurship and need for flexible, 8; working across, 205–207, 219–228

Organizational capacity building, 79

Organizational control systems, 33

Organizational culture: description of, 151–152; how top management influences, 180; risk aversion, 155; social intrapreneurship barrier due to embeddedness of, 157; as social intrapreneurship internal antecedent, 150*fig*, 152

Organizational dashboards, 100–101, 102*fig*

Organizational performance: Balanced Scorecard to evaluate, 98–100; comparing commercial versus social entrepreneurship measurement of, 7; organizational dashboards to evaluate, 100–101, 102*fig*; relationship between entrepreneurial orientation (EO) and, 33–34; social intrapreneurship impact on, 150*fig*, 154

Organizational structure: collective impact (CI) impact on centralized and decentralized, 219; formalization of, 150*fig*, 151; implications for entrepreneurial orientation (EO), 33; scaling through affiliated structures, 114; scaling through branching, 114

Organizational turnarounds innovation, 176

Organizations: alignment with social value, 8; established, 164–166, 255–256; hybrid, 61–62, 220, 221*fig*, 222, 223*t*; social entrepreneurship conceptualized as behavior of, 27–44

Osberg, S., 5*t*

Osborne, D., 188

Outcome evaluation: description and five areas of, 103–104; monetizing outcome, 107–110; research designs used for, 104–107*fig*; social return on investment (SROI), 109

Outcomes: comparing for-profit, public, and nonprofit, 38; description of, 73*fig*, 74; evaluation of impact and, 101–107*fig*; "If...then" statements about, 74; logic model and evaluation of, 93*fig*–94

Outputs: description of, 73*fig*, 74; "If...then" statements about, 74

P

Panera Bread, 148

Panera Cares Café, 148

PaperSeed, 176

PaperSeed Foundation: founding and description of, 25–26; innovativeness of, 29–30; proactiveness of, 30

Participant governed networks, 215

Partners in Christ International (PICI), 143–144

Patagonia, 230

Paton, R., 100

Pattern recognition: factors that contribute to, 59–60; how prior experience contributes to, 59, 60–62; social entrepreneurship opportunities created by, 58–59

Pepper's Dragons (Bjarnason), 176–177

Peredor, A. M., 6*t*

Peters, T., 154–155

Pew Research Center's Internet & American Life Project, 240

Pfizer, 21

Philanthropy: attention, 245–250, 258; funding through, 126*t*, 128–130; venture, 130–131

Pick n' Pay (South Africa), 144

Pinchot, E., 146

Pinchot, G., 146

Pizza Hut, 36

public and private/nonprofit sectors, 21; lessons learned from failed, 257; moving from action to impact of, 89–114; moving to action from opportunity, 67–88; *new entry* nature of, 26; as opportunity driven, 255; as possible for established organizations and not just start-ups, 255–256; as possible in for-profit, public, and nonprofit sectors, 256; possible pitfalls of hybridization of, 257; in the public sector, 17–19; Shalman's PCDO model implications of, 8; similarities and differences between commercial and, 7, 37–38, 54–55; social intrapreneurship subset of, 145–158; social mission as the compass of, 254; social value, alignment, and boundaries concerns of, 8. *See also* Opportunities

Social entrepreneurship drivers: demographics, 13–14; globalization, 15–16; opportunity as, 255; overview of, 11*fig*–13; potential to contribute, 16–17; technological factors, 14–15

Social impact: approaches to evaluate effectiveness and, 94–101; description of, 73*fig*, 74; evaluation for outcome and, 101, 103–107*fig*; framework for venture evaluation of, 91–94; "If...then" statements about, 74, 93; monetizing outcome and, 107–110; process of establishing and expanding, 91*fig*; scaling to increase, 110–114; social venture effectiveness as, 90–94

Social impact bonds (SIBs), 139, 200

Social impact model, 79

Social impact theory: description of, 69; elaborating opportunity using, 69*fig*–72

Social Innovation Fund (SIF), 131

"Social innovation" school of thought, 7

Social Innovators Institute, 199

Social intrapreneurship: clarifying the concept of, 145–146; cognitive, network, and cultural embeddedness barrier to, 156–157; definitions of, 145, 146–147*t*; dimensions of, 147–149; external antecedents of, 150*fig*, 153–154; internal antecedents of, 150*fig*–152; management challenges of, 154–158; managing the process of, 161–180; other labels of, 146; performance consequences of, 150*fig*, 154; strategies for overcoming challenges to, 157–158. *See also* Innovation

Social intrapreneurship dimensions: new business venturing, 147–148; product and service innovation, 148; self-renewal, 148–149

Social intrapreneurship process: Burgelman's model of strategy-making process to understand, 164–166; examining the management of, 163–164; initiators of innovations in public and nonprofit organizations, 174–176; of M-Pesa financial services in Kenya, 161–162; Ren and Guo's two-phase model of the, 166–174; role of frontline managers in the, 176–177; role of middle managers in the, 177–179; role of top managers in the, 179–180

Social media: board definition of, 236; fundraising through, 240–241; global participation in, 234–235; how social entrepreneurship is impacted by, 15; information sharing through, 239–240; *Kony 2012: Part II–Beyond Famous* video limited success through, 234; *Kony 2012* video viral success through, 233–234, 247, 250; media and social dimensions of, 236–237*fig*; myths and realities about,

V

Value chains: creating social value in the, 75–76; definition of, 75

Value proposition: blending economic and social, 70; centrality in social entrepreneurship, 71*fig*; description of, 70; social, 70–71

Values-based models: competing values framework or New Change model, 95–97; stakeholder satisfaction model, 97

Van de Ven, A. H., 253

Venkataraman, S., 60

Venture philanthropy, 130–131

Ventures. *See* Social ventures

Vermeulen, S., 29

Virtuous behavior, 9

VisionSpring, 15

Vital Spark Foundation, 21

VMware, 145

Vodafone, 161–162

Volunteer Louisiana Commission, 198

W

Walker, R., 150

Waterman, R., 154–155

Web 2.0 tools, 235, 236, 237, 241. *See also* Social media

Weerawardena, J., 5*t*, 28, 29, 39

Wei-Skillern, J., 4*t*, 7, 8, 52*t*, 93, 134

Weiss, L., 162

Wharton San Francisco, 14

"Wheels from Above" program (PICI), 144

Wikipedia, 236, 237*fig*

Wiklund, J., 33

William and Flora Hewlett Foundation's Expected Return, 110

Wireless Foundation, 240

Wolk, A., 78

Women: increasing numbers of social entrepreneurs among, 14; micro loans provided to those living in developing countries, 22

Wooldridge, B., 168

Working Today, 57, 61

World Bank's Development Marketplace, 193

World of Warcraft, 237*fig*

Worldchanging, 248, 249, 250

Y

Year Up: Balanced Scorecard on, 100; branching used as scaling technique by, 114; cost-benefit analysis of, 109; description of the, 89; evaluation of internal processes and results of, 94; examining move from action to impact by, 90–114; experimental design used to evaluate, 105; organizational dashboard for, 101, 102*fig*; social return on investment (SROI) of, 109; stakeholder satisfaction model for evaluating impact of, 97; three-phase growth plan (2000–2011) of, 89–90. *See also* Social venture evaluation

Yen, J., 8

Yoplait, 54

Young, D., 127

Young, D. R., 6*t*, 9

YouTube, 237*fig*

Yunus, M., 8, 22, 47–49, 59

Yusuf, J., 247*t*

Z

Zahra, S., 65

Zidisha, 15